Other Books and Series by Jeff Bowen

Applications for Enrollment of Chickasaw Newborn Act of 1905
Volumes I thru VII

Cherokee Intermarried White 1906 Volume I thru X

Applications for Enrollment of Creek Newborn Act of 1905
Volumes I thru XIV

Applications for Enrollment of Choctaw Newborn Act of 1905
Volume I, II, III, IV, V, VI, VII, VIII, IX, X, XI, XII, XIII & XIV

Visit our website at **www.nativestudy.com** to learn more about these and other books and series by Jeff Bowen

APPLICATIONS FOR ENROLLMENT OF CHOCTAW NEWBORN ACT OF 1905

VOLUME XV

TRANSCRIBED BY
JEFF BOWEN
NATIVE STUDY
Gallipolis, Ohio
USA

Other Books and Series by Jeff Bowen

1901-1907 Native American Census Seneca, Eastern Shawnee, Miami, Modoc, Ottawa, Peoria, Quapaw, and Wyandotte Indians (Under Seneca School, Indian Territory)

1932 Census of The Standing Rock Sioux Reservation with Births And Deaths 1924-1932

Census of The Blackfeet, Montana, 1897- 1901 Expanded Edition

Eastern Cherokee by Blood, 1906-1910, Volumes I thru XIII

Choctaw of Mississippi Indian Census 1929-1932 with Births and Deaths 1924-1931   Volume I
Choctaw of Mississippi Indian Census 1933, 1934 & 1937, Supplemental Rolls to 1934 & 1935 with Births and Deaths 1932-1938, and Marriages 1936-1938 Volume II

Eastern Cherokee Census Cherokee, North Carolina 1930-1939 Census 1930-1931 with Births And Deaths 1924-1931 Taken By Agent L. W. Page Volume I
Eastern Cherokee Census Cherokee, North Carolina 1930-1939 Census 1932-1933 with Births And Deaths 1930-1932 Taken By Agent R. L. Spalsbury   Volume II
Eastern Cherokee Census Cherokee, North Carolina 1930-1939 Census 1934-1937 with Births and Deaths 1925-1938 and Marriages 1936 & 1938 Taken by Agents R. L. Spalsbury And Harold W. Foght Volume III

Seminole of Florida Indian Census, 1930-1940 with Birth and Death Records, 1930-1938

Texas Cherokees 1820-1839 A Document For Litigation 1921

Choctaw By Blood Enrollment Cards 1898-1914 Volumes I thru XVII

Starr Roll 1894 (Cherokee Payment Rolls) Districts: Canadian, Cooweescoowee, and Delaware Volume One
Starr Roll 1894 (Cherokee Payment Rolls) Districts: Flint, Going Snake, and Illinois   Volume Two
Starr Roll 1894 (Cherokee Payment Rolls) Districts: Saline, Sequoyah, and Tahlequah; Including Orphan Roll   Volume Three

Cherokee Intruder Cases Dockets of Hearings 1901-1909 Volumes I & II

Indian Wills, 1911-1921 Records of the Bureau of Indian Affairs Books One thru Seven;
Native American Wills & Probate Records 1911-1921

Other Books and Series by Jeff Bowen

Turtle Mountain Reservation Chippewa Indians 1932 Census with Births & Deaths, 1924-1932

Chickasaw By Blood Enrollment Cards 1898-1914 Volume I thru V

Cherokee Descendants East An Index to the Guion Miller Applications Volume I
Cherokee Descendants West An Index to the Guion Miller Applications Volume II (A-M)
Cherokee Descendants West An Index to the Guion Miller Applications Volume III (N-Z)

Applications for Enrollment of Seminole Newborn Freedmen, Act of 1905

Eastern Cherokee Census, Cherokee, North Carolina, 1915-1922, Taken by Agent James E. Henderson   Volume I (1915-1916)
Volume II (1917-1918)
Volume III (1919-1920)
Volume IV (1921-1922)

Complete Delaware Roll of 1898

Eastern Cherokee Census, Cherokee, North Carolina, 1923-1929, Taken by Agent James E. Henderson   Volume I (1923-1924)
Volume II (1925-1926)
Volume III (1927-1929)

Applications for Enrollment of Seminole Newborn Act of 1905 Volumes I & II

North Carolina Eastern Cherokee Indian Census 1898-1899, 1904, 1906, 1909-1912, 1914 Revised and Expanded Edition

1932 Hopi and Navajo Native American Census with Birth & Death Rolls (1925-1931) Volume 1 - Hopi
1932 Hopi and Navajo Native American Census with Birth & Death Rolls (1930-1932) Volume 2 - Navajo

Western Navajo Reservation Navajo, Hopi and Paiute 1933 Census with Birth & Death Rolls 1925-1933

Cherokee Citizenship Commission Dockets 1880-1884 and 1887-1889 Volumes I thru V

Copyright © 2013
by Jeff Bowen

ALL RIGHTS RESERVED
No part of this publication may be reproduced
or used in any form or manner whatsoever
without previous written permission from the
copyright holder or publisher.

Originally published:
Baltimore, Maryland
2013

Reprinted by:

Native Study LLC
Gallipolis, OH
www.nativestudy.com
2020

Library of Congress Control Number: 2020918113

ISBN: 978-1-64968-108-9

Made in the United States of America.

This series is dedicated to the descendants of the
Choctaw newborn listed in these applications.

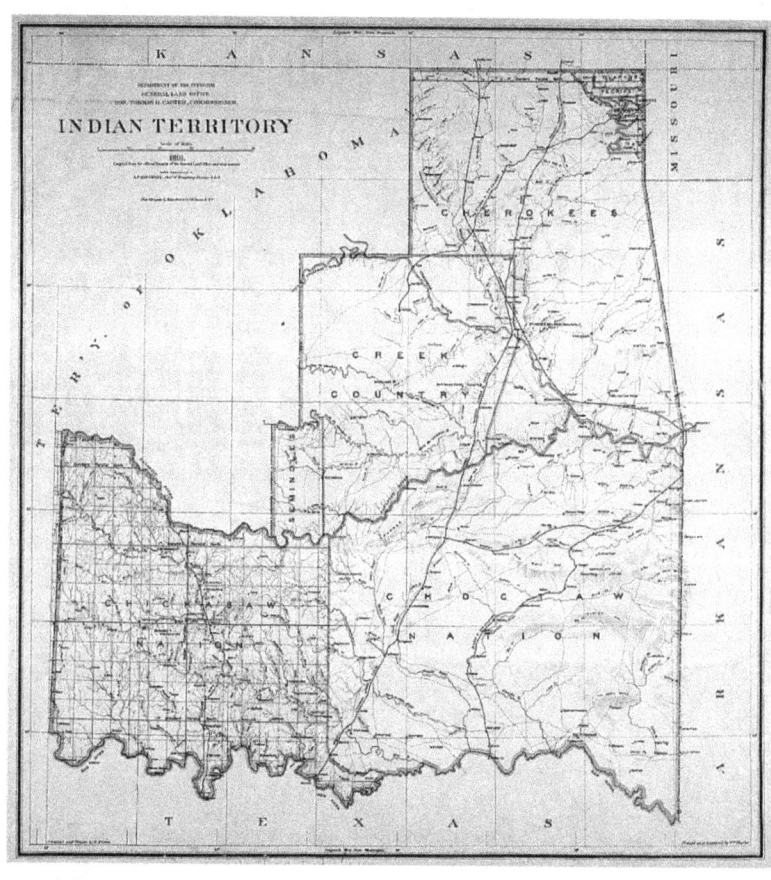

This map of Indian Territory shows how large the Choctaw and Chickasaw Nations' land base was that contained huge deposits of asphalt and coal. Just the size and territory involved was flooded with the "Grafters".

DEPARTMENT OF THE INTERIOR.
Commissioner to the Five Civilized Tribes.

NOTICE.

Opening of Land Office at Wewoka,
IN THE SEMINOLE NATION, INDIAN TERRITORY.

Notice is hereby given that on Monday, September 4, 1905, the Commissioner to the Five Civilized Tribes will establish a land office at Wewoka, in the Seminole Nation, Indian Territory, for the purpose of allowing citizens and freedmen of the Seminole Nation to select allotments of land for their minor children enrolled under the Act of Congress approved March 3, 1905 (33 Stat. L. 1060), and for the further purpose of allowing citizens and freedmen of the Seminole Nation, whose allotments are incomplete, to select additional land in order to bring the value of their allotments up to the standard of $309.09, as nearly as may be practicable.

Each child whose enrollment in accordance with the Act of March 3, 1905, has been duly approved by the Secretary of the Interior, is entitled to receive an alllotment of forty acres without regard to the character or value of the land selected.

Selection of allotments for minor children must be made by their citizen or freedmen parents or by a duly appointed guardian, or curator, or by a duly appointed administrator.

TAMS BIXBY,
Commissioner.

Muskogee, Indian Territory,
July 29, 1905.

This particular notice for the Seminole and Creek Newborn makes mention of the Act of 1905. It is likely that a similar notice was posted in the Choctaw and Chickasaw Nations for the registration of newborn children.

DEPARTMENT OF THE INTERIOR.
Commission to the Five Civilized Tribes.

Rules and Regulations Governing the Selection of Allotments and the Designation of Homesteads in the Choctaw and Chickasaw Nations.

1. Selections of allotments and designations of homesteads for adult citizens and selections of allotments for adult freedmen must be made in person except as herein otherwise provided.
2. Applications to have land set apart and homesteads designated for duly identified Mississippi Choctaws must be made personally before the Commission to the Five Civilized Tribes. Fathers may apply for their minor children and if the father be dead the mother may apply. Husbands may apply for wives. Applications for orphans, insane persons and persons of unsound mind may be made by duly appointed guardian or curator, and for aged and infirm persons and prisoners by agents duly authorized thereunto by power of attorney, in the discretion of said Commission.
3. At the time of the selection of allotment each citizen and duly identified Mississippi Choctaw shall designate as a homestead out of said selection land equal in value to one hundred and sixty acres of the average allottable land of the Choctaw and Chickasaw Nations, as nearly as may be.
4. Each Choctaw and Chickasaw freedman, at the time of selection shall designate as his or her allotment of the lands of the Choctaw and Chickasaw Nations, land equal in value to forty acres of the average allottable land of the Choctaw and Chickasaw Nations.
5. Citizens, freedmen and identified Mississippi Choctaws who are married, whether they have attained their majority or not, will be regarded as of age for the purpose of making selections.
6. Selections may be made by citizen and freedman parents for unmarried male children under twenty-one years of age and for unmarried female children under eighteen years of age, and a male citizen or freedman may make selection for his wife, if she is entitled to make selection, unless she shall, at the time or previously thereto, protest in writing.
7. Where the father of an unmarried minor citizen, freedman or identified Mississippi Choctaw is a non-citizen, the citizen, freedman or identified Mississippi Choctaw mother of such children must make selection in person in behalf of said children.
8. Selections of allotments and designations of homesteads for minor citizens and selections of allotments for minor freedmen may be made by the citizen father or mother or freedman father or mother, as the case may be, or by a guardian, curator, or an administrator having charge of their estate, in the order named.
9. Selections of allotments and designations of homesteads for citizen, and selections of allotment for freedmen, prisoners, convicts, aged and infirm persons and soldiers and sailors of the United States on duty outside of Indian Territory, may be made by duly appointed agents under power of attorney, and for incompetents by guardians, curators, or other suitable person akin to them.
10. Selections may be made and homesteads designated by duly identified Mississippi Choctaws, who have, within one year after the date of their identification as such, made satisfactory proof of bona fide settlement within the Choctaw-Chickasaw country, at any time within six months after the date of their said identification.
11. Persons authorized to make selections by power of attorney, as provided in rules 2 and 9 hereof, must be the husband or wife, or a relative not further removed than a cousin of the first degree of the person for whom such selection is made.
12. It shall be the duty of the Commission to the Five Civilized Tribes to see that selections of allotments and designations of homesteads for the classes of persons mentioned in rules 2, 6, 7, 8 and 9 hereof, are made for the best interests of such persons.
13. Selections of allotments for citizens, freedmen and identified Mississippi Choctaws who have died subsequent to September 25, 1902, and before making a selection of allotment, shall be made by a duly appointed administrator or executor. If, however, such administrator or executor be not duly and expeditiously appointed, or fails to act promptly when appointed, or for any other cause such selections be not so made within a reasonable and practicable time, the Commission to the Five Civilized Tribes shall designate the lands thus to be allotted.
14. In determining the value of a selection the appraised value of the land selected shall be increased by the appraised value of such pine timber on such land as has heretofore been estimated by the Commission to the Five Civilized Tribes.
15. Selections of allotments may be made only by citizens and freedmen whose enrollment has been approved by the Secretary of the Interior, and by persons duly identified by the Commission to the Five Civilized Tribes as Mississippi Choctaws, and by none others.
16. When a selection of land has been made by a citizen, freedman or identified Mississippi Choctaw, and the land so selected is claimed by a person whose rights as a citizen or freedman have not been finally determined, contest for the land so selected may be instituted by the person claiming the land, formal application for the land being first made as is required by the Rules of Practice in Choctaw and Chickasaw allotment contest cases.

THE COMMISSION TO THE FIVE CIVILIZED TRIBES.

TAMS BIXBY, Chairman.

Muskogee, Indian Territory, March 24, 1903.

The above statement published prior to 1905, was established for what was supposed to be a set of guidelines when it came to allotments. But with supplemental agreements and Congressional legislation, time frames as well as rules and regulations often changed and were not the same for every tribe.

INTRODUCTION

The *Applications for Enrollment of Choctaw Newborn Act of 1905*, National Archive film M-1301, Rolls 50-57, are found under the heading of Applications for Enrollment of the Commission to the Five Civilized Tribes. For this series, I have transcribed the application forms filled out by individuals applying for enrollment in the Five Civilized Tribes under the Dawes Commission. These applications contain considerably more information than stated on the census cards found in series M-1186. M-1301 possesses its own numerical sequence, separate from M-1186. To find each party's roll number you would have to reference M-1186.

The Choctaw as well as the Chickasaw allotments were likely some of the most sought after properties in Indian Territory. There was supposed to be a 25-year restriction on the sale or lease of any Indian lands so as to insure that the owners wouldn't be swindled, but that isn't what happened. This fact is borne out in the Dawes Commission General Allotment Act, of February 8, 1887, Section 5, which "Provides that after an Indian person is allotted land, the United States will hold the land 'in trust [1] for the sole use and benefit of the Indian' (or his heirs if the Indian landowner dies) for a period of 25 years. (Land held in trust by the United States government cannot be sold or in anyway alienated by the Indian landowner, since the United States government considers the underlying ownership of the land held by itself and not the tribe. After the period of trust ends, the Indian landowner is free to sell the land and is free from any encumbrance from the United States.)"[1] Instead, Native Americans were exploited by the devious. The Choctaw and Chickasaw Districts both had huge asphalt and coal deposits, so there was pressure from outsiders to acquire them from the minute they were discovered. After repeated attacks throughout the years and many legislative changes, President "Roosevelt finally signed the Five Tribes Bill at noon on April 26, 1906, the forces seeking to end all restrictions were disappointed. Section 19 removed restrictions from the sale of all inherited land but directed that no full-bloods could sell their land for twenty-five years. The Act also prohibited leases for more than one year without the approval of the Secretary of the Interior."[2]

Angie Debo described the opportunists that wanted these Native American allotments as, "Grafters". The parents of the newborns enumerated within this series would no sooner receive the approval for their child's allotment than there would be someone there with cash in hand holding a new deed or lease for the parents to sign their child's birthright away. Angie Debo said it best, "As the business incapacity of the allottees became apparent, a horde of despoilers fastened themselves upon their property." According to Debo, "The term 'grafter' was applied as a matter of course to dealers in Indian land, and was frankly accepted by them. The speculative fever also affected Government employees so that it was almost impossible to prevent them from making personal investments."[3]

---

[1] General Allotment Act, Act of Feb. 8, 1887 (24 Stat. 388, ch. 119, 25 USCA 331)
[2] The Dawes Commission and the Allotment of the Five Civilized Tribes, 1893-1914 by Kent Carter, pg. 173
[3] And Still the Waters Run, Angie Debo, p. 92.

INTRODUCTION

According to the Department of Interior in 1905, "It is estimated that there will be added to the final rolls of the citizens and freedmen of the Choctaw and Chickasaw nations the names of 2,000 persons, including 1,500 new-born children to be enrolled under the provisions of the act of Congress approved March 3, 1905."[4]

The quote below explains, in detail, the requirements for qualifying as a newborn Choctaw, "By the act of Congress approved March 3, 1905 (H.R. 17474), entitled 'An act making appropriations for the current and contingent expenses of the Indian Department and for fulfilling treaty stipulations with various Indian tribes for the fiscal year ending June 30, 1906, and for other purposes,' it was provided as follows:

'That the Commission to the Five Civilized Tribes is hereby authorized for sixty days after the date of the approval of this act to receive and consider applications for enrollment of infant children born prior to September twenty-fifth, nineteen hundred and two, and who were living on said date, to citizens by blood of the Choctaw and Chickasaw tribes of Indians whose enrollment has been approved by the Secretary of the Interior prior to the date of the approval of this act; and to enroll and make allotments to such children.'

'That the Commission to the Five Civilized Tribes is authorized for sixty days after the date of the approval of this act to receive and consider applications for enrollment of children born subsequent to September twenty-fifth, nineteen hundred and two, and prior to March fourth, nineteen hundred and five, and who were living on said latter date, to citizens by blood of the Choctaw and Chickasaw tribes of Indians whose enrollment has been approved by the Secretary of the Interior prior to the date of the approval of this act; and to enroll and make allotments to such children.'

"Notice is hereby given that the Commission to the Five Civilized Tribes will, up to and inclusive of midnight, May 2, 1905, receive applications for the enrollment of infant children born prior to September 25, 1902, and who were living on said date, to citizens by blood of the Choctaw and Chickasaw tribes of Indians whose enrollment has been approved by the Secretary of the Interior prior to March 3, 1905."[5]

Following is the scope of these transcriptions: Besides the applications themselves, researchers will find the identities of other individuals within these applications -- doctors, lawyers, mid-wives, and other relatives -- that may help with you genealogical research.

Jeff Bowen
Gallipolis, Ohio
NativeStudy.com

---

[4] Annual Reports of the Department of the Interior For the Fiscal Year Ended June 30, 1905, p. 609.
[5] Annual Reports of the Department of the Interior For the Fiscal Year Ended June 30, 1905, p. 593.

Applications for Enrollment of Choctaw Newborn
Act of 1905   Volume XV

Choc New Born 1064
    Porter J. Lewis
    (Born September 3, 1903)

AFFIDAVIT OF ATTENDING PHYSICIAN OR MIDWIFE

UNITED STATES OF AMERICA
INDIAN TERRITORY
_____DISTRICT

I, Minerva Hicks   a   midwife on oath state that I attended on Mrs. Mary Lewis *known as Seaton* wife of Calvin Lewis on the 3rd day of September, 190 3, that there was born to her on said date a male child, that said child is now living, and is said to have been named Porter John Lewis

                                Minervia[sic] Hicks

Subscribed and sworn to before me this, the   17th day of Jan   190 5

WITNESSETH:
Must be two witnesses who are citizens
{ Sampson Brown
  Lewis Carnes }

      L.C. Tuey   Notary Public.

We hereby certify that we are well acquainted with Minerva Hicks a midwife and know her to be reputable and of good standing in the community.

    Sampson Brown   _____

    Lewis Carnes   _____

NEW-BORN AFFIDAVIT.

    Number................

...Choctaw Enrolling Commission...

IN THE MATTER OF THE APPLICATION FOR ENROLLMENT, as a citizen of the Choctaw Nation, of Porter John Lewis born on the 3rd day of ___September___ 190 3

Applications for Enrollment of Choctaw Newborn
Act of 1905   Volume XV

Name of father   Calvin Lewis   a citizen of   Chickasaw Freedman
Nation final enrollment No.   3891
Name of mother   Mary Lewis *known as Sexton*   a citizen of   Choctaw
Nation final enrollment No.   8322

Postoffice   Kinta IT

AFFIDAVIT OF MOTHER.

UNITED STATES OF AMERICA
INDIAN TERRITORY
   Western   DISTRICT

I   Mary Lewis *known as Sexton*   , on oath state that I am 31   years of age and a citizen by   blood   of the   Choctaw   Nation, and as such have been placed upon the final roll of the   Choctaw   Nation, by the Honorable Secretary of the Interior my final enrollment number being   8322 ; that I am the lawful wife of   Calvin Lewis   , who is a citizen of the   Chickasaw   Nation, and as such has been placed upon the final roll of said Nation by the Honorable Secretary of the Interior, his final enrollment number being   3891   and that a   Male   child was born to me on the 3rd   day of   September   190 3; that said child has been named   Porter John Lewis   , *known as Sexton* and is now living.

                                    Mary Lewis
Witnesseth.   *per Calvin Lewis*

Must be two   ⎫   Sampson Brown
Witnesses who ⎬
are Citizens. ⎭   Lewis Carnes

Subscribed and sworn to before me this   6"   day of   Jan   190 5

                                    L.C. Tuey
                                       Notary Public.
My commission expires: Jan 17-1907

BIRTH AFFIDAVIT.
DEPARTMENT OF THE INTERIOR.
COMMISSION TO THE FIVE CIVILIZED TRIBES.

IN RE APPLICATION FOR ENROLLMENT, as a citizen of the   Choctaw   Nation, of   Porter J Lewis   , born on the 3rd   day of   Sept   , 1903

Name of Father: Calvin Lewis   a citizen of the   Choctaw   Nation.
Name of Mother: Mary Sexton   a citizen of the   Choctaw   Nation.

                     Postoffice   Kinta I.T.

Applications for Enrollment of Choctaw Newborn
Act of 1905   Volume XV

AFFIDAVIT OF MOTHER.

UNITED STATES OF AMERICA, Indian Territory, }
  Western   DISTRICT.

I, Mary Sexton, on oath state that I am 32 years of age and a citizen by blood, of the Choctaw Nation; that I am the lawful wife of Calvin Lewis, who is a ~~citizen, by~~ Freedman of the Choctaw Nation; that a male child was born to me on 3rd day of September, 1903; that said child has been named Porter J. Lewis, and was living March 4, 1905.

                                                                her
                                             Mary x Sexton
Witnesses To Mark: mark
{ J W Lyle
  C.W. Wilson

Subscribed and sworn to before me this 22 day of Mch, 1905

                                   (Name Illegible)
                                    Notary Public.
                       My com expires 2/2 of 1909

AFFIDAVIT OF ATTENDING PHYSICIAN OR MID-WIFE.

UNITED STATES OF AMERICA, Indian Territory, }
  Western   DISTRICT.

I, Minervia Hicks, a midwife, on oath state that I attended on Mrs. Mary Sexton, wife of Calvin Lewis on the 3rd day of Sept, 1903; that there was born to her on said date a male child; that said child was living March 4, 1905, and is said to have been named Porter J. Lewis

                                       Minervia Hicks
Witnesses To Mark:
{

Subscribed and sworn to before me this 22 day of Mch, 1905

                                   (Name Illegible)
                                    Notary Public.
                       My com expires 2/2 of 1909

Applications for Enrollment of Choctaw Newborn
Act of 1905   Volume XV

Muskogee, Indian Territory, March 29, 1905.

Calvin Lewis,
    Kinta, Indian Territory.

Dear Sir:

    Receipt is hereby acknowledged of the affidavits of Mary Sexton and Minervia Hicks to the birth of Porter J. Lewis son of Calvin Lewis and Mary Sexton, September 3, 1903.

    It appears from the affidavits of the mother that she is a citizen by blood of the Choctaw Nation and if this is correct you are requested to state the names of her parents, the names of her other children if any, and such other information as will enable the Commission to identify her upon its records. The matter of the affidavits referred to will then receive further consideration.

                   Respectfully,

                             Chairman.

7-2830

Muskogee, Indian Territory, April 19, 1905.

Calvin Lewis,
    Kinta, Indian Territory.

Dear Sir:

    Receipt is hereby acknowledged of your letter of April 3, 1905 in which you state that your wife Mary Lewis was Mary Sexton, daughter of Okemah and Jack Riddle, and the information contained therein has enabled the Commission to identify her as having been enrolled as a citizen by blood of the Choctaw Nation.

    The affidavits heretofore forwarded to the birth of Porter J. Lewis, son of Calvin Lewis and Mary Sexton September 30, 1903, have been filed with our records as an application for the enrollment of said child.

                   Respectfully,

                             Chairman.

Applications for Enrollment of Choctaw Newborn
Act of 1905   Volume XV

Choc New Born 1065
    Willie Stidham
    (Born Jan. 4, 1903)

BIRTH AFFIDAVIT.

DEPARTMENT OF THE INTERIOR,
COMMISSION TO THE FIVE CIVILIZED TRIBES.

IN RE Application for Enrollment, as a citizen of the   Choctaw   Nation, of   Willie Stidham , born on the 4th day of Jan, 1903

Name of Father: Zachariah Stidham   a citizen of the Choctaw Nation.
Name of Mother: Laura Stidham   a citizen of the undecided ~~Nation.~~

Post-Office: Atlee Ind Ter

AFFIDAVIT OF MOTHER.

UNITED STATES OF AMERICA,
    INDIAN TERRITORY.
Southern   District.

    I,   Laura Stidham , on oath state that I am   30   years of age and a citizen by   Blood , of the U.S. Nation; that I am the lawful wife of   Zachariah Stidham , who is a citizen, by   Blood   of the Choctaw Nation; that a   male   child was born to me on 4th day of Jan, 1903, that said child has been named   Willie Stidham , and is now living.

                                     Laura Stidham

WITNESSES TO MARK:

    Subscribed and sworn to before me this   16th *day of*   March , *1905*.

                                     W.A. Wilson
                                         NOTARY PUBLIC.

Applications for Enrollment of Choctaw Newborn
Act of 1905 Volume XV

AFFIDAVIT OF ATTENDING PHYSICIAN OR MID-WIFE.

UNITED STATES OF AMERICA,
  INDIAN TERRITORY.
  Southern   District.

I, Alice[sic] Driskell[sic], a Female, on oath state that I attended on Mrs. Laura Stidham, wife of Zachariah Stidham on the 4th day of Jan, 1903 ; that there was born to her on said date a male child; that said child is now living and is said to have been named Willie

Allice Driskill

WITNESSES TO MARK:
{

Subscribed and sworn to before me this 21st *day of* March, 1905.

W A Wilson
NOTARY PUBLIC.

Choctaw 248.

Muskogee, Indian Territory, April 20, 1905.

Zachariah Stidham,
  Atlee, Indian Territory.

Dear Sir:

Receipt is hereby acknowledged of the affidavits of Laura Stidham and Allice Driskill to the birth of Willie Stidham, son of Zachariah and Laura Stidham, January 4, 1903, and the same have been filed with our records as an application for the enrollment of said child.

Respectfully,

Chairman.

Choc New Born 1066
  Bassie Robert
  (Born Dec. 15, 1902)

Applications for Enrollment of Choctaw Newborn
Act of 1905 Volume XV

BIRTH AFFIDAVIT.

DEPARTMENT OF THE INTERIOR.
COMMISSION TO THE FIVE CIVILIZED TRIBES.

IN RE APPLICATION FOR ENROLLMENT, as a citizen of the Choctaw Nation, of Bassie Robert, born on the 15 day of Dec, 1902

Name of Father: Daniel Robert   a citizen of the Choctaw Nation.
Name of Mother: Artemissa Robert   a citizen of the Choctaw Nation.

Postoffice Beach I.T.

AFFIDAVIT OF MOTHER.

UNITED STATES OF AMERICA, Indian Territory, }
    Central   DISTRICT. }

I, Artemissa Robert, on oath state that I am 20 years of age and a citizen by Blood, of the Choctaw Nation; that I am the lawful wife of Daniel Robert, who is a citizen, by Blood of the Choctaw Nation; that a female child was born to me on 15 day of Dec, 1902; that said child has been named Bassie Robert, and was living March 4, 1905.

                                              her
                                 Artemissa x Robert
Witnesses To Mark: mark
  { Robinson Jones
    JW Perkins

Subscribed and sworn to before me this 8 day of April, 1905.

                                 C.L. Lester
                                   Notary Public.

AFFIDAVIT OF ATTENDING PHYSICIAN OR MID-WIFE.

UNITED STATES OF AMERICA, Indian Territory, }
    Central   DISTRICT. }

I, Lucinda Bohanon, a mid wife, on oath state that I attended on Mrs. Artemissa Robert, wife of Daniel Robert on the 15 day of Dec, 1902; that there was born to her on said date a female child; that said child was living March 4, 1905, and is said to have been named Bassie Robert

                                       her
                               Lucinda x Bohanon
                                    mark

Applications for Enrollment of Choctaw Newborn
Act of 1905 Volume XV

Witnesses To Mark:
{ Robinson Jones
{ JW Perkins

Subscribed and sworn to before me this 8 day of April , 1905

C.L. Lester
Notary Public.

Choc New Born 1067
Deborah Anderson
(Born Jan. 2, 1904)

BIRTH AFFIDAVIT.

DEPARTMENT OF THE INTERIOR,
COMMISSION TO THE FIVE CIVILIZED TRIBES.

IN RE Application for Enrollment, as a citizen of the Chocktaw[sic] Nation, of Deborah Anderson , born on the 2 day of Jan , 1904

Name of Father: Mack Anderson   a citizen of the Chocktaw Nation.
Name of Mother: Ella Anderson   a citizen of the Chocktaw Nation.

Post-Office: Pontotoc Ind Ter

AFFIDAVIT OF MOTHER.

UNITED STATES OF AMERICA, }
   INDIAN TERRITORY. }
Southern District. }

I, Ella Anderson , on oath state that I am 29 years of age and a citizen by Blood , of the Chocktaw Nation; that I am the lawful wife of Mack Anderson , who is a citizen, by Blood of the Chocktaw Nation; that a Girl child was born to me on 2 day of Jan , 1904 , that said child has been named Deborah Anderson , and is now living.

Ella Anderson

WITNESSES TO MARK:
{
{

Applications for Enrollment of Choctaw Newborn
Act of 1905   Volume XV

Subscribed and sworn to before me this 13   *day of*   Jan   , 1905.

M.S. Bradford
NOTARY PUBLIC.

AFFIDAVIT OF ATTENDING PHYSICIAN OR MID-WIFE.

UNITED STATES OF AMERICA,
 INDIAN TERRITORY.
.... District.

  I,   Dora Whistler   , a mid wife , on oath state that I attended on Mrs.   Ella Anderson   , wife of   Mack Anderson   on the   2   day of Jan   , 1904; that there was born to her on said date a   Girl   child; that said child is now living and is said to have been named   Deborah Anderson

Dora Whistler

WITNESSES TO MARK:

{

Subscribed and sworn to before me this 13   *day of*   Jan   , 1905.

M.S. Bradford
NOTARY PUBLIC.

BIRTH AFFIDAVIT.

DEPARTMENT OF THE INTERIOR.
COMMISSION TO THE FIVE CIVILIZED TRIBES.

  IN RE APPLICATION FOR ENROLLMENT, as a citizen of the   Chocktaw[sic]   Nation, of   Deborah Anderson   , born on the   2   day of   Jan   , 1904

Name of Father: Mack Anderson   a citizen of the   Chocktaw   Nation.
Name of Mother: Ella Anderson   a citizen of the   Chocktaw   Nation.

Postoffice   Connerville I.T.

AFFIDAVIT OF MOTHER.

UNITED STATES OF AMERICA, Indian Territory,
  Southern   **DISTRICT.**

  I,   Ella Anderson   , on oath state that I am   29   years of age and a citizen by   Blood   , of the   Chocktaw   Nation; that I am the lawful wife of   Mack

9

Applications for Enrollment of Choctaw Newborn
Act of 1905 Volume XV

Anderson   , who is a citizen, by Blood   of the   Chocktaw   Nation; that a female   child was born to me on   2   day of   January   , 1904; that said child has been named   Deborah Anderson   , and was living March 4, 1905.

                                                Ella Anderson

Witnesses To Mark:
{

    Subscribed and sworn to before me this 12   day of   April   , 1905

                                         M.S. Bradford
                                         Notary Public.

AFFIDAVIT OF ATTENDING PHYSICIAN OR MID-WIFE.

UNITED STATES OF AMERICA, Indian Territory, }
  Southern   **DISTRICT.**

    I,   Dora Whistler   , a   Mid wife   , on oath state that I attended on Mrs. Ella Anderson   , wife of   Mack Anderson   on the 2   day of   Jan   , 1904; that there was born to her on said date a   female   child; that said child was living March 4, 1905, and is said to have been named Deborah Anderson

                                              Dora Whistler

Witnesses To Mark:
{

    Subscribed and sworn to before me this 12   day of   April   , 1905

                                         M.S. Bradford
                                         Notary Public.

Choc New Born 1068
    Joseph Billy
    (Born July 24, 1904)

Applications for Enrollment of Choctaw Newborn
Act of 1905 Volume XV

BIRTH AFFIDAVIT.

DEPARTMENT OF THE INTERIOR.
COMMISSION TO THE FIVE CIVILIZED TRIBES.

IN RE APPLICATION FOR ENROLLMENT, as a citizen of the Choctaw Nation, of Joseph Billy, born on the 24th day of July, 1904

Name of Father: Wilkin Billy   a citizen of the Choctaw Nation.
Name of Mother: Emily Billy nee Moore   a citizen of the Choctaw Nation.

Postoffice   Goodwater I.T.

AFFIDAVIT OF MOTHER.

UNITED STATES OF AMERICA, Indian Territory,
Central   DISTRICT.

I, Emily Billy, on oath state that I am 21 years of age and a citizen by Blood, of the Choctaw Nation; that I am the lawful wife of Wilkin Billy, who is a citizen, by Blood of the Choctaw Nation; that a male child was born to me on 24th day of July, 1904; that said child has been named Joseph Billy, and was living March 4, 1905.

           her
     Emily x Billy
Witnesses To Mark: mark
   { LG Battiest
     Nelson Kemp

Subscribed and sworn to before me this 10th day of April, 1905

       C.J. Paudlum
          Notary Public.

AFFIDAVIT OF ATTENDING PHYSICIAN OR MID-WIFE.

UNITED STATES OF AMERICA, Indian Territory,
Central   DISTRICT.

I, Yahoke Sampson, a mid-wife, on oath state that I attended on Mrs. Emily Billy, wife of Wilkin Billy on the 24th day of July, 1904; that there was born to her on said date a male child; that said child was living March 4, 1905, and is said to have been named Joseph Billy

           her
    Yahoke x Sampson
        mark

Applications for Enrollment of Choctaw Newborn
Act of 1905   Volume XV

Witnesses To Mark:
- LG Battiest
- Wilkin Billy

Subscribed and sworn to before me this 12th day of April, 1905

C.J. Paudlum
Notary Public.

Choc New Born 1069
  Calvin Hudson
  (Born Feb. 14, 1905)
  Cleo Hudson
  (Born June 28, 1903)

BIRTH AFFIDAVIT.

DEPARTMENT OF THE INTERIOR.
COMMISSION TO THE FIVE CIVILIZED TRIBES.

IN RE APPLICATION FOR ENROLLMENT, as a citizen of the Choctaw Nation, of Calvin Hudson, born on the 14th day of February, 1905

Name of Father: Roar Hudson   a citizen of the Choctaw Nation.
Name of Mother: Alice Hudson   a citizen of the Choctaw Nation.

Postoffice   Eagletown, Ind. Ter.

AFFIDAVIT OF MOTHER.

UNITED STATES OF AMERICA, Indian Territory,
Central DISTRICT.

I, Alice Hudson, on oath state that I am 29 years of age and a citizen by blood, of the Choctaw Nation; that I am the lawful wife of Roar Hudson, who is a citizen, by blood of the Choctaw Nation; that a male child was born to me on 14th day of February, 1905; that said child has been named Calvin Hudson, and was living March 4, 1905.

Alice Hudson

Witnesses To Mark:

Applications for Enrollment of Choctaw Newborn
Act of 1905   Volume XV

Subscribed and sworn to before me this 13th day of   April   , 1905

                        Wirt Franklin
                        Notary Public.

AFFIDAVIT OF ATTENDING PHYSICIAN OR MID-WIFE.

UNITED STATES OF AMERICA, Indian Territory,
  Central   DISTRICT.

I,   Martha Ann Burris   , a mid-wife   , on oath state that I attended on Mrs.   Alice Hudson   , wife of   Roar Hudson   on the 14th day of   February , 1905; that there was born to her on said date a   male   child; that said child was living March 4, 1905, and is said to have been named Calvin Hudson

                        her
                  Martha Ann x Burris
Witnesses To Mark: mark
  { Robert Anderson
    Vester W Rose

Subscribed and sworn to before me this 13th day of   April   , 1905

                        Wirt Franklin
                        Notary Public.

BIRTH AFFIDAVIT.

DEPARTMENT OF THE INTERIOR.
COMMISSION TO THE FIVE CIVILIZED TRIBES.

IN RE APPLICATION FOR ENROLLMENT, as a citizen of the   Choctaw   Nation, of   Cleo Hudson   , born on the 28th   day of   June , 1903

Name of Father: Roar Hudson   a citizen of the   Choctaw   Nation.
Name of Mother: Alice Hudson   a citizen of the   Choctaw   Nation.

                  Postoffice   Eagletown, Ind. Ter.

AFFIDAVIT OF MOTHER.

UNITED STATES OF AMERICA, Indian Territory,
  Central   DISTRICT.

I,   Alice Hudson   , on oath state that I am 29   years of age and a citizen by blood   , of the   Choctaw   Nation; that I am the lawful wife of   Roar Hudson   ,

Applications for Enrollment of Choctaw Newborn
Act of 1905   Volume XV

who is a citizen, by blood   of the   Choctaw   Nation; that a   female   child was born to me on   28th   day of   June   , 1903; that said child has been named Cleo Hudson   , and was living March 4, 1905.

                                            Alice Hudson

Witnesses To Mark:
{

    Subscribed and sworn to before me this 13th   day of   April   , 1905

                                          Wirt Franklin
                                              Notary Public.

AFFIDAVIT OF ATTENDING PHYSICIAN OR MID-WIFE.

UNITED STATES OF AMERICA, Indian Territory, }
  Central   DISTRICT. }

    I,   Lucy Burris   , a   mid-wife   , on oath state that I attended on Mrs.   Alice Hudson   , wife of   Roar Hudson   on the 28th   day of   June , 1903; that there was born to her on said date a   female   child; that said child was living March 4, 1905, and is said to have been named Cleo Hudson

                                            her
                                    Lucy x Burris
Witnesses To Mark: mark
  { Simeon Going
  { H.L. Stiff

    Subscribed and sworn to before me this 29th   day of   April   , 1905

                                        J.W. Costelow
                                            Notary Public.

Applications for Enrollment of Choctaw Newborn
Act of 1905   Volume XV

COMMISSIONERS:
TAMS BIXBY,
THOMAS B. NEEDLES,
C.R. BRECKINRIDGE.

WM. O. BEALL
SECRETARY

DEPARTMENT OF THE INTERIOR
COMMISSION TO THE FIVE CIVILIZED TRIBES

W.H.A.

REFER IN REPLY TO THE FOLLOWING:
7-----675
Roll-1617

ADDRESS ONLY THE
COMMISSION TO THE FIVE CIVILIZED TRIBES.

Atoka, Indian Territory, June 17, 1904.

Roar Hudson,
    Eagletown, Indian Territory.

Dear Sir:

    There is returned herewith Marriage Certificate issued to Allis McCoy and yourself. Certified copies of same having been made and filed with the records of the Commission.

                    Respectfully,
                    Tams Bixby
                      Chairman.

Enc LTM 17/3.

Choc New Born 1070
    John O. Baggett
    (Born March 2, 1903)

BIRTH AFFIDAVIT.

DEPARTMENT OF THE INTERIOR.
COMMISSION TO THE FIVE CIVILIZED TRIBES.

IN RE APPLICATION FOR ENROLLMENT, as a citizen of the   Choctaw   Nation, of John O. Baggett   , born on the 2nd day of M^{ch} , 1903

Name of Father: John L Baggett   a citizen of the   United States
Name of Mother: Mattie Baggett   a citizen of the   Choctaw   Nation.

                Postoffice   Tuskahoma I.T.

Applications for Enrollment of Choctaw Newborn
Act of 1905 Volume XV

AFFIDAVIT OF MOTHER.

UNITED STATES OF AMERICA, Indian Territory,
Central DISTRICT.

I, Mattie Baggett, on oath state that I am 38 years of age and a citizen by blood, of the Choctaw Nation; that I am the lawful wife of John L Baggett, who is a citizen, by —— of the United States Nation; that a male child was born to me on 2nd day of March, 1903; that said child has been named John O. Baggett, and was living March 4, 1905.

                                        Mattie Baggett

Witnesses To Mark:

Subscribed and sworn to before me this 14 day of April, 1905

                                        OL Johnson
                                            Notary Public.

AFFIDAVIT OF ATTENDING PHYSICIAN OR MID-WIFE.

UNITED STATES OF AMERICA, Indian Territory,
Central DISTRICT.

I, Mary Hunter, a midwife, on oath state that I attended on Mrs. Mattie Baggett, wife of John Baggett on the 2nd day of March, 1903; that there was born to her on said date a male child; that said child was living March 4, 1905, and is said to have been named John O Baggett

                                        her
                                Mary x Hunter
Witnesses To Mark: mark
   Albert Myrick
   Price Self

Subscribed and sworn to before me this 13 day of April, 1905

                                       Chas W Self
                                         Notary Public.

Applications for Enrollment of Choctaw Newborn
Act of 1905   Volume XV

Choc New Born 1071
    Cicero Spring
    (Born Dec. 23, 1903)

NEW-BORN AFFIDAVIT.

Number..............

Choctaw Enrolling Commission.

IN THE MATTER OF THE APPLICATION FOR ENROLLMENT, as a citizen of the Choctaw   Nation, of   Cicero Spring

born on the   23rd day of   Dec   190 3

Name of father   Joel Spring   a citizen of   Choctaw Nation final enrollment No   3874
Name of mother   Winnie R Spring   a citizen of   Choctaw Nation final enrollment No   3875

Postoffice   Hugo Ind Ter

AFFIDAVIT OF MOTHER.

UNITED STATES OF AMERICA, ⎫
   INDIAN TERRITORY,   ⎬
  Central   DISTRICT   ⎭

I   Winnie R. Spring   on oath state that I am   37   years of age and a citizen by   Blood   of the   Choctaw   Nation, and as such have been placed upon the final roll of the   Choctaw   Nation, by the Honorable Secretary of the Interior my final enrollment number being   3875   ; that I am the lawful wife of   Joel Spring   , who is a citizen of the   Choctaw   Nation, and as such has been placed upon the final roll of said Nation by the Honorable Secretary of the Interior, his final enrollment number being   3874   and that a   male   child was born to me on the   23rd day of   Dec   190 3 ; that said child has been named   Cicero Spring   , and is now living.

                                                      her
                                           Winnie x R Spring

WITNESSETH: mark

  Must be two   ⎫   Sue Denison
  Witnesses who   ⎬
  are Citizens.   ⎭   Henry Spring

Subscribed and sworn to before me this   19   day of   Jan   190 5

                                            Chas G. Shull
                                                  Notary Public.

My commission expires   Dec - 14 - 1906

Applications for Enrollment of Choctaw Newborn
Act of 1905   Volume XV

Affidavit of Attending Physician or Midwife

UNITED STATES OF AMERICA, }
INDIAN TERRITORY,
Central   DISTRICT

I, Mary Brown   a   Mid Wife   on oath state that I attended on Mrs. Winnie Spring   wife of Joel Spring on the 23 day of December, 190 3, that there was born to her on said date a male child, that said child is now living, and is said to have been named Cicero Spring

Mary Brown   M. D.

Subscribed and sworn to before me this the   18   day of   January   1905

James Bower
Notary Public.

WITNESSETH:
Must be two witnesses who are citizens and know the child.
{ Sue Denison
  Henry Spring

We hereby certify that we are well acquainted with   Mary Brown   a   Midwife   and know   her   to be reputable and of good standing in the community.

Must be two citizen witnesses.
{ Sue Denison
  Henry Spring

BIRTH AFFIDAVIT.

DEPARTMENT OF THE INTERIOR.
COMMISSION TO THE FIVE CIVILIZED TRIBES.

IN RE APPLICATION FOR ENROLLMENT, as a citizen of the   Choctaw   Nation, of Cicero Spring, born on the 23^d day of December, 1903

Name of Father: Joel Spring   a citizen of the Choctaw Nation.
Name of Mother: Winnie R. Spring   a citizen of the Choctaw Nation.

Postoffice   Hugo Ind. Ter.

Applications for Enrollment of Choctaw Newborn
Act of 1905 Volume XV

AFFIDAVIT OF MOTHER.

UNITED STATES OF AMERICA, Indian Territory, }
    Central   DISTRICT. }

    I, Winnie R. Spring, on oath state that I am 37 years of age and a citizen by blood, of the Choctaw Nation; that I am the lawful wife of Joel Spring, who is a citizen, by blood of the Choctaw Nation; that a male child was born to me on 23^d day of December, 1903; that said child has been named Cicero Spring, and was living March 4, 1905.

                                              her
                                  Winnie R x Spring
Witnesses To Mark: mark
{ Joel Spring Jr
  A. A. McDonald

    Subscribed and sworn to before me this 17 day of April, 1905

                                    A. A. McDonald
                                    Notary Public.

AFFIDAVIT OF ATTENDING PHYSICIAN OR MID-WIFE.

UNITED STATES OF AMERICA, Indian Territory, }
    Central   DISTRICT. }

    I, G.B. Green M.D., a Physician, on oath state that I attended on Mrs. Winnie R Spring, wife of Joel Spring on the 23^d day of December, 1903; that there was born to her on said date a male child; that said child was living March 4, 1905, and is said to have been named Cicero Spring

                                  G.B. Green M.D.
Witnesses To Mark:

{

    Subscribed and sworn to before me this 17th day of April, 1905

                                    Wirt Franklin
                                    Notary Public.

Applications for Enrollment of Choctaw Newborn
Act of 1905   Volume XV

7-NB-1071

Muskogee, Indian Territory, July 27, 1905.

Joel Spring,
    Hugo, Indian Territory.

Dear Sir:

Receipt is hereby acknowledged of your letter of July 22, 1905, asking if your child Cisero[sic] Spring has been approved.

In reply to your letter you are advised that the name of your child Cicero Spring has been placed upon a schedule of citizens by blood of the Choctaw Nation which has been forwarded the Secretary of the Interior and you will be notified when his enrollment is approved by the Department.

Respectfully,

Commissioner.

Choc New Born 1072
    Solomon Homer
    (Born March 10, 1904)

BIRTH AFFIDAVIT.

DEPARTMENT OF THE INTERIOR.
COMMISSION TO THE FIVE CIVILIZED TRIBES.

IN RE APPLICATION FOR ENROLLMENT, as a citizen of the Choctaw Nation, of Solomon Homer, born on the 10th day of March, 1904

Name of Father: Silan Homer   a citizen of the Choctaw Nation.
Name of Mother: Sissie Homer   a citizen of the Choctaw Nation.

Postoffice   Soper, Ind. Ter.

Applications for Enrollment of Choctaw Newborn
Act of 1905   Volume XV

AFFIDAVIT OF MOTHER.

UNITED STATES OF AMERICA, Indian Territory, }
  Central   DISTRICT.

    I, Sissie Homer, on oath state that I am about 35 years of age and a citizen by blood, of the Choctaw Nation; that I am the lawful wife of Silan Homer, who is a citizen, by blood of the Choctaw Nation; that a male child was born to me on 10th day of March, 1904; that said child has been named Solomon Homer, and was living March 4, 1905.

                            her
                        Sissie x Homer
Witnesses To Mark: mark
  { Robert Anderson
    Vester W. Rose

    Subscribed and sworn to before me this 17th day of April, 1905

                        Wirt Franklin
                        Notary Public.

AFFIDAVIT OF ATTENDING PHYSICIAN OR MID-WIFE.

UNITED STATES OF AMERICA, Indian Territory, }
  Central   DISTRICT.

    I, Lina Hotinlubbee, a mid-wife, on oath state that I attended on Mrs. Sissie Homer, wife of Silan Homer on the 10th day of March, 1904; that there was born to her on said date a male child; that said child was living March 4, 1905, and is said to have been named Solomon Homer

                        her
                      Lina x Hotinlubbee
Witnesses To Mark: mark
  { Robert Anderson
    Vester W. Rose

    Subscribed and sworn to before me this 17th day of April, 1905

                        Wirt Franklin
                        Notary Public.

Applications for Enrollment of Choctaw Newborn
Act of 1905   Volume XV

Choc New Born 1073
    James Nelson
    (Born Sept. 6, 1903)

(The affidavit below typed as given.)

Indian Territory   }   In matter of enrollment of
Central District   James Nelson

We   J.D. Brown and B A Nelson   do hereby certify that James Nelson was born to Isaac Nelson & wife Emma Nelson on Sept 6th 1903, That said child was living on Mch 4th 1905 and is living yet. That Emma Nelson, Indian Territory deceased was said childs mother; That we are disinterest parties hereto and are not in any way related to the parties herein above mentioned.

    Witness my hand this the 9th day of June A. D. 1905

                                      B A Nelson

                                      J D Brown

    Subscribed & sworn to before me this the _____ day June A. D. 1905.

                                      C W Hill
                                            Notary Public.

BIRTH AFFIDAVIT.
DEPARTMENT OF THE INTERIOR.
COMMISSION TO THE FIVE CIVILIZED TRIBES.

IN RE APPLICATION FOR ENROLLMENT, as a citizen of the   Choctaw   Nation, of James Nelson   , born on the   6   day of   Sept   , 1903

Name of Father: Isaac Nelson   a citizen of the   Choctaw   Nation.
Name of Mother: Emma Nelson   a citizen of the   Nation.

                            Postoffice   Grant I.T.

Applications for Enrollment of Choctaw Newborn
Act of 1905   Volume XV

AFFIDAVIT OF ATTENDING PHYSICIAN OR MID-WIFE.

UNITED STATES OF AMERICA, Indian Territory,　}
　　Central　　　　　　　　　DISTRICT.

　　　I,　J D Brown　　, a　physician　, on oath state that I attended on Mrs.　Emma Nelson　, wife of　Isaac Nelson　on the 6　day of　Sept　, 1903; that there was born to her on said date a　male　child; that said child was living March 4, 1905, and is said to have been named　James Nelson

　　　　　　　　　　　　　　　　　　J.D. Brown, M.D.
Witnesses To Mark:
{

　　　Subscribed and sworn to before me this　15th　day of　April　, 1905

　　　　　　　　　　　　　　　　CW Hill
　　　　　　　　　　　　　　　　　　Notary Public.

　　　　　　　　　　　　　　　　　　　　　　　7--NB--1073

　　　　　　　Muskogee, Indian Territory, June 2, 1905.

Isaac Nelson,
　　　Grant, Indian Territory.

Dear Sir:

　　　Referring to the application for the enrollment of your infant child, James Nelson, born September 6, 1903, it is noted from the affidavits heretofore filed in this office that the mother of the child is dead.

　　　In this event it will be necessary that the affidavits of two persons, who are disinterested and not related to the applicant, who have actual knowledge of the facts that the child was born, the date of his birth; that he was living on March 4, 1905, and that Emma Nelson was his mother be filed with the Commission.

　　　This matter should receive your immediate attention as no further action can be taken relative to the enrollment of this child until the Commission has been furnished these affidavits.

　　　　　　　　　Respectfully,

　　　　　　　　　　　　　　　　　　　　　　　[sic]

Applications for Enrollment of Choctaw Newborn
Act of 1905   Volume XV

7 NB 1073

Muskogee, Indian Territory, June 14, 1905

Isaac Nelson,
    Grant, Indian Territory.

Dear Sir:

Receipt is hereby acknowledged of the joint affidavit of B. A. Nelson and J. D. Brown to the birth of James Nelson, son of Isaac and Emma Nelson, September 6, 1903, and the same have been filed in the matter of the enrollment of said child.

Respectfully,

Chairman.

Choc New Born 1074
    Elbert Homer Loring
    (Born May 28, 1904)

NEW-BORN AFFIDAVIT.

Number............

Choctaw Enrolling Commission.

IN THE MATTER OF THE APPLICATION FOR ENROLLMENT, as a citizen of the Choctaw   Nation, of   Albert Homer Loring

born on the   28th   day of   May   190 4

Name of father   William H. Loring   a citizen of   Choctaw
Nation final enrollment No   4594
Name of mother   Sallie Loring   a citizen of ....
Nation final enrollment No ....

Postoffice   Bennington I T

Applications for Enrollment of Choctaw Newborn
Act of 1905 Volume XV

AFFIDAVIT OF MOTHER.

UNITED STATES OF AMERICA,
INDIAN TERRITORY,
Central   DISTRICT

  I   Sallie Loring   on oath state that I am 34 years of age and a citizen by Blood of the Choctaw Nation, and as such have been placed upon the final roll of the Choctaw Nation, by the Honorable Secretary of the Interior my final enrollment number being .... ; that I am the lawful wife of William H Loring , who is a citizen of the Choctaw Nation, and as such has been placed upon the final roll of said Nation by the Honorable Secretary of the Interior, his final enrollment number being 4594 and that a male child was born to me on the 28th day of May 190 4 ; that said child has been named Albert Homer Loring , and is now living.

                 Sallie Loring

WITNESSETH:
 Must be two Witnesses who are Citizens.   W F Durant
         Frank Lacey

  Subscribed and sworn to before me this   18   day of   Jan   190 5

               W. A. Shoney
                  Notary Public.

My commission expires   Jan 10, 1909

Affidavit of Attending Physician or Midwife

UNITED STATES OF AMERICA,
INDIAN TERRITORY,
Central   DISTRICT

  I, Dr. J. H. Hargave[sic]   a   Physician on oath state that I attended on Mrs. Sallie Loring wife of William H Loring on the 28th day of May , 190 4, that there was born to her on said date a male child, that said child is now living, and is said to have been named Albert Homer Loring

            J.H. Hargrave   M. D.

  Subscribed and sworn to before me this the   27   day of   January   1905

             J.C. Parker
                Notary Public.

WITNESSETH:
 Must be two witnesses who are citizens and know the child.   (Name Illegible)
         Ross Frazier

Applications for Enrollment of Choctaw Newborn
Act of 1905   Volume XV

We hereby certify that we are well acquainted with   Dr J.H. Hargave   a   Physician   and know   him   to be reputable and of good standing in the community.

Must be two citizen witnesses. { Frank Lacey / W.F. Durant

BIRTH AFFIDAVIT.

DEPARTMENT OF THE INTERIOR.
COMMISSION TO THE FIVE CIVILIZED TRIBES.

IN RE APPLICATION FOR ENROLLMENT, as a citizen of the   Choctaw   Nation, of   Elbert Homer Loring   , born on the 28th day of   May   , 1904

Name of Father: William H. Loring   a citizen of the   Choctaw   Nation.
(by marriage)
Name of Mother: Sallie Loring   a citizen of the   Choctaw   Nation.

Postoffice   Bennington I.T.

AFFIDAVIT OF MOTHER.

UNITED STATES OF AMERICA, Indian Territory,
   Cent   DISTRICT.

I,   Sallie Loring   , on oath state that I am   30   years of age and a citizen by ...., of the .... Nation; that I am the lawful wife of   William H Loring   , who is a citizen, by blood   of the   Choctaw   Nation; that a male   child was born to me on   28th day of   May   , 1904; that said child has been named   Elbert Homer Loring   , and was living March 4, 1905.

                              Sallie Loring

Witnesses To Mark:
{

Subscribed and sworn to before me this   10th   day of   April   , 1905

                              B.W. Williams
                                 Notary Public.

Applications for Enrollment of Choctaw Newborn
Act of 1905   Volume XV

AFFIDAVIT OF ATTENDING PHYSICIAN OR MID-WIFE.

UNITED STATES OF AMERICA, Indian Territory, }
Cent   DISTRICT.

I, R.M. Parish, a Physician, on oath state that I attended on Mrs. Sallie Loring, wife of William H Loring on the 28th day of May, 1904; that there was born to her on said date a _____ child; that said child was living March 4, 1905, and is said to have been named Elbert Homer Loring

R M Parish

Witnesses To Mark:
{

Subscribed and sworn to before me this 10th day of April, 1905

B.W. Williams
Notary Public.

Choc New Born 1075
Bertie May Stiles
(Born Aug 31, 1904)

BIRTH AFFIDAVIT.

DEPARTMENT OF THE INTERIOR.
COMMISSION TO THE FIVE CIVILIZED TRIBES.

IN RE APPLICATION FOR ENROLLMENT, as a citizen of the Choctaw Nation, of Bertie May Stiles, born on the 31 day of August, 1904

Name of Father: H.R. Stiles   a citizen of the United States Nation.
Name of Mother: Ara D. Stiles nee Folsom   a citizen of the Choctaw Nation.

Postoffice   Edwards, I.T.

Applications for Enrollment of Choctaw Newborn
Act of 1905   Volume XV

AFFIDAVIT OF MOTHER.

UNITED STATES OF AMERICA, Indian Territory, }
Central   DISTRICT.

I, Ara D. Stiles, on oath state that I am 16 years of age and a citizen by blood, of the Choctaw Nation; that I am the lawful wife of H.R. Stiles, who is a citizen, by —— of the United States ~~Nation~~; that a female child was born to me on 31st day of August, 1904; that said child has been named Bertie May Stiles, and was living March 4, 1905.

Ara D Stiles

Witnesses To Mark:

Subscribed and sworn to before me this 7th day of April, 1905

W.H. Angell
Notary Public.

AFFIDAVIT OF ATTENDING PHYSICIAN OR MID-WIFE.

UNITED STATES OF AMERICA, Indian Territory, }
Central   DISTRICT.

I, Laura Rushing, a midwife, on oath state that I attended on Mrs. Ara D. Stiles, wife of H.R. Stiles on the 31st day of August, 1904; that there was born to her on said date a female child; that said child was living March 4, 1905, and is said to have been named Bertie May Stiles

Laura Rushing

Witnesses To Mark:

Subscribed and sworn to before me this 7th day of April, 1905

W.H. Angell
Notary Public.

Applications for Enrollment of Choctaw Newborn
Act of 1905 Volume XV

7-NB-1075.

Muskogee, Indian Territory, June 1, 1905.

W. H. Angell,
    Choctaw Land Office,
        Atoka, Indian Territory.

Dear Sir:

    There is enclosed herewith application for the enrollment of Bertie May Stiles.

    In the affidavit of the midwife, which was executed by you, the date of the applicant's birth is given as August 31, 1905, which is apparently an error. You will please correct this affidavit and return it to this office.

                Respectfully,

VR 1-4.   Chairman.

Choc New Born 1076
    Julia Lee Spring
    (Born Sept. 28, 1904)

BIRTH AFFIDAVIT.
DEPARTMENT OF THE INTERIOR.
COMMISSION TO THE FIVE CIVILIZED TRIBES.

    IN RE APPLICATION FOR ENROLLMENT, as a citizen of the Choctaw Nation, of Julia Lee Spring, born on the 28th day of Sept, 1904

Name of Father: Willie Spring   a citizen of the Choctaw Nation.
Name of Mother: Hattie Spring   a citizen of the Choctaw Nation.

                Postoffice   Hugo, Ind. Ter.

Applications for Enrollment of Choctaw Newborn
Act of 1905   Volume XV

AFFIDAVIT OF MOTHER.

UNITED STATES OF AMERICA, Indian Territory,
Central   DISTRICT.

    I, Hattie Spring, on oath state that I am 38 years of age and a citizen by marriage, of the Choctaw Nation; that I am the lawful wife of Willie Spring, who is a citizen, by blood of the Choctaw Nation; that a female child was born to me on 28th day of September, 1904; that said child has been named Julia Lee Spring, and was living March 4, 1905.

                                 Hattie Spring

Witnesses To Mark:

    Subscribed and sworn to before me this 17th day of April, 1905

                                Wirt Franklin
                                   Notary Public.

AFFIDAVIT OF ATTENDING PHYSICIAN OR MID-WIFE.

UNITED STATES OF AMERICA, Indian Territory,
Central   DISTRICT.

    I, T.W. Simmons, a physician, on oath state that I attended on Mrs. Hattie Spring, wife of Willie Spring on the 28th day of September, 1904; that there was born to her on said date a female child; that said child was living March 4, 1905, and is said to have been named Julia Lee Spring

                                 Thos W Simmons M.D.

Witnesses To Mark:

    Subscribed and sworn to before me this 17th day of April, 1905

                                Wirt Franklin
                                   Notary Public.

Applications for Enrollment of Choctaw Newborn
Act of 1905   Volume XV

NEW-BORN AFFIDAVIT.

Number............

...Choctaw Enrolling Commission...

IN THE MATTER OF THE APPLICATION FOR ENROLLMENT, as a citizen of the Choctaw   Nation, of   Julia Lee Spring

born on the 28th day of September 190 4

Name of father   Willie Spring   a citizen of   Choctaw
Nation final enrollment No. 4229
Name of mother   Hattie Spring   a citizen of   Choctaw
Nation final enrollment No. 76

Postoffice   Hugo, I.T.

AFFIDAVIT OF MOTHER.

UNITED STATES OF AMERICA
INDIAN TERRITORY
Central   DISTRICT

I   Hattie Spring   , on oath state that I am 38   years of age and a citizen by Interm   of the   Choctaw   Nation, and as such have been placed upon the final roll of the   Choctaw   Nation, by the Honorable Secretary of the Interior my final enrollment number being   76 ; that I am the lawful wife of   Willie Spring   , who is a citizen of the   Choctaw   Nation, and as such has been placed upon the final roll of said Nation by the Honorable Secretary of the Interior, his final enrollment number being   4229   and that a   female   child was born to me on the 28   day of   September   190 4; that said child has been named   Julia Lee Spring   , and is now living.

Hattie Spring

Witnesseth.

Must be two ⎫   Tom Griggs, Jr
Witnesses who ⎬
are Citizens. ⎭   Chas E Bearden

Subscribed and sworn to before me this   11   day of   Feby   190 5

(Name Illegible)
Notary Public.

My commission expires: Oct - 8 - 08

Applications for Enrollment of Choctaw Newborn
Act of 1905   Volume XV

AFFIDAVIT OF ATTENDING PHYSICIAN OR MIDWIFE

UNITED STATES OF AMERICA
INDIAN TERRITORY
  Central   DISTRICT

I, T.W. Simmons   a   Practicing Physician on oath state that I attended on Mrs. Hattie Spring   wife of   Willie Spring on the 28 day of September, 190 4, that there was born to her on said date a   female child, that said child is now living, and is said to have been named   Julia Lee Spring

Thos W Simmons   M.D.

WITNESSETH:
Must be two witnesses who are citizens and know the child.
  John McIntosh
  Chas E Bearden

Subscribed and sworn to before me this, the   11th   day of Feby   190 5

(Name Illegible)   Notary Public.

We hereby certify that we are well acquainted with   Thos W Simmons a   Practicing Physician   and know   him   to be reputable and of good standing in the community.

  John McIntosh
  Cha E Bearden

Choc New Born 1077
  Beulah Bell[sic] Bearden
  (Born Nov. 12, 1903)

Applications for Enrollment of Choctaw Newborn
Act of 1905   Volume XV

NEW-BORN AFFIDAVIT.

Number..............

Choctaw Enrolling Commission.

IN THE MATTER OF THE APPLICATION FOR ENROLLMENT, as a citizen of the Choctaw Nation, of Beulah Belle Bearden

born on the 12 day of November 190 3

Name of father Chas. E. Bearden   a citizen of   Choctaw Intermarried
Nation final enrollment No 233
Name of mother Bessie Bearden   a citizen of   Choctaw
Nation final enrollment No 4020

Postoffice Grant I.T.

AFFIDAVIT OF MOTHER.

UNITED STATES OF AMERICA,
  INDIAN TERRITORY,
  Central   DISTRICT

I Bessie Bearden on oath state that I am 25 years of age and a citizen by Blood of the Choctaw Nation, and as such have been placed upon the final roll of the Choctaw Nation, by the Honorable Secretary of the Interior my final enrollment number being 4020 ; that I am the lawful wife of Chas E. Bearden , who is a citizen of the Choctaw Nation, and as such has been placed upon the final roll of said Nation by the Honorable Secretary of the Interior, his final enrollment number being 233 and that a Female child was born to me on the 12 day of November 190 3 ; that said child has been named Beulah Belle Bearden , and is now living.

Bessie Bearden

WITNESSETH:
  Must be two Witnesses who are Citizens.   L E Oakes
                                             Joseph Collins

Subscribed and sworn to before me this 19 day of Jany 190 5

J.P. Ward
Notary Public.

My commission expires April 28/08

Applications for Enrollment of Choctaw Newborn
Act of 1905 Volume XV

Affidavit of Attending Physician or Midwife

UNITED STATES OF AMERICA,
INDIAN TERRITORY,
Central DISTRICT

I, Martha J Jeffreys   a   Mid wife on oath state that I attended on Mrs. Bessie Bearden   wife of   Chas E Bearden on the   12   day of   November , 190 3, that there was born to her on said date a   Female child, that said child is now living, and is said to have been named   Beulah Belle Bearden

Martha J Jeffreys   ~~M. D.~~ *midwife*

Subscribed and sworn to before me this the   19   day of   Jany   1905

J.P. Ward
Notary Public.

WITNESSETH:
Must be two witnesses who are citizens and know the child.   { L E Oakes
Joseph Collins

We hereby certify that we are well acquainted with   Martha J Jeffreys   a   Mid wife   and know   her   to be reputable and of good standing in the community.

Must be two citizen witnesses.   { L E Oakes
Joseph Collins

BIRTH AFFIDAVIT.

DEPARTMENT OF THE INTERIOR.
COMMISSION TO THE FIVE CIVILIZED TRIBES.

IN RE APPLICATION FOR ENROLLMENT, as a citizen of the   Choctaw   Nation, of Beulah Belle Bearden   , born on the   12th   day of   November , 1903

Name of Father: Chas E Bearden   a citizen of the   Choctaw   Nation.
Name of Mother: Bessie Bearden   a citizen of the   Choctaw   Nation.

Postoffice   Hugo, Ind. Ter.

Applications for Enrollment of Choctaw Newborn
Act of 1905   Volume XV

AFFIDAVIT OF MOTHER.

UNITED STATES OF AMERICA, Indian Territory, }
Central   DISTRICT.

I,   Bessie Bearden   , on oath state that I am   24   years of age and a citizen by   blood   , of the   Choctaw   Nation; that I am the lawful wife of   Chas E. Bearden   , who is a citizen, by marriage   of the   Choctaw   Nation; that a female   child was born to me on   12th   day of   November   , 1903; that said child has been named   Beulah Belle Bearden   , and was living March 4, 1905.

Bessie Bearden

Witnesses To Mark:
{

Subscribed and sworn to before me this   17th   day of   April   , 1905

Wirt Franklin
Notary Public.

AFFIDAVIT OF ATTENDING PHYSICIAN OR MID-WIFE.

UNITED STATES OF AMERICA, Indian Territory, }
Central   DISTRICT.

I,   Martha J Jeffreys   , a   mid-wife   , on oath state that I attended on Mrs.   Bessie Bearden   , wife of   Chas E Bearden   on the   12th day of November   , 1903; that there was born to her on said date a   female   child; that said child was living March 4, 1905, and is said to have been named   Beulah Belle Bearden

Martha J Jeffreys

Witnesses To Mark:
{

Subscribed and sworn to before me this   17th   day of   April   , 1905

Wirt Franklin
Notary Public.

Applications for Enrollment of Choctaw Newborn
Act of 1905   Volume XV

Choc New Born 1078
    Martha Ellen Oakes
    Born Sept. 3, 1903

BIRTH AFFIDAVIT.

DEPARTMENT OF THE INTERIOR.
COMMISSION TO THE FIVE CIVILIZED TRIBES.

IN RE APPLICATION FOR ENROLLMENT, as a citizen of the   Choctaw   Nation, of Martha Ellen Oakes   , born on the 3rd day of Sept , 1903

Name of Father: Charles D. Oakes   a citizen of the   Choctaw   Nation.
Name of Mother: Margaret A Oakes   a citizen of the   Choctaw   Nation.

               Postoffice   Grant, Ind. Ter.

AFFIDAVIT OF MOTHER.

UNITED STATES OF AMERICA, Indian Territory, }
    Central   DISTRICT.   }

    I,   Margaret A. Oakes   , on oath state that I am 38 years of age and a citizen by   marriage   , of the   Choctaw   Nation; that I am the lawful wife of Charles D. Oakes   , who is a citizen, by blood   of the   Choctaw   Nation; that a   female   child was born to me on 3rd   day of September , 1903; that said child has been named   Martha Ellen Oakes   , and was living March 4, 1905.

                                    Margaret Oakes
Witnesses To Mark:

    Subscribed and sworn to before me this 17th day of   April   , 1905

                                Wirt Franklin
                                Notary Public.

AFFIDAVIT OF ATTENDING PHYSICIAN OR MID-WIFE.

UNITED STATES OF AMERICA, Indian Territory, }
    Central   DISTRICT.   }

    I,   Rosie Oakes   , a   mid-wife   , on oath state that I attended on Mrs.   Margaret A. Oakes   , wife of   Charles D. Oakes   on the   3rd day of

Applications for Enrollment of Choctaw Newborn
Act of 1905   Volume XV

September   , 1903; that there was born to her on said date a   female   child; that said child was living March 4, 1905, and is said to have been named Martha Ellen Oakes

Rosie Oakes

Witnesses To Mark:
{

    Subscribed and sworn to before me this 17th day of   April   , 1905

Wirt Franklin
Notary Public.

Choc New Born 1079
    George Sanders
    (Born Sept. 21, 1904)

Affidavit of Attending Physician or Midwife

UNITED STATES OF AMERICA,
    INDIAN TERRITORY,
  Central   DISTRICT

    I, Lena Fulsom   a   Mid-wife
on oath state that I attended on Mrs. Susan Willis   wife of   Robert Sanders
on the 21st   day of Sept , 190 4, that there was born to her on said date a   male   child, that said child is now living, and is said to have been named   George Sanders

her
Lena x Fulsom   M. D.
mark

Subscribed and sworn to before me this the   18th   day of   Jan   1905

W.E. Larecy
Notary Public.

WITNESSETH:
  Must be two witnesses { Joseph Cole
  who are citizens and
  know the child.   J O Nail

Applications for Enrollment of Choctaw Newborn
Act of 1905   Volume XV

We hereby certify that we are well acquainted with   Lena Fulsom a   Mid-wife   and know   her   to be reputable and of good standing in the community.

        Must be two citizen { J O Nail
        witnesses.   { Joseph Cole

BIRTH AFFIDAVIT.

DEPARTMENT OF THE INTERIOR.
COMMISSION TO THE FIVE CIVILIZED TRIBES.

IN RE APPLICATION FOR ENROLLMENT, as a citizen of the   Choctaw   Nation, of   George Sanders   , born on the 21st day of Sept , 1904

Name of Father: Robert Sanders   a citizen of the Choctaw Nation.
Name of Mother: Susan Sanders   a citizen of the Choctaw Nation.

      Postoffice   Soper, Ind. Ter.

AFFIDAVIT OF MOTHER.

UNITED STATES OF AMERICA, Indian Territory, }
   Central   DISTRICT. }

I, Susan Sanders , on oath state that I am about 35 years of age and a citizen by   blood , of the   Choctaw   Nation; that I am the lawful wife of Robert Sanders , who is a citizen, by blood   of the   Choctaw   Nation; that a   male   child was born to me on 21st   day of   September , 1904; that said child has been named George Sanders , and was living March 4, 1905.

                her
        Susan x Sanders
Witnesses To Mark: mark
  { Robert Anderson
  { Vester W. Rose

Subscribed and sworn to before me this 17th day of   April   , 1905

                Wirt Franklin
                Notary Public.

Applications for Enrollment of Choctaw Newborn
Act of 1905   Volume XV

AFFIDAVIT OF ATTENDING PHYSICIAN OR MID-WIFE.

UNITED STATES OF AMERICA, Indian Territory,
Central   DISTRICT.

I, Lena Folsom[sic] , a mid-wife , on oath state that I attended on Mrs. Susan Sanders , wife of Robert Sanders on the 21st day of September , 1904; that there was born to her on said date a male child; that said child was living March 4, 1905, and is said to have been named George Sanders

             her
           Lena x Folsom
Witnesses To Mark: mark
 { Robert Anderson
   Vester W. Rose

Subscribed and sworn to before me this 17th day of April , 1905

          Wirt Franklin
           Notary Public.

NEW-BORN AFFIDAVIT.

     Number............

Choctaw Enrolling Commission.

IN THE MATTER OF THE APPLICATION FOR ENROLLMENT, as a citizen of the Choctaw Nation, of George Sanders

born on the 21st day of September 190 4

Name of father   Robert Sanders   a citizen of   Choctaw
Nation final enrollment No 10902
Name of mother   Susan Willis   a citizen of   Choctaw
Nation final enrollment No 5021

       Postoffice   Soper

AFFIDAVIT OF MOTHER.

UNITED STATES OF AMERICA,
 INDIAN TERRITORY,
 Central   DISTRICT

I   Susan Willis   on oath state that I am 21 years of age and a citizen by Blood of the Choctaw Nation, and as such have been placed upon the final roll of the Choctaw Nation, by the Honorable Secretary of the Interior my final enrollment number being 5021 ; that I am the lawful

39

Applications for Enrollment of Choctaw Newborn
Act of 1905   Volume XV

wife of   Robert Sanders   , who is a citizen of the   Choctaw   Nation, and as such has been placed upon the final roll of said Nation by the Honorable Secretary of the Interior, his final enrollment number being   10902   and that a   Male   child was born to me on the   21st   day of   September   190 4 ; that said child has been named   George Sanders   , and is now living.

Susan x Willis (her mark)

WITNESSETH:
Must be two Witnesses who are Citizens.   } Joseph Cole
                                              J O Nail

Subscribed and sworn to before me this   18   day of   Jan   190 5

WE Larecy
Notary Public.

My commission expires   July 9th 1908

7-NB-1079

Muskogee, Indian Territory, July 10, 1905.

Robert Sanders,
    Soper, Indian Territory.

Dear Sir:

   Receipt is hereby acknowledged of your letter of July 4, 1905, asking if your child George Sanders has been approved.

   In reply to your letter you are advised that the name of your son George Sanders has been placed upon a schedule of citizens by blood of the Choctaw Nation which has been prepared for forwarding to the Secretary of the Interior but this office has not yet been advised of Departmental action thereon.

   You will be advised when his enrollment has been approved by the Secretary of the Interior.

Respectfully,

Commissioner.

Applications for Enrollment of Choctaw Newborn
Act of 1905   Volume XV

Choc New Born 1080
    Sweeney Folsom
    (Born Feb. 2, 1905)

BIRTH AFFIDAVIT.

DEPARTMENT OF THE INTERIOR.
COMMISSION TO THE FIVE CIVILIZED TRIBES.

IN RE APPLICATION FOR ENROLLMENT, as a citizen of the Choctaw Nation, of Sweeney Folsom, born on the 2nd day of February, 1905

Name of Father: Sim Folsom   a citizen of the Choctaw Nation.
Name of Mother: Lena Folsom   a citizen of the Choctaw Nation.

Postoffice   Soper, Ind. Ter.

AFFIDAVIT OF MOTHER.

UNITED STATES OF AMERICA, Indian Territory,
Central   DISTRICT.

    I, Lena Folsom, on oath state that I am about 30 years of age and a citizen by blood, of the Choctaw Nation; that I am the lawful wife of Sim Folsom, who is a citizen, by blood of the Choctaw Nation; that a male child was born to me on 2nd day of February, 1905; that said child has been named Sweeney Folsom, and was living March 4, 1905.

                                      her
                              Lena x Folsom
Witnesses To Mark: mark
    Robert Anderson
    Vester W Rose

    Subscribed and sworn to before me this 17th day of April, 1905

                            Wirt Franklin
                                Notary Public.

Applications for Enrollment of Choctaw Newborn
Act of 1905   Volume XV

AFFIDAVIT OF ATTENDING PHYSICIAN OR MID-WIFE.

UNITED STATES OF AMERICA, Indian Territory,
Central   DISTRICT.

I, Susan Sanders, a mid-wife, on oath state that I attended on Mrs. Lena Folsom, wife of Sim Folsom on the 2nd day of February, 1905; that there was born to her on said date a male child; that said child was living March 4, 1905, and is said to have been named Sweeney Folsom

                               her
                        Susan x Sanders
Witnesses To Mark: mark
  { Robert Anderson
    Vester W Rose

Subscribed and sworn to before me this 17th day of April, 1905

                        Wirt Franklin
                        Notary Public.

Choc New Born 1081
    Davis Wesley
    (Born Nov. 24, 1903)

NEW-BORN AFFIDAVIT.

    Number............

...Choctaw Enrolling Commission...

IN THE MATTER OF THE APPLICATION FOR ENROLLMENT, as a citizen of the Choctaw Nation, of Davis Wesley

born on the 24 day of November 190 3

Name of father Joseph Wesley   a citizen of Choctaw
Nation final enrollment No. 3110
Name of mother Eliza Wesley   a citizen of Choctaw
Nation final enrollment No. 3111

                        Postoffice   Fort Towson, I.T.

Applications for Enrollment of Choctaw Newborn
Act of 1905   Volume XV

AFFIDAVIT OF MOTHER.

UNITED STATES OF AMERICA
INDIAN TERRITORY
Central   DISTRICT

I   Eliza Wesley   , on oath state that I am 27 years of age and a citizen by blood of the Choctaw Nation, and as such have been placed upon the final roll of the Choctaw Nation, by the Honorable Secretary of the Interior my final enrollment number being 3111 ; that I am the lawful wife of Joseph Wesley , who is a citizen of the Choctaw Nation, and as such has been placed upon the final roll of said Nation by the Honorable Secretary of the Interior, his final enrollment number being 3110 and that a Male child was born to me on the 24th day of November 190 3; that said child has been named Davis Wesley , and is now living.

              her
             Eliza x Wesley
Witnesseth.   mark

Must be two Witnesses who are Citizens. } H B Jacob
       Jesse Christy

Subscribed and sworn to before me this 22 day of Feb 190 5

         W.A. Shoney
           Notary Public.
My commission expires:

AFFIDAVIT OF ATTENDING PHYSICIAN OR MIDWIFE

UNITED STATES OF AMERICA
INDIAN TERRITORY
Central   DISTRICT

I, Sibbie Haiopatubbi a midwife on oath state that I attended on Mrs. Eliza Wesley wife of Joseph Wesley on the 24th day of November , 190 3, that there was born to her on said date a male child, that said child is now living, and is said to have been named Davis Wesley

        Sibbie Haiopatubbi M.D.

WITNESSETH:
Must be two witnesses who are citizens and know the child. { H B Jacob
       Jesse Christy

Subscribed and sworn to before me this, the 22 day of Feb 190 5

       W A Shoney Notary Public.

Applications for Enrollment of Choctaw Newborn
Act of 1905 Volume XV

We hereby certify that we are well acquainted with Sibbie Haiopatubbi a midwife and know her to be reputable and of good standing in the community.

{ H B Jacob
{ Jesse Christy

BIRTH AFFIDAVIT.

DEPARTMENT OF THE INTERIOR.
COMMISSION TO THE FIVE CIVILIZED TRIBES.

IN RE APPLICATION FOR ENROLLMENT, as a citizen of the Choctaw Nation, of Davis Wesley, born on the 24th day of November, 1903

Name of Father: Joseph Wesley — a citizen of the Choctaw Nation.
Name of Mother: Eliza Wesley — a citizen of the Choctaw Nation.

Postoffice Fort Towson, Ind. Ter.

AFFIDAVIT OF MOTHER.

UNITED STATES OF AMERICA, Indian Territory, }
Central DISTRICT. }

I, Eliza Wesley, on oath state that I am 27 years of age and a citizen by blood, of the Choctaw Nation; that I am the lawful wife of Joseph Wesley, who is a citizen, by blood of the Choctaw Nation; that a male child was born to me on 24th day of November, 1903; that said child has been named Davis Wesley, and was living March 4, 1905.

                        her
               Eliza x Wesley
Witnesses To Mark: mark
{ Robert Anderson
{ Vester W Rose

Subscribed and sworn to before me this 17th day of April, 1905.

                Wirt Franklin
                  Notary Public.

Applications for Enrollment of Choctaw Newborn
Act of 1905   Volume XV

AFFIDAVIT OF ATTENDING PHYSICIAN OR MID-WIFE.

UNITED STATES OF AMERICA, Indian Territory,
Central   DISTRICT.

I, Elizabeth Loman , a mid-wife , on oath state that I attended on Mrs. Eliza Wesley , wife of Joseph Wesley on the 24th day of November , 1903; that there was born to her on said date a male child; that said child was living March 4, 1905, and is said to have been named Davis Wesley

                                               her
Witnesses To Mark: Elizabeth x Loman
  { Robert Anderson   mark
    Vester W Rose

Subscribed and sworn to before me this 17th day of April , 1905

                                   Wirt Franklin
                                   Notary Public.

Choc New Born 1082
    Thomas S[sic]. E. Combs
    (Born July 27, 1903)

BIRTH AFFIDAVIT.
DEPARTMENT OF THE INTERIOR.
COMMISSION TO THE FIVE CIVILIZED TRIBES.

IN RE APPLICATION FOR ENROLLMENT, as a citizen of the Choctaw Nation, of Thomas L.E. Combs , born on the 27th day of July , 1904

Name of Father: Edward Combs   a citizen of the Choctaw Nation.
Name of Mother: Sarah Combs   a citizen of the Choctaw Nation.

                     Postoffice   Hugo, Ind. Ter.

Applications for Enrollment of Choctaw Newborn
Act of 1905   Volume XV

AFFIDAVIT OF MOTHER.

UNITED STATES OF AMERICA, Indian Territory, }
Central   DISTRICT.

I, Sarah Combs, on oath state that I am 41 years of age and a citizen by blood, of the Choctaw Nation; that I am the lawful wife of Edward Combs, who is a citizen, by marriage of the Choctaw Nation; that a male child was born to me on 27th day of July, 1903; that said child has been named Thomas L.E. Combs, and was living March 4, 1905.

Sarah Combs

Witnesses To Mark:
{

Subscribed and sworn to before me this 17th day of April, 1905

Wirt Franklin
Notary Public.

AFFIDAVIT OF ATTENDING PHYSICIAN OR MID-WIFE.

UNITED STATES OF AMERICA, Indian Territory, }
Central   DISTRICT.

I, Perry E.A. Fling, a physician, on oath state that I attended on Mrs. Sarah Combs, wife of Edward Combs on the 27th day of July, 1903; that there was born to her on said date a male child; that said child was living March 4, 1905, and is said to have been named Thomas L.E. Combs

Perry E.A. Fling

Witnesses To Mark:
{

Subscribed and sworn to before me this 17th day of April, 1905

Wirt Franklin
Notary Public.

Applications for Enrollment of Choctaw Newborn
Act of 1905   Volume XV

NEW-BORN AFFIDAVIT.

Number..............

Choctaw Enrolling Commission.

IN THE MATTER OF THE APPLICATION FOR ENROLLMENT, as a citizen of the Choctaw Nation, of   Thomas Lee Edward Combs

born on the 27th day of July   190 3

Name of father   Edward Combs   a citizen of   Choctaw
Nation final enrollment No 703
Name of mother   Sarah Combs   a citizen of   Choctaw
Nation final enrollment No 3939

Postoffice   Hugo, I.T.

AFFIDAVIT OF MOTHER.

UNITED STATES OF AMERICA,
INDIAN TERRITORY,
Central   DISTRICT

I   Sarah Combs   on oath state that
I am 41 years of age and a citizen by blood   of the Choctaw   Nation, and as such have been placed upon the final roll of the   Choctaw   Nation, by the Honorable Secretary of the Interior my final enrollment number being   3939   ; that I am the lawful wife of   Edward Combs   , who is a citizen of the   Choctaw   Nation, and as such has been placed upon the final roll of said Nation by the Honorable Secretary of the Interior, his final enrollment number being   703   and that a   male   child was born to me on the   27   day of   July   190 3 ; that said child has been named Thos Lee Edward Combs   , and is now living.

Sarah Combs

WITNESSETH:
Must be two Witnesses who are Citizens.   *(Name Illegible)*
                 H J Bohanan

Subscribed and sworn to before me this   17   day of   Jan   190 5

W A Shoney
Notary Public.

My commission expires   Jan 10, 1909

47

Applications for Enrollment of Choctaw Newborn
Act of 1905   Volume XV

Affidavit of Attending Physician or Midwife

UNITED STATES OF AMERICA,
INDIAN TERRITORY,
Central   DISTRICT

I, Perry Fling   a   Physician   on oath state that I attended on Mrs. Sarah Combs   wife of   Edward Combs   on the 27th day of July, 190 3, that there was born to her on said date a   male   child, that said child is now living, and is said to have been named   Thomas Lee Edward Combs

Perry Fling   M. D.

Subscribed and sworn to before me this the   17th day of   January   1905

My commission expires   R E Rowells
December 14-1907   Notary Public.

WITNESSETH:
Must be two witnesses who are citizens and know the child.   { Sam R. Oliver
Josie Oliver

We hereby certify that we are well acquainted with   Dr Perry Fling   a   Physician   and know   him   to be reputable and of good standing in the community.

Must be two citizen witnesses.   { Sam R Oliver
Josie Oliver

Choc New Born 1083
   Ada Ann James
   (Born April 1, 1903)

NEW-BORN AFFIDAVIT.

Number............

Choctaw Enrolling Commission.

IN THE MATTER OF THE APPLICATION FOR ENROLLMENT, as a citizen of the Choctaw   Nation, of   Ada Anna[sic] James

born on the   1st day of   April   190 3

Applications for Enrollment of Choctaw Newborn
Act of 1905 Volume XV

Name of father Benjamen James   a citizen of   Choctaw
Nation final enrollment No   4620
Name of mother   Winnie James   a citizen of   Choctaw
Nation final enrollment No   4621

Postoffice   Soper IT

AFFIDAVIT OF MOTHER.

UNITED STATES OF AMERICA,
INDIAN TERRITORY,
Central   DISTRICT

I   Winnie James   on oath state that I am 24 years of age and a citizen by blood of the Choctaw Nation, and as such have been placed upon the final roll of the Choctaw Nation, by the Honorable Secretary of the Interior my final enrollment number being 4621 ; that I am the lawful wife of Benjamen James , who is a citizen of the Choctaw Nation, and as such has been placed upon the final roll of said Nation by the Honorable Secretary of the Interior, his final enrollment number being 4620 and that a female child was born to me on the 1st day of April 190 3 ; that said child has been named Ada Anna James , and is now living.

Winnie James x mark
her

WITNESSETH:
Must be two   Wilson Thomas
Witnesses who   her
are Citizens.   Susan x Thomas
                    mark

Subscribed and sworn to before me this 17 day of Jan 190 5

W A Shoney
Notary Public.

My commission expires Jan 10, 1909

Affidavit of Attending Physician or Midwife

UNITED STATES OF AMERICA,
INDIAN TERRITORY,
Central   DISTRICT

I, Susan Thomas a midwife on oath state that I attended on Mrs. Winnie James wife of Benjamen James on the 1st day of April , 190 3, that there was born to her on said date a female child, that said child is now living, and is said to have been named Ada Anna James

M.D.

Applications for Enrollment of Choctaw Newborn
Act of 1905 Volume XV

Subscribed and sworn to before me this the 23 day of January 1905

G.A. Reynolds
Notary Public.
my commission expires
June 29th 1908

WITNESSETH:
Must be two witnesses who are citizens and know the child.
{ Wilson Thomas
  her
  Susan x Thomas
  mark }

We hereby certify that we are well acquainted with Susan Thomas a midwife and know her to be reputable and of good standing in the community.

Must be two citizen witnesses.
{ Nancy Reynolds
  Thompson Coleman }

BIRTH AFFIDAVIT.

DEPARTMENT OF THE INTERIOR.
COMMISSION TO THE FIVE CIVILIZED TRIBES.

IN RE APPLICATION FOR ENROLLMENT, as a citizen of the Choctaw Nation, of Ada Ann James, born on the 1st day of April, 1903

Name of Father: Benjamin James   a citizen of the Choctaw Nation.
Name of Mother: Winnie James   a citizen of the Choctaw Nation.

Postoffice   Soper, Ind. Ter.

AFFIDAVIT OF MOTHER.

UNITED STATES OF AMERICA, Indian Territory, }
Central   DISTRICT. }

I, Winnie James, on oath state that I am 23 years of age and a citizen by blood, of the Choctaw Nation; that I am the lawful wife of Benjamin James, who is a citizen, by blood of the Choctaw Nation; that a female child was born to me on 1st day of April, 1903; that said child has been named Ada Ann James, and was living March 4, 1905.

her
Winnie x James
mark

Witnesses To Mark:
{ Robert Anderson
  Vester Rose

Applications for Enrollment of Choctaw Newborn
Act of 1905   Volume XV

Subscribed and sworn to before me this 17th day of April, 1905

                         Wirt Franklin
                         Notary Public.

AFFIDAVIT OF ATTENDING PHYSICIAN OR MID-WIFE.

UNITED STATES OF AMERICA, Indian Territory,
  Central   DISTRICT.

    I, Susan Thomas, a mid-wife, on oath state that I attended on Mrs. Winnie James, wife of Benjamin James on the 1st day of April, 1903; that there was born to her on said date a female child; that said child was living March 4, 1905, and is said to have been named Ada Ann James

                                           her
                              Susan x Thomas
Witnesses To Mark: mark
  { Robert Anderson
  { Vester Rose

Subscribed and sworn to before me this 17th day of April, 1905

                         Wirt Franklin
                         Notary Public.

Choc New Born 1084
     Agnes Watkins
     (Born March 29, 1903)

BIRTH AFFIDAVIT.

DEPARTMENT OF THE INTERIOR.
COMMISSION TO THE FIVE CIVILIZED TRIBES.

    IN RE APPLICATION FOR ENROLLMENT, as a citizen of the Choctaw Nation, of Agnes Watkins, born on the 29th day of March, 1903

Name of Father: Joseph Watkins   a citizen of the Choctaw Nation.
Name of Mother: Eliza Watkins   a citizen of the Choctaw Nation.
                                                            by Blood
                         Postoffice

Applications for Enrollment of Choctaw Newborn
Act of 1905   Volume XV

AFFIDAVIT OF ATTENDING PHYSICIAN OR MID-WIFE.

UNITED STATES OF AMERICA, Indian Territory,
.... DISTRICT.

We Isaac Jones and Hampton Joel , on oath state that ~~I attended on~~ *we personally acquainted with* Mrs. Eliza Watkins , wife of Joseph Watkins *and that* on *or about* the 29th day of March , 1903; that there was born to her on said date a female child; that said child was living March 4, 1905, and is said to have been named Agnes Watkins

Witnesses To Mark: Isaac Jones
{ _____   Hampton Joel
  _____

Subscribed and sworn to before me this 3 day of August , 1905

My commission expires   W.P. Burwell
April 10th 1909   Notary Public.

BIRTH AFFIDAVIT.

DEPARTMENT OF THE INTERIOR.
COMMISSION TO THE FIVE CIVILIZED TRIBES.

IN RE APPLICATION FOR ENROLLMENT, as a citizen of the Choctaw Nation, of Agnes Watkins , born on the 29th day of March , 1903

Name of Father: Joseph Watkins   a citizen of the Choctaw Nation.
Name of Mother: Eliza Watkins   a citizen of the Choctaw Nation.

Postoffice   Alikchi, Ind. Ter.

AFFIDAVIT OF MOTHER.

Child present
W.F.

UNITED STATES OF AMERICA, Indian Territory,
Central   DISTRICT.

I, Eliza Watkins , on oath state that I am about 29 years of age and a citizen by blood , of the Choctaw Nation; that I am the lawful wife of Joseph Watkins , who is a citizen, by blood of the Choctaw Nation; that a female child was born to me on 29th day of March , 1903; that said child has been named Agnes Watkins , and was living March 4, 1905.

Applications for Enrollment of Choctaw Newborn
Act of 1905   Volume XV

                                         her
                                 Eliza x Watkins

Witnesses To Mark: mark
{ Robert Anderson
{ Vester W Rose

Subscribed and sworn to before me this   17th day of   April   , 1905

                                       Wirt Franklin
                                           Notary Public.

AFFIDAVIT OF ATTENDING PHYSICIAN OR MID-WIFE.

UNITED STATES OF AMERICA, Indian Territory, }
  Central   DISTRICT.   }

     I,   Joseph Watkins   , a................................., on oath state that I attended on Mrs.   Eliza Watkins   , ~~wife of~~   *my wife*   on the   29th day of   March   , 1903; that there was born to her on said date a   female   child; that said child was living March 4, 1905, and ~~is said to have~~ *has* been named   Agnes Watkins

                                   Joseph Watkins

Witnesses To Mark:

{

Subscribed and sworn to before me this   17th day of   April   , 1905

                                       Wirt Franklin
                                          Notary Public.

United States of America,   )
)
Indian Territory,   ) ss.
)
Central District.   )

     I, Sinsie Watkins, on oath state that I am twenty-five years of age and a citizen by blood of the Choctaw Nation; that my post office address is Alikchi, Indian Territory; that I am personally acquainted with Eliza Watkins, wife of Joseph Watkins, and have known said parties for about nine years; that since they were married about seven years ago I have lived within one mile of where they have lived and have visited them often at their home; that I know of my own knowledge that on or about the 29th of March, 1903, there was born to the said Eliza Watkins a female child; that said child is now living and is said to have been named Agnes Watkins.

Applications for Enrollment of Choctaw Newborn
Act of 1905   Volume XV

           her
         Sinsie x Watkins
           mark

subscribed[sic] and sworn to before me this 17th day of April, 1905.

          Wirt Franklin
          Notary Public.

Witnesses to mark.
 Robert Anderson
 Vester W Rose

7--NB--1084

Muskogee, Indian Territory, June 2, 1905.

Joseph Watkins,
 Alikchi, Indian Territory.

Dear Sir:

  Referring to the application for the enrollment of your infant child, Agnes Watkins, born March 29, 1903, it is noted from the affidavits heretofore filed in this office that you were the only one in attendance upon your wife at the time of the birth of the applicant.

  In this event it will be necessary that the affidavits of two persons, who are disinterested and not related to the applicant, who have actual knowledge of the facts that the child was born, the date of birth; that she was living on March 4, 1905, and that Eliza Watkins is her mother be filed in this office.

  The affidavit of Sinsie Watkins to these facts has been filed. It will, therefore, be necessary that you secure a similar affidavit from another person.

  This matter should receive your immediate attention as no further action can be taken relative to the enrollment of said child until the Commission has been furnished this affidavit.

       Respectfully,

              [sic]

Applications for Enrollment of Choctaw Newborn
Act of 1905 Volume XV

7-NB-1084

Muskogee, Indian Territory, August 9, 1905.

Joseph Watkins,
    Alikchi, Indian Territory.

Dear Sir:

    Receipt is hereby acknowledged of your letter of August 4, 1905, transmitting affidavits of Isaac Jones and Hampton Joel to the birth of Agnes Watkins, daughter of Joseph and Eliza Watkins, March 29, 1903, and the same have been filed with the records of this office in the matter of the enrollment of said child.

        Respectfully,

        Acting Commissioner.

Choc New Born 1085
    Aaron Watkins
    (Born April 17, 1903)

BIRTH AFFIDAVIT.

DEPARTMENT OF THE INTERIOR.
COMMISSION TO THE FIVE CIVILIZED TRIBES.

IN RE APPLICATION FOR ENROLLMENT, as a citizen of the Choctaw Nation, of Aaron Watkins, born on the 17th day of April, 1903

Name of Father: Simon Watson   a citizen of the Choctaw Nation.
Name of Mother: Zona Watkins   a citizen of the Choctaw Nation.

        Postoffice   Alikchi, Ind. Ter.

Applications for Enrollment of Choctaw Newborn
Act of 1905 Volume XV

AFFIDAVIT OF MOTHER.

UNITED STATES OF AMERICA, Indian Territory, }
Central DISTRICT.

I, Zona Watkins, on oath state that I am 22 years of age and a citizen by blood, of the Choctaw Nation; that I am ~~not~~ the lawful wife of Simon Watson, who is a citizen, by blood of the Choctaw Nation; that a male child was born to me on 17th day of April, 1904; that said child has been named Aaron Watkins, and was living March 4, 1905.

                                        her
                                Zona x Watkins
Witnesses To Mark: mark
{ Robert Anderson
{ Vester W Rose

Subscribed and sworn to before me this 17th day of April, 1905

                            Wirt Franklin
                            Notary Public.

AFFIDAVIT OF ATTENDING PHYSICIAN OR MID-WIFE.

UNITED STATES OF AMERICA, Indian Territory, }
Central DISTRICT.

I, Ennissie Watkins, a mid-wife, on oath state that I attended on Mrs. Zona Watkins, ~~wife of~~ on the 17th day of April, 1903; that there was born to her on said date a male child; that said child was living March 4, 1905, and is said to have been named Aaron Watkins

                                        her
                                Ennissie x Watkins
Witnesses To Mark: mark
{ Robert Anderson
{ Vester W Rose

Subscribed and sworn to before me this 17th day of April, 1905

                            Wirt Franklin
                            Notary Public.

Applications for Enrollment of Choctaw Newborn
Act of 1905   Volume XV

Choc New Born 1086
    Louisa Willis
    (Born July 22, 1904)

BIRTH AFFIDAVIT.

DEPARTMENT OF THE INTERIOR.
COMMISSION TO THE FIVE CIVILIZED TRIBES.

IN RE APPLICATION FOR ENROLLMENT, as a citizen of the Choctaw Nation, of Louisa Willis, born on the 22nd day of July, 1904

Name of Father: Emerson D. Willis   a citizen of the Choctaw Nation.
Name of Mother: Martha Willis   a citizen of the Choctaw Nation.

    Postoffice   Alikchi, Ind. Ter.

AFFIDAVIT OF MOTHER.

UNITED STATES OF AMERICA, Indian Territory,
    Central   DISTRICT.

    I, Martha Willis, on oath state that I am 19 years of age and a citizen by blood, of the Choctaw Nation; that I am the lawful wife of Emerson D. Willis, who is a citizen, by blood of the Choctaw Nation; that a female child was born to me on 22nd day of July, 1904; that said child has been named Louisa Willis, and was living March 4, 1905.

                                    her
                               Martha x Willis
Witnesses To Mark: mark
   { Robert Anderson
     Vester W Rose

    Subscribed and sworn to before me this 17th day of April, 1905

                           Wirt Franklin
                              Notary Public.

Applications for Enrollment of Choctaw Newborn
Act of 1905   Volume XV

AFFIDAVIT OF ATTENDING PHYSICIAN OR MID-WIFE.

UNITED STATES OF AMERICA, Indian Territory,
Central   DISTRICT.

I, Elizabeth Loman , a mid-wife , on oath state that I attended on Mrs. Martha Willis , wife of Emerson D Willis on the 22nd day of July , 1904; that there was born to her on said date a female child; that said child was living March 4, 1905, and is said to have been named Louisa Willis

                              her
                        Elizabeth x Loman
Witnesses To Mark: mark
  { Robert Anderson
    Vester W Rose

Subscribed and sworn to before me this 17th day of April , 1905

                            Wirt Franklin
                            Notary Public.

Choc New Born 1087
    Lillie Byington
    (Born Jan. 8, 1905)

NEW BORN AFFIDAVIT

No ....

CHOCTAW ENROLLING COMMISSION

IN THE MATTER OF THE APPLICATION FOR ENROLLMENT as a citizen of the Choctaw Nation, of Mary[sic] Byington born on the 18th day of January 190 5

Name of father Moody Byington   a citizen of Choctaw Nation, final enrollment No. 3321
Name of mother Annie Byington   a citizen of Choctaw Nation, final enrollment No. 3322

                          Norwood I.T.   Postoffice.

Applications for Enrollment of Choctaw Newborn
Act of 1905   Volume XV

AFFIDAVIT OF MOTHER

UNITED STATES OF AMERICA
   INDIAN TERRITORY
DISTRICT   Central

I   Annie Byington   , on oath state that I am   25   years of age and a citizen by   blood   of the   Choctaw   Nation, and as such have been placed upon the final roll of the   Choctaw   Nation, by the Honorable Secretary of the Interior my final enrollment number being   3322   ; that I am the lawful wife of   Moody Byington   , who is a citizen of the   Choctaw   Nation, and as such has been placed upon the final roll of said Nation by the Honorable Secretary of the Interior, his final enrollment number being   3321   and that a   female   child was born to me on the   18th day of   January   190 5; that said child has been named   Mary[sic] Byington   , and is now living.

WITNESSETH: Annie Byington
   Must be two witnesses   Thomas Byington
   who are citizens   Arlington King

Subscribed and sworn to before me this, the   14th day of   March   , 190 5

                               W A Shoney
                                  Notary Public.

My Commission Expires:

Affidavit of Attending Physician or Midwife

UNITED STATES OF AMERICA,
   INDIAN TERRITORY,
Central   DISTRICT

I,   Maimie James   a   midwife on oath state that I attended on Mrs.   Annie Byington   wife of   Moody Byington   on the   18th day of   January   , 190 5, that there was born to her on said date a   female   child, that said child is now living, and is said to have been named   Mary[sic] Byington

                            Maimie James   ~~M. D.~~

Subscribed and sworn to before me this the   14th day of   March   1905

                            W A Shoney
                              Notary Public.

WITNESSETH:
   Must be two witnesses   Thomas Byington
   who are citizens and
   know the child.

Applications for Enrollment of Choctaw Newborn
Act of 1905   Volume XV

We hereby certify that we are well acquainted with   Maimie James
a   midwife   and know   her   to be reputable and of good standing in the community.

                                    Must be two citizen   Thomas Byington
                                    witnesses.   Arlington King

Moody Byington,
Roll No. 3321

Annie Byington,
Roll No. 3322

United States of America,)
)
Indian Territory,   ) ss.
)
Central District.   )

    I, Joel Logan, on oath state that I am forty years of age and a citizen by blood of the Choctaw Nation; that my post office address is Goodwater, Indian Territory; that I am personally acquainted with Annie Byington, wife of Moody Byington, and have known said parties for about ten years; that since their marriage about eight years ago I have lived within four miles of them; that I know of my own knowledge that on or about the 8th[sic] day of January 1905, there was born to the said Annie Byington a female child; that said child is now living and is said to have been named Lillie Byington.

                                                        Joel Logan

Subscribed and sworn to before me this 14th day of April, 1905.

                                                        Wirt Franklin
                                                            Notary Public.

Applications for Enrollment of Choctaw Newborn
Act of 1905 Volume XV

BIRTH AFFIDAVIT.

DEPARTMENT OF THE INTERIOR.
COMMISSION TO THE FIVE CIVILIZED TRIBES.

IN RE APPLICATION FOR ENROLLMENT, as a citizen of the Choctaw Nation, of Lillie Byington, born on the 8th[sic] day of January, 1905

Name of Father: Moody Byington   a citizen of the Choctaw Nation.
Name of Mother: Annie Byington   a citizen of the Choctaw Nation.

Postoffice   Norwood, Ind. Ter.

AFFIDAVIT OF MOTHER.

Child present
W.F.

UNITED STATES OF AMERICA, Indian Territory, }
Central   DISTRICT.

     I, Annie Byington, on oath state that I am 25 years of age and a citizen by blood, of the Choctaw Nation; that I am the lawful wife of Moody Byington, who is a citizen, by blood of the Choctaw Nation; that a female child was born to me on 8th[sic] day of January, 1905; that said child has been named Lillie Byington, and was living March 4, 1905. *and that no one but my said husband was present when said child was born*

                                       Annie Byington

Witnesses To Mark:
{

     Subscribed and sworn to before me this 14th day of April, 1905

                                     Wirt Franklin
                                     Notary Public.

AFFIDAVIT OF ATTENDING PHYSICIAN OR MID-WIFE.

UNITED STATES OF AMERICA, Indian Territory, }
Central   DISTRICT.

     I, Moody Byington, a ~~...~~, on oath state that I attended on Mrs. Annie Byington, ~~wife of~~ *my wife* on the 8th day of January, 1905; that there was born to her on said date a female child; that said child was living March 4, 1905, and is said to have been named Lillie Byington

                                     Moody Byington

Applications for Enrollment of Choctaw Newborn
Act of 1905   Volume XV

Witnesses To Mark:
{

    Subscribed and sworn to before me this   14th day of   April   , 1905

Wirt Franklin
Notary Public.

BIRTH AFFIDAVIT.

DEPARTMENT OF THE INTERIOR.
COMMISSION TO THE FIVE CIVILIZED TRIBES.

    IN RE APPLICATION FOR ENROLLMENT, as a citizen of the   Choctaw   Nation, of Lillie Byington , born on the 18 day of Jan , 1905

Name of Father: Moody Byington   Roll 3321   a citizen of the   Choctaw   Nation.
Name of Mother: Annie Byington   " 3322   a citizen of the   Choctaw   Nation.

Postoffice   Norwood, I.T.

AFFIDAVIT OF MOTHER.

UNITED STATES OF AMERICA, Indian Territory, }
   Central   DISTRICT. }

    I,   Annie Byington   , on oath state that I am   25   years of age and a citizen by   blood   , of the   Choctaw   Nation; that I am the lawful wife of   Moody Byington , who is a citizen, by blood   of the   Choctaw   Nation; that a female   child was born to me on   18   day of   Jan   , 1905; that said child has been named   Lillie Byington   , and was living March 4, 1905.

Annie Byington

Witnesses To Mark:
{

    Subscribed and sworn to before me this   2nd   day of   Sept   , 1905

MJ Whiteman
Notary Public.

Applications for Enrollment of Choctaw Newborn
Act of 1905   Volume XV

AFFIDAVIT OF ATTENDING PHYSICIAN OR MID-WIFE.

UNITED STATES OF AMERICA, Indian Territory,
.... DISTRICT.

I, Allington[sic] King, a ...., on oath state that I ~~attended on~~ am acquainted with Mrs. Annie Byington, wife of Moody Byington on the 18 day of Jan, 1905; that there was born to her on said date a female child; that said child was living March 4, 1905, and is said to have been named Lillie Byington

Arlington King

Witnesses To Mark:

Subscribed and sworn to before me this 2nd day of Sept, 1905

MJ Whiteman
Notary Public.

7-NB-1087.

Muskogee, Indian Territory, June 5, 1905.

Moody Byington,
    Norwood, Indian Territory.

Dear Sir:

There is enclosed you herewith for execution application for the enrollment of your infant child.

In the affidavits of March 14, 1905, heretofore filed in this office, the name of the applicant is given as Mary Byington, while in those of April 14, 1905, the name is given as Lillie Byington. In the enclosed application the name of the applicant is left blank. Please insert the correct name and when the affidavits are properly executed return them to this office.

It is also noted that there was no one, excepting yourself, in attendance upon your wife at the time of birth of the applicant. In this event it will be necessary that the affidavits of two persons, who are disinterested and not related to the applicant, who have actual knowledge of the facts that the child was born, the date of her birth; that she was living on March 4, 1905, and that Annie Byington is her mother, be filed in this office.

The affidavit of Joel Logan to the above mentioned facts is on file. It will, therefore, be necessary that you secure a similar affidavit from another person.

Applications for Enrollment of Choctaw Newborn
Act of 1905 Volume XV

This matter should receive your immediate attention, as no further action can be taken until this affidavit is filed with the Commission.

Respectfully

VR 3-6. [sic]

7-NB-1087

Muskogee, Indian Territory, July 25, 1905.

Moody Byington,
    Norwood, Indian Territory.

Dear Sir:

    Your attention is called to a communication addressed to you under date of June 5, 1905, by the Commission to the Five Civilized Tribes, with which was inclosed application for the enrollment of your infant child.

    In said letter you were advised that the affidavits of March 14, 1905, gave the name of applicant as Mary Byington, while those of April 14, 1905, gave the name as Lillie Byington. You were requested to insert the correct name of the child and after having the affidavits properly executed to forwarded them to this office. No reply to this letter has been received.

    You were also advised that in the affidavits of March 14, 1905, the date of birth of applicant was given as January 18, 1905, while in those of April 14, 1905, the date was given as January 8, 1905.

    You are requested to insert in the affidavits heretofore forwarded you the correct date of birth of applicant together with the correct name and when properly executed return to this office immediately, as no further action can be taken relative to the enrollment of said child until the evidence requested has been supplied.

Respectfully,

Commissioner.

Applications for Enrollment of Choctaw Newborn
Act of 1905 Volume XV

7-NB-1087

Muskogee, Indian Territory, September 7, 1905.

Moody Byington,
    Norwood, Indian Territory.

Dear Sir:

    Receipt is hereby acknowledged of the affidavits of Annie Byington, the mother, and Arlington King, executed September 2, 1905, to the birth of your infant child, Lillie Byington, born January 18, 1905, offered in support of the application for the enrollment of the said child as a citizen by blood of the Choctaw Nation. Said affidavit has been filed with the record in this case.

                  Respectfully,

                                    Acting Commissioner.

7-NB-1087

Muskogee, Indian Territory, March 2, 1906.

E. W. Usher,
    Atoka, Indian Territory.

Dear Sir:

    Receipt is hereby acknowledged of your letter of February 27, 1906, asking the status of the enrollment of Lillie Byington, child of Moody and Annie Byington as a new born citizen of the Choctaw Nation.

    In reply to your letter you are advised that the name of Lillie Byington has been placed upon a schedule of new born citizens of the Choctaw Nation which has been forwarded the Secretary of the Interior, but this office has not yet been notified of Departmental action thereon.

                  Respectfully,

                                    Acting Commissioner.

Applications for Enrollment of Choctaw Newborn
Act of 1905   Volume XV

Choc New Born 1088
    Mary Gertrude Hibben
    (Born April 9, 1903)

(The affidavit below typed as given.)

NEW-BORN AFFIDAVIT.

    Number..................

Choctaw Enrolling Commission.

    IN THE MATTER OF THE APPLICATION FOR ENROLLMENT, as a citizen of the Chocktaw   Nation, of   Mary Gertrude Hibben

born on the   19   day of   April   190 3

Name of father   Thomas D Hibben   a citizen of Chocktaw Nation Ind mag
Nation final enrollment No   231
Name of mother   Mary Hibben   a citizen of Chocktaw Nation By Blood
Nation final enrollment No   3930

    Postoffice   Frogville Ind Ter

AFFIDAVIT OF MOTHER.

UNITED STATES OF AMERICA,
  INDIAN TERRITORY,
  Centrel   DISTRICT

    I   Mary Hibben   on oath state that I am   41   years of age and a citizen by   Blood   of the   Choctaw   Nation, and as such have been placed upon the final roll of the   Chocktaw   Nation, by the Honorable Secretary of the Interior my final enrollment number being   3930   ; that I am the lawful wife of   Thomas D Hibben   , who is a citizen of the   Chocktaw   Nation, and as such has been placed upon the final roll of said Nation by the Honorable Secretary of the Interior, his final enrollment number being   231   and that a   Female   child was born to me on the   19   day of   April   190 3 ; that said child has been named   Mary Gertrude , and is now living.

    Mary Hibben

WITNESSETH:
  Must be two
  Witnesses who   } Willie Wechabibie
  are Citizens.   Sophie Payne nee Hibben

Applications for Enrollment of Choctaw Newborn
Act of 1905 Volume XV

Subscribed and sworn to before me this 14 day of March 190 5

Sam C Payne
Notary Public.

My commission expires April 18 1907

(The affidavit below typed as given.)

Affidavit of Attending Physician or Midwife

UNITED STATES OF AMERICA,
    INDIAN TERRITORY,
  Centrel   DISTRICT

I, Faney Frasher a Mid Wife on oath state that I attended on Mrs. Mary Hibben wife of Tomas D Hibben on the 19 day of April , 190 3, that there was born to her on said date a Female child, that said child is now living, and is said to have been named Mary Gertrude Hibben

Faney Frasher   M. W.

Subscribed and sworn to before me this the 14 day of March 1905

Sam C Payne
Notary Public.

WITNESSETH:
Must be two witnesses who are citizens and know the child. { Willie Wechabibie
Sophie Payne nee Hibben

We hereby certify that we are well acquainted with Faney Frasher a Mid Wife and know her to be reputable and of good standing in the community.

Must be two citizen witnesses. { Willie Wechabibie
Sophie Payne nee Hibben

Applications for Enrollment of Choctaw Newborn
Act of 1905   Volume XV

BIRTH AFFIDAVIT.

DEPARTMENT OF THE INTERIOR.
COMMISSION TO THE FIVE CIVILIZED TRIBES.

IN RE APPLICATION FOR ENROLLMENT, as a citizen of the   Choctaw   Nation, of Mary Gertrude Hibben   , born on the   19th   day of   April   , 1903

Name of Father: Thomas D Hibben   a citizen of the   Choctaw   Nation.
Name of Mother: Mary Hibben   a citizen of the   Choctaw   Nation.

Postoffice   Frogville Ind. Ter.

AFFIDAVIT OF MOTHER.

UNITED STATES OF AMERICA, Indian Territory, }
Central   DISTRICT.

I,   Mary Hibben   , on oath state that I am   41   years of age and a citizen by blood   , of the   Choctaw   Nation; that I am the lawful wife of   Thomas D. Hibben   , who is a citizen, by   marriage   of the   Choctaw   Nation; that a   female   child was born to me on   19th   day of   April   , 1903; that said child has been named   Mary Gertrude Hibben   , and was living March 4, 1905.

Mary Hibben

Witnesses To Mark:
{

Subscribed and sworn to before me this   17th   day of   April   , 1905

Wirt Franklin
Notary Public.

AFFIDAVIT OF ATTENDING PHYSICIAN OR MID-WIFE.

UNITED STATES OF AMERICA, Indian Territory, }
Central   DISTRICT.

I,   Fannie Frazier   , a   mid-wife   , on oath state that I attended on Mrs.   Mary Hibben   , wife of   Thomas D Hibben   on the   19th day of April , 1903; that there was born to her on said date a   female   child; that said child was living March 4, 1905, and is said to have been named   Mary Gertrude Hibben

her
Fannie x Frazier
mark

Applications for Enrollment of Choctaw Newborn
Act of 1905   Volume XV

Witnesses To Mark:
  { Robert Anderson
  { Vester W Rose

Subscribed and sworn to before me this 17th day of April , 1905

Wirt Franklin
Notary Public.

Choc New Born 1089
  Josephine Thomas
  (Born March 31, 1904)

BIRTH AFFIDAVIT.

DEPARTMENT OF THE INTERIOR.
COMMISSION TO THE FIVE CIVILIZED TRIBES.

IN RE APPLICATION FOR ENROLLMENT, as a citizen of the   Choctaw   Nation, of Josephine Thomas , born on the 31st day of March , 1904

Name of Father: Wilson Thomas   a citizen of the United States Nation.
Name of Mother: Susan Thomas   a citizen of the   Choctaw   Nation.

Postoffice   Soper, Ind. Ter.

AFFIDAVIT OF MOTHER.

UNITED STATES OF AMERICA, Indian Territory, }
  Central   DISTRICT. }

I, Susan Thomas , on oath state that I am about 30 years of age and a citizen by blood , of the Choctaw Nation; that I am the lawful wife of Wilson Thomas , who is a citizen, ~~by~~ .... of the United States Nation; that a female child was born to me on 31st day of March , 1904; that said child has been named Josephine Thomas , and was living March 4, 1905.

                                        her
                                Susan x Thomas
Witnesses To Mark: mark
  { Vester Rose
  { Robert Anderson

Applications for Enrollment of Choctaw Newborn
Act of 1905   Volume XV

Subscribed and sworn to before me this 17th day of April, 1905

Wirt Franklin
Notary Public.

AFFIDAVIT OF ATTENDING PHYSICIAN OR MID-WIFE.

UNITED STATES OF AMERICA, Indian Territory, }
Central   DISTRICT.

I, Emily Allen, a mid-wife, on oath state that I attended on Mrs. Susan Thomas, wife of Wilson Thomas on the 31st day of March, 1904; that there was born to her on said date a female child; that said child was living March 4, 1905, and is said to have been named Josephine Thomas

Emily Allen

Witnesses To Mark:
{

Subscribed and sworn to before me this 17th day of April, 1905

Wirt Franklin
Notary Public.

Choc New Born 1090
    Willie Arthur Crawford
    (Born March 3, 1905)

BIRTH AFFIDAVIT.

DEPARTMENT OF THE INTERIOR.
COMMISSION TO THE FIVE CIVILIZED TRIBES.

IN RE APPLICATION FOR ENROLLMENT, as a citizen of the Choctaw Nation, of Willie Arthur Crawford, born on the 3^d day of March, 1905

Name of Father: Barnett Crawford Roll 14370   a citizen of the Choctaw Nation.
Name of Mother: Lizzie Crawford   a citizen of the Choctaw Nation.

Postoffice

Applications for Enrollment of Choctaw Newborn
Act of 1905   Volume XV

AFFIDAVIT OF ATTENDING PHYSICIAN OR MID-WIFE.

UNITED STATES OF AMERICA, Indian Territory, }
.... DISTRICT.

    I,   L.T. Jackson   , a   Physician   , on oath state that I attended on Mrs.   Lizzie Crawford   , wife of   Barnett Crawford   on the   3^d day of   March   , 1905; that there was born to her on said date a   male   child; that said child was living March 4, 1905, and is said to have been named Willie Arthur Crawford

                                      L.T. Jackson
Witnesses To Mark:
{

    Subscribed and sworn to before me this   Eighth   day of   June   , 1905

                                      J M Gryder
                                      Notary Public.

BIRTH AFFIDAVIT.

DEPARTMENT OF THE INTERIOR.
COMMISSION TO THE FIVE CIVILIZED TRIBES.

    IN RE APPLICATION FOR ENROLLMENT, as a citizen of the   Choctaw   Nation, of Willie Arthur Crawford   , born on the   3^d day of   March   , 1905

Name of Father: Barnett Crawford   Roll 14370   a citizen of the   Choctaw   Nation.
Name of Mother: Lizzie Crawford   a citizen of the   Choctaw   Nation.

                      Postoffice   Wade Ind Ter

AFFIDAVIT OF ATTENDING PHYSICIAN OR MID-WIFE.

UNITED STATES OF AMERICA, Indian Territory, }
.... DISTRICT.

    I,   M J Taylor   , a   Midwife   , on oath state that I attended on Mrs.   Lizzie Crawford   , wife of   Barnett Crawford   on the   3^d day of   March   , 1905; that there was born to her on said date a   male   child; that said child was living March 4, 1905, and is said to have been named Willie Arthur Crawford

                                      M J Taylor
Witnesses To Mark:
{

Applications for Enrollment of Choctaw Newborn
Act of 1905 Volume XV

Subscribed and sworn to before me this Eighth day of June, 1905

J M Gryder
Notary Public.

BIRTH AFFIDAVIT.

DEPARTMENT OF THE INTERIOR.
COMMISSION TO THE FIVE CIVILIZED TRIBES.

IN RE APPLICATION FOR ENROLLMENT, as a citizen of the Choctaw Nation, of Willie Arthur Crawford, born on the 3rd day of March, 1905

Name of Father: Barnett Crawford a citizen of the Choctaw Nation.
Name of Mother: Lizzie Crawford a citizen of the United States ~~Nation~~.

Postoffice Wade Ind Ter

AFFIDAVIT OF MOTHER.

UNITED STATES OF AMERICA, Indian Territory,
Central DISTRICT.

I, Lizzie Crawford, on oath state that I am 31 years of age and a citizen ~~by~~ _____, of the United States ~~Nation~~; that I am the lawful wife of Barnett Crawford, who is a citizen, by blood of the Choctaw Nation; that a male child was born to me on 3rd day of March, 1905; that said child has been named Willie Arthur Crawford, and was living March 4, 1905.

Lizzie Crawford

Witnesses To Mark:

Subscribed and sworn to before me this 17th day of April, 1905

Wirt Franklin
Notary Public.

**Applications for Enrollment of Choctaw Newborn
Act of 1905 Volume XV**

No. 559

Certificate of Record of Marriages.

DEPARTMENT OF THE INTERIOR,
Commission to the Five Civilized Tribes.
FILED

APR 20 1905 Tams Bixby CHAIRMAN.

UNITED STATES OF AMERICA,
INDIAN TERRITORY, } SCT:
Central DISTRICT.

I, E.J. Fannin , Clerk of the United States Court in the Indian Territory and District aforesaid, do hereby CERTIFY, that the License for and Certificate of the Marriage of

Mr. G.B. Crawford and

M Lizzie Jolly was

filed in my office in said Territory and District the 1 day of April A.D., 190 4 and duly recorded in Book I of Marriage Record, Page 280

WITNESS my hand and seal of said Court, at Summit , this 1 day of April , A.D. 190 4

E.J. Fannin
Clerk.
By WB Stone *Deputy.*

Applications for Enrollment of Choctaw Newborn
Act of 1905 Volume XV

No.

MARRIAGE LICENSE

United States of America,   The Indian Territory,
   Central DISTRICT, SS.

To any Person Authorized by Law to Solemnize Marriage, Greeting:

You are hereby commanded to Solemnize the Rite and publish the Banns of Matrimony between Mr. G.B. Crawford of Wade in the Indian Territory, aged 22 years, and Miss Lizzie Jolley of Wade in the Indian Territory., aged 25 years, according to law, and do you officially sign and return this License to the parties therein named.

WITNESS my hand and official seal, this 21st day of March A. D. 190 4

E.J. Fannin
Clerk of the United States Court.

WB Stone   Deputy

Certificate of Marriage.

United States of America, }
  The Indian Territory, } ss.
            District.   }   I,   J.W. Posey

a Minister of Gospel, do hereby certify, that on the 22 day of March A. D. 190 4, I did, duly and according to law, as commanded in the foregoing License, solemnize the Rite and publish the Banns of Matrimony between the parties therein named.

Witness my hand, this 22 day of March A. D. 190 4

My credentials are recorded in the office of the Clerk of
  the United States Court in the Indian Territory,
  Central District, Book B , Page 36

J.W. Posey
a Minister of Gospel

Note—This License and Certificate of Marriage must be returned to the Office of the Clerk of the United States Court of the Indian Territory, from whence it was issued, within sixty days from the date thereof, or the party to whom the License was issued will be liable in the amount of the One Hundred Dollars ($100.00)

Applications for Enrollment of Choctaw Newborn
Act of 1905   Volume XV

(The affidavits below typed as given.)

Nurses Affidavit

This is to certify that I attended Mrs Lizzie Crawford during the birth of her son Willie Arthur Crawford on March 3rd 1905

                Mrs M J Taylor
P.O.   Wade I.T.

Sworn to and subscribed to before me a Notary Public For the Central district Durant Division Ind. Ter. This April 14th 1905.

                J.M. Gryder
                Notary Public

Physicians Affidavit

This is to certify that I attended Mrs Lizzie Crawford during the birth of her son Willie Arthur Crawford on March 3rd 1905

                L.T. Jackson M.D.
P.O.   Wade, I.T.

Sworn to and subscribed before me a Notary Public For the Central District Durant Division Ind. Terr. This the 14th day of April 1905.

                J M. Gryder
                Notary Public

---

                7 NB 1090

Muskogee, Indian Territory, June 13, 1905.

Barnett Crawford,
    Wade, Indian Territory.

Dear Sir:

Receipt is hereby acknowledged of the affidavits of L. T. Jackson and M. J. Taylor to the birth of Willie Arthur Crawford, son of Barnett and Lizzie Crawford, March 3, 1905, and the same have been filed in the matter of the enrollment of said child.

                Respectfully

                      Chairman.

Applications for Enrollment of Choctaw Newborn
Act of 1905   Volume XV

7--NB--1090

Muskogee, Indian Territory, June 3, 1905.

Barnett Crawford,
    Wade, Indian Territory.

Dear Sir:

    Referring to the application for the enrollment of your infant child, Willie Arthur Crawford, born March 3, 1905, it is noted that the affidavits of attending physician and midwife do not show that applicant was living on March 4, 1905. It is necessary, for the child to be enrolled, that he was living on March 4, 1905. For the purpose of showing this there are enclosed you herewith affidavits to be executed by attending physician and mid-wife. In the event the child died prior to March 4, 1905, you are requested to erase the words "was living March 4, 1905."

    In having these affidavits executed care should be exercised to see that all names are written in full, as they appear in the body of the affidavit, and in the event that either of the persons signing the affidavit are unable to write, signatures by mark must be attested by two witnesses. Each affidavit must be executed before a Notary Public and the notarial seal and signature of the officer must be attached to each separate affidavit.

    This matter should receive your immediate attention as no further action can be taken relative to the enrollment of said child until the Commission has been furnished these affidavits.

                        Respectfully,

Enc-FVK-28.   [sic]

<u>Choc New Born 1091</u>
    Julius Arthur Wood
    Born Jan. 29, 1905

Applications for Enrollment of Choctaw Newborn
Act of 1905 Volume XV

BIRTH AFFIDAVIT.

DEPARTMENT OF THE INTERIOR.
COMMISSION TO THE FIVE CIVILIZED TRIBES.

IN RE APPLICATION FOR ENROLLMENT, as a citizen of the Choctaw Nation, of Julius Arthur Wood, born on the 29th day of January, 1905

Name of Father: John W Wood   a citizen of the Choctaw Nation.
Name of Mother: Margaret Wood   a citizen of the Choctaw Nation.

Postoffice   Shoals, Ind. Ter.

AFFIDAVIT OF MOTHER.

UNITED STATES OF AMERICA, Indian Territory,
Central   DISTRICT.

I, Margaret Wood, on oath state that I am 18 years of age and a citizen by blood, of the Choctaw Nation; that I am the lawful wife of John W Wood, who is a citizen, by marriage of the Choctaw Nation; that a male child was born to me on 29th day of January, 1905; that said child has been named Julius Arthur Wood, and was living March 4, 1905.

Margaret Wood

Witnesses To Mark:

Subscribed and sworn to before me this 17th day of April, 1905.

Wirt Franklin
Notary Public.

AFFIDAVIT OF ATTENDING PHYSICIAN OR MID-WIFE.

UNITED STATES OF AMERICA, Indian Territory,
Central   DISTRICT.

I, Nannie Day, a mid-wife, on oath state that I attended on Mrs. Margaret Wood, wife of John W Wood on the 29th day of January, 1905; that there was born to her on said date a male child; that said child was living March 4, 1905, and is said to have been named Julius Arthur Wood

Nannie Day

Witnesses To Mark:

Applications for Enrollment of Choctaw Newborn
Act of 1905   Volume XV

Subscribed and sworn to before me this   17th day of   April   , 1905

Wirt Franklin
Notary Public.

Choc New Born 1092
    Susie M. Gardner
    (Born Nov. 19, 1903)

NEW-BORN AFFIDAVIT.

Number..................

...Choctaw Enrolling Commission...

IN THE MATTER OF THE APPLICATION FOR ENROLLMENT, as a citizen of the Choctaw   Nation, of   Susie Mattie Gardner

born on the   19th day of   November   190 3

Name of father   Alfred Gardner   a citizen of   Choctaw
Nation final enrollment No.   3572
Name of mother Mattie Gardner   a citizen of   Choctaw
Nation final enrollment No. 68

Postoffice   Parsons I.T.

AFFIDAVIT OF MOTHER.

UNITED STATES OF AMERICA
INDIAN TERRITORY
  Central   DISTRICT

    I   Mattie Gardner   , on oath state that I am   25   years of age and a citizen by   Intermarriage   of the   Choctaw   Nation, and as such have been placed upon the final roll of the   Choctaw   Nation, by the Honorable Secretary of the Interior my final enrollment number being   68 ; that I am the lawful wife of   Alfred Gardner   , who is a citizen of the   Choctaw   Nation, and as such has been placed upon the final roll of said Nation by the Honorable Secretary of the Interior, his final enrollment number being   3572   and that a   female   child was born to me on the   19th day of   November   190 3; that said child has been named   Susie Mattie Gardner   , and is now living.

Applications for Enrollment of Choctaw Newborn
Act of 1905   Volume XV

               her
            Mattie x Gardner
Witnesseth.   mark
 Must be two William W Swink
 Witnesses who
 are Citizens.   W E Watkins

   Subscribed and sworn to before me this 24th day of Feb   190 5

              W.A. Shoney
                 Notary Public.
My commission expires: Jan 10, 1909

AFFIDAVIT OF ATTENDING PHYSICIAN OR MIDWIFE

UNITED STATES OF AMERICA
INDIAN TERRITORY
 Central   DISTRICT

   I, C.L. Wright   a   Physician
on oath state that I attended on Mrs. Mattie Gardner wife of Alfred Gardner
on the 19th day of November , 190 3, that there was born to her on said date a female
child, that said child is now living, and is said to have been named Susie Mattie Gardner

            C.L. Wright   M.D.

WITNESSETH:
 Must be two witnesses William W Swink
 who are citizens and
 know the child.   W E Watkins

     Subscribed and sworn to before me this, the 24 day of
  Feb   190 5

             W.A. Shoney   Notary Public.

   We hereby certify that we are well acquainted with C.L. Wright
a physician   and know him to be reputable and of good standing in the
community.

             William W Swink

             W E Watkins

Applications for Enrollment of Choctaw Newborn
Act of 1905   Volume XV

BIRTH AFFIDAVIT.

DEPARTMENT OF THE INTERIOR.
COMMISSION TO THE FIVE CIVILIZED TRIBES.

IN RE APPLICATION FOR ENROLLMENT, as a citizen of the Choctaw Nation, of Susie M. Gardner, born on the 19th day of November, 1903

Name of Father: Alfred Gardner   a citizen of the Choctaw Nation.
Name of Mother: Mattie Gardner   a citizen of the Choctaw Nation.

Postoffice   Valliant I.T.

AFFIDAVIT OF MOTHER.

UNITED STATES OF AMERICA, Indian Territory,
Central   DISTRICT.

I, Mattie Gardner, on oath state that I am 25 years of age and a citizen by intermarriage, of the Choctaw Nation; that I am the lawful wife of Alfred Gardner, who is a citizen, by Blood of the Choctaw Nation; that a female child was born to me on 19th day of November, 1903; that said child has been named Susie M. Gardner, and was living March 4, 1905.

                                her
                        Mattie x Gardner
Witnesses To Mark: mark
  { Louie Austin
  { Jackson Baker

Subscribed and sworn to before me this 14th day of April, 1905.

E.J. Gardner
Notary Public.

AFFIDAVIT OF ATTENDING PHYSICIAN OR MID-WIFE.

UNITED STATES OF AMERICA, Indian Territory,
DISTRICT.

I, C.L. Wright, a Physician, on oath state that I attended on Mrs. Mattie Gardner, wife of Alfred Gardner on the 19th day of November, 1903; that there was born to her on said date a female child; that said child was living March 4, 1905, and is said to have been named Susie M. Gardner

C.L. Wright M.D.

Applications for Enrollment of Choctaw Newborn
Act of 1905   Volume XV

Witnesses To Mark:
{

    Subscribed and sworn to before me this   14th   day of   April   , 1905

                                     E.J. Gardner
                                     Notary Public.

Choc New Born 1093
     Gensie Hopson
   (Born April 2, 1904)

DEPARTMENT OF THE INTERIOR,
COMMISSIONER TO THE FIVE CIVILIZED TRIBES.

In the matter of the application for the enrollment as a citizen by blood of the Choctaw Nation of................

                        GENSIE HOPSON........7-NB-1093.

BIRTH AFFIDAVIT.
                 DEPARTMENT OF THE INTERIOR.
       COMMISSION TO THE FIVE CIVILIZED TRIBES.

     IN RE APPLICATION FOR ENROLLMENT, as a citizen of the   Chocktaw[sic]   Nation, of   Gensie Hopson   , born on the 2   day of April   , 1904

Name of Father: Reyson Hopson   a citizen of the   Chocktaw   Nation.
Name of Mother: Lena Hopson   a citizen of the   Chocktaw   Nation.

                 Postoffice   Corinne[sic] Ind. T.

                 AFFIDAVIT OF MOTHER.

UNITED STATES OF AMERICA, Indian Territory, }
    Central   **DISTRICT.**

    I,   Lena Hopson   , on oath state that I am   23   years of age and a citizen by Blood   , of the   Chocktaw   Nation; that I am the lawful wife of   Reyson Hopson , who is a citizen, by Blood   of the   Chocktaw   Nation; that a   Female

Applications for Enrollment of Choctaw Newborn
Act of 1905   Volume XV

child was born to me on   second   day of   April   , 1904; that said child has been named   Gensie Hopson   , and was living March 4, 1905.

                her
             ~~Ray~~ Lena x Hopson

Witnesses To Mark: mark
 { Lymon Billy (her mark)
  Susan x Billy (mark)

  Subscribed and sworn to before me this   10 day of   April   , 1905

            Jno E Talbert
My Com expires   Notary Public.
Dec 12 1908

AFFIDAVIT OF ATTENDING PHYSICIAN OR MID-WIFE.

UNITED STATES OF AMERICA, Indian Territory, }
 Central   DISTRICT.

  I,   Reyson Hopson   , a   midwife   , on oath state that I attended on ~~Mrs.~~ *my wife* Lena Hopson , wife of   Reyson Hopson   on the second day of April , 1904; that there was born to her on said date a   Female   child; that said child was living March 4, 1905, and is said to have been named Gensie Hopson

               his
            Reyson x Hopson
Witnesses To Mark: mark
 { Lymon Billy (her mark)
  Susan x Billy (mark)

  Subscribed and sworn to before me this   10 day of   April   , 1905

            Jno E Talbert
My Com expires   Notary Public.
Dec 12 1908

Applications for Enrollment of Choctaw Newborn
Act of 1905   Volume XV

BIRTH AFFIDAVIT.

DEPARTMENT OF THE INTERIOR.
COMMISSION TO THE FIVE CIVILIZED TRIBES.

IN RE APPLICATION FOR ENROLLMENT, as a citizen of the Chocktaw[sic] Nation, of Gensie Hopson, born on the 2d day of April, 1904

Name of Father: Reason Hopson   a citizen of the Chocktaw Nation.
Name of Mother: Lena Hopson   a citizen of the Chocktaw Nation.

Postoffice   Corinne[sic] Ind. Ter.

AFFIDAVIT OF MOTHER.

UNITED STATES OF AMERICA, Indian Territory,
Central   DISTRICT.

I, Lena Nehka, on oath state that I am 23 years of age and a citizen by Blood, of the Chocktaw Nation; that I am the lawful wife of Reason Hopson, who is a citizen, by Blood of the Chocktaw Nation; that a Female child was born to me on second day of April, 1904; that said child has been named Gensie Hopson, and was living March 4, 1905.

             her
       Lena x Nehka
Witnesses To Mark: mark
   { Columbus Tims
   { Morris Tom

Subscribed and sworn to before me this 28 day of April, 1905

         Jno E Talbert
My Com expires   Notary Public.
Dec 12 1908

AFFIDAVIT OF ATTENDING PHYSICIAN OR MID-WIFE.

UNITED STATES OF AMERICA, Indian Territory,
Central   DISTRICT.

I, Reason Hopson, a midwife, on oath state that I attended on Mrs. Lena Hopson, wife of Reason Hopson on the second day of April, 1904; that there was born to her on said date a Female child; that said child was living March 4, 1905, and is said to have been named Gensie Hopson

Applications for Enrollment of Choctaw Newborn
Act of 1905   Volume XV

Witnesses To Mark:
{ Columbus Tims
  Morris Tom

Reason x Hopson
(his mark)

Subscribed and sworn to before me this 28 day of April, 1905

Jno E Talbert
Notary Public.

My Com expires
Dec 12 1908

DEPARTMENT OF THE INTERIOR,
COMMISSION TO THE FIVE CIVILIZED TRIBES.

Valliant, Indian Territory, April 16, 1906.

In the matter of the death of Gensie Hopson, Choctaw New Born, Card Number 1093.

Testimony taken six miles northwest of Rufe, Indian Territory, April 11, 1906.

REASON HOPSON, being first duly sworn, testified, through interpreter Jacob Homer, as follows:

BY THE COMMISSIONER:

Q What is your name? A Reason Hopson.
Q How old are you? A About 40 years old.
Q What is your post office address? A Corinne[sic], I T.
Q Are you a citizen by blood of the Choctaw Nation? A Yes, a full-blood Choctaw.

Witness is here identified as a Choctaw by blood, Roll Number 2488.

Q Are you the father of Gensie Hopson?
A Yes, sir.
Q When was Gensie Hopson born?
A The 2nd day of April.
Q What year?
A Year before last (1904).
Q Is the child now living?
A No, she is dead.
Q When did Gensie Hopson die?
A She died six days after she was born.
Q The records of the Commission to the Five Civilized Tribes show that on April 28, 1905, before John E. Tolbert, Notary Public, you, as mid-wife, affirmed that this child,

Applications for Enrollment of Choctaw Newborn
Act of 1905   Volume XV

Gensie Hopson, was born on the 2nd of April 1904 and was living March 4, 1905; you have just testified that the child was born the 2nd of April, 1904 and died on the 8th of April 1904 when only six days old: why did you affirm the child to be living March 4, 1905 when it died April 8, 1904?
A I guess that's a mistake, I do not know anything about how they fixed it; I can't read nor write.
Q Did the Notary Public before whom you appeared to have Gensie Hopson enrolled ask you whether or not the child was living March 4, 1905.
A He did not ask me anything about whether the child was living or dead.
Q Do you state upon oath and as a matter of fact that you are the father of Gensie Hopson; that she was born the 2nd of April 1904 and died on or about the 8th of April 1904 and was about one week old at the time of her death?
A Yes.

Witness Excused.

Testimony taken six miles northwest of Rufe, Indian Territory, April 11, 1906.

Jacob Homer, Interpreter.

<u>BY THE COMMISSIONER:</u>

Q What is your name? A Lena Hopson.
Q What is your post office? A Corinne[sic], I. T.
Q What is your age? A About 25 years old.
Q Are you a citizen by blood of the Choctaw Nation?
A Yes, sir.
Q What was your maiden name? A Lena Nehka.

The witness is here identified as a Choctaw by blood, Roll Number 2481.

Q Are you the mother of Gensie Hopson?
A Yes.
Q When was Gensie Hopson born?
A The 2nd day of April 1904.
Q Is the child living or dead? A Dead.
Q When did she die?
A About six days after she was born.
Q From the records of the Commission to the Five Civilized Tribes it appears that on the 28th day of April 1905, before John E. Tolbert, Notary Public, you affirmed that you were the mother of a female child named Gensie Hopson, born on the 2nd of April 1904 and living March 4, 1905; you now state Gensie Hopson was born the 2nd of April 1904 and died about six days afterwards; when you make affidavit regarding the birth of this child, did you know you swore the child was living eleven months afterwards?
A The child died when it was six days old; I never noticed how they fixed the papers.
Q Can you read or write? A No, sir.

Applications for Enrollment of Choctaw Newborn
Act of 1905   Volume XV

Q Did the Notary Public ask you regarding whether or not the child was dead or living when you appeared before him?
A No, sir.

Witness Excused.

W. P. Covington, being first duly sworn, states that the above and foregoing is a full true and correct transcript of his stenographic notes taken in said case on said date.

W.P. Covington

Subscribed and sworn to before me, this 16th day of April, 1906.

Lacey P. Bobo
Notary Public.

7-NB-1093.

DEPARTMENT OF THE INTERIOR,
COMMISSIONER TO THE FIVE CIVILIZED TRIBES.

In the matter of the application for the enrollment of Gensie Hopson as a citizen by blood of the Choctaw Nation.

DECISION.

It appears from the record herein that on April 17, 1905, application was made to the Commission to the Five Civilized Tribes for the enrollment of Gensie Hopson as a citizen by blood of the Choctaw Nation.

It appears from the record herein and from the records of the Commission to the Five Civilized Tribes that the applicant was born on April 2, 1904; that he[sic] is the son of Lena Hopson, a recognized and enrolled citizen by blood of the Choctaw Nation, whose name (as Lena Nekha[sic]) appears as number 2481 upon the final roll of citizens by blood of the Choctaw Nation approved by the Secretary of the Interior December 12, 1902, and Reason Hopson, a recognized and enrolled citizen by blood of the Choctaw Nation, whose name appears as number 2488 upon the final roll of citizens by blood of the Choctaw Nation approved by the Secretary of the Interior December 12, 1902; and that said applicant died on April 8, 1904.

The Act of Congress approved March 3, 1905 (33 Stats., 1070) provides:

> "That the Commission to the Five Civilized Tribes is authorized for sixty days after the date of the approval of this act to receive and consider applications for enrollment of children born subsequent to September twenty-fifth, nineteen hundred and two, and prior to March fourth, nineteen hundred and five, and who were living on said latter date, to citizens by blood of the Choctaw and Chickasaw tribes of Indians whose enrollment has been approved by the

Applications for Enrollment of Choctaw Newborn
Act of 1905   Volume XV

Secretary of the Interior prior to the date of the approval of this act; and to enroll and make allotments to such children."

It is, therefore, ordered that the application for the enrollment of Gensie Hopson as a citizen by blood of the Choctaw Nation be, and the same is hereby dismissed.

Tams Bixby Commissioner.

Muskogee, Indian Territory.
JUN 21 1906

7-NB-1093

Muskogee, Indian Territory, June 21, 1906.

COPY

Lena Hopson,
    Corinne[sic], Indian Territory.

Dear Madam:

Inclosed herewith you will find a copy of the order of the Commissioner to the Five Civilized Tribes, dated June 21, 1906, dismissing the application for the enrollment of Gensie Hopson as a citizen by blood of the Choctaw Nation.

Respectfully,
SIGNED

Tams Bixby
Chairman.

Registered.
Incl. 7-NB-1093.

Applications for Enrollment of Choctaw Newborn
Act of 1905   Volume XV

7-NB-1903
F-NB-1093
7-NB-1093

Muskogee, Indian Territory, June 21, 1906.

Mansfield, McMurray & Cornish,
    Attorneys for the Choctaw and Chickasaw Nations,
        South McAlester, Indian Territory.

Gentlemen:

    Inclosed herewith you will find a copy of the order of the Commissioner to the Five Civilized Tribes, dated June 21, 1906, dismissing the application for the enrollment of Gensie Hopson as a citizen by blood of the Choctaw Nation.

        Respectfully,
        SIGNED

        Tams Bixby
        Chairman.

Incl. F-NB-1093.

Choctaw 925.

Muskogee, Indian Territory, April 20, 1905.

Reyson Hopson,
    Corinne[sic], Indian Territory.

Dear Sir:

    Receipt is hereby acknowledged of the affidavits of Lena Hopson and Rayson[sic] Hopson to the birth of Ginsie[sic] Hopson, daughter of Reyson and Lena Hopson, April 2, 1904.

    It is stated in the affidavit of the mother that she is a citizen by blood of the Choctaw Nation, and if this is correct you are requested to give the name under which she was enrolled, the names of her parents and if she has taken an allotment of the lands of the Choctaw and Chickasaw Nations, give her roll number as the same appears upon her allotment certificate.

    You are also requested to state your age, the names of your parents, and if you have selected an allotment, your roll number as the same appears upon your allotment certificate.

Applications for Enrollment of Choctaw Newborn
Act of 1905   Volume XV

This matter should receive your immediate attention in order that proper disposition may be made of the application for the enrollment of your child.

Respectfully,

Chairman.

---

7 NB 1093

Muskogee, Indian Territory, May 5, 1905.

Reason Hopson,
    Corrine, Indian Territory.

Dear Sir:

Receipt is hereby acknowledged of the affidavits of Lena Nehka and Reason Hopson to the birth of Gensie Hopson, a daughter of Reason and Lena Hopson, April 2, 1904, and the same have been filed with our records as an application for the enrollment of said child.

Respectfully,

Commissioner in Charge.

7--NB--1093

Muskogee, Indian Territory, June 2, 1906.

Reason Hopson,
    Corrine, Indian Territory.

Dear Sir:

Referring to the application for the enrollment of your infant child, Gensie Hopson, born April 2, 1904, it is noted from the affidavits heretofore filed in this office that you were the only one in attendance upon your wife at the time of the birth of the applicant.

In this event it will be necessary that the affidavits of two persons, who are disinterested and not related to the applicant, who have actual knowledge of the facts that the child was born, the date of her birth; that she was living on March 4, 1905, and that Lena Hopson is her mother be filed in this office.

Applications for Enrollment of Choctaw Newborn
Act of 1905   Volume XV

This matter should receive your immediate attention as no further action relative to the enrollment of said child can be taken until the Commission has been furnished these affidavits.

                       Respectfully,

                                      [sic]

7-NB-1093

                 Muskogee, Indian Territory, July 25, 1905.

Reason Hopson,
    Corinne[sic], Indian Territory.

Dear Sir:

Your attention is called to a communication addressed to you by the Commission to the Five Civilized Tribes under date of June 2, 1905, requesting additional evidence in the matter of the enrollment of your infant child, Gensie Hopson, born April 2, 1904, in which you were advised that the affidavits heretofore filed in this office show that you were the only one in attendance upon you wife at the time of the birth of the applicant and you were requested to furnish the affidavits of two persons who are disinterested and not related to the applicant, who have actual knowledge of the facts; that the child was born, the date of her birth, that she was living on March 4, 1905, and that Lena Hopson is her mother. No reply to this letter has been received.

The matter should receive your immediate attention as no further action can be taken relative to the enrollment of your said child until evidence requested is supplied.

                       Respectfully,

                                Commissioner.

<u>Choc New Born 1094</u>
    Sidney Milton
    (Born Sept. 17, 1903)

Applications for Enrollment of Choctaw Newborn
Act of 1905   Volume XV

(The affidavit below typed as given.)

BIRTH AFFIDAVIT.

DEPARTMENT OF THE INTERIOR,
COMMISSION TO THE FIVE CIVILIZED TRIBES.

IN RE Application for Enrollment, as a citizen of the   Choctaw   Nation, of   Sidney Billy , born on the   19   day of   December , 1903

Name of Father: Thomas Quinn   a citizen of the   Choctaw   Nation.
Name of Mother: Mily Billy   a citizen of the   Choctaw   Nation.

Post-Office: Wister I.T.

AFFIDAVIT OF MOTHER.

UNITED STATES OF AMERICA,
  INDIAN TERRITORY.
  Central   District.

I,   Mily Billy , on oath state that I am   30   years of age and a citizen by Blood , of the   Choctaw   Nation; that I am *not* the lawful wife of   Thomas Quinn , who is a citizen, by   Blood   of the Choctaw   Nation; that a   male   child was born to me on 19   day of   December , 1901, that said child has been named   Sidney Billy , and is now living.

                                        her
                                  Mily x Billy
WITNESSES TO MARK: mark
  { Roberson Perry
  { H J Jackson

Subscribed and sworn to before me this   2   day of   June , 1904.

                              J.J. Riggs
                                  NOTARY PUBLIC.

Applications for Enrollment of Choctaw Newborn
Act of 1905   Volume XV

AFFIDAVIT OF ATTENDING PHYSICIAN OR MID-WIFE.

UNITED STATES OF AMERICA,
   INDIAN TERRITORY.
...............................District.

I, Liza Perry, a ...., on oath state that I attended on Mrs. Milly Billy, wife of Eastman Billy on the 19 day of December, 1903 ; that there was born to her on said date a male child; that said child is now living and is said to have been named Sidney Billy

                      her
                 Liza x Perry
WITNESSES TO MARK: mark
  { Roberson Perry
    H J Jackson

Subscribed and sworn to before me this 2 *day of* June, 1904.

                      J.J. Riggs
                        NOTARY PUBLIC.

7-6594

BIRTH AFFIDAVIT.

DEPARTMENT OF THE INTERIOR.
COMMISSION TO THE FIVE CIVILIZED TRIBES.

IN RE APPLICATION FOR ENROLLMENT, as a citizen of the Choctaw Nation, of Sidney Milton, born on the 17 day of September, 1903

Name of Father: Thomas Quinn   a citizen of the Choc Nation.
Name of Mother: Mila Milton   a citizen of the Choc Nation.

               Postoffice   Wister I.T.

AFFIDAVIT OF MOTHER.

UNITED STATES OF AMERICA, Indian Territory,
  Central   DISTRICT.

I, Mila Milton, on oath state that I am 30 years of age and a citizen by blood, of the Choctaw Nation; that I am *not* the lawful wife of Thomas Quinn, who is a citizen, by blood of the Choctaw Nation; that a male child was born to me on 17 day of September, 1903; that said child has been named Sidney Milton, and was living March 4, 1905.

Applications for Enrollment of Choctaw Newborn
Act of 1905 Volume XV

                              her
                           Mila x Milton
Witnesses To Mark: mark
  { Chas. T. Difendafer
    OL Johnson

    Subscribed and sworn to before me this 18 day of   April , 1905

                                    OL Johnson
                                    Notary Public.

AFFIDAVIT OF ATTENDING PHYSICIAN OR MID-WIFE.

UNITED STATES OF AMERICA, Indian Territory, }
  Central   DISTRICT. }

    I,   Liza Perry , a midwife , on oath state that I attended on Mrs. Mila Milton , wife of Thomas Quinn on the 17 day of September, 1903; that there was born to her on said date a male child; that said child was living March 4, 1905, and is said to have been named Sidney Milton

                              her
                       Liza x Perry
Witnesses To Mark: mark
  { Chas. T. Difendafer
    OL Johnson

    Subscribed and sworn to before me this 18 day of   April , 1905

                                    OL Johnson
                                    Notary Public.

Applications for Enrollment of Choctaw Newborn
Act of 1905   Volume XV

$W^m O.B.$

COMMISSIONERS:
TAMS BIXBY,
THOMAS B. NEEDLES,
C.R. BRECKINBRIDGE.

WM. O. BEALL
Secretary

DEPARTMENT OF THE INTERIOR,
COMMISSIONER TO THE FIVE CIVILIZED TRIBES.

REFER IN REPLY TO THE FOLLOWING:
_____

ADDRESS ONLY THE
COMMISSION TO THE FIVE CIVILIZED TRIBES.

Muskogee, Indian Territory, December 7, 1904.

Roberson Perry,
    Wister, Indian Territory.

Dear Sir:

    On June 18, 1904, there was received at this office the affidavits of Mily Billy and Liza Perry relative to the birth of Sidney Billy, infant son of Thomas Quinn and Mily Billy December 19, 1903.

    It appears from the affidavits that you were a witness to the signature by mark must be attested by two witnesses of Mily Billy to her affidavit relative to the birth of her child. It is stated in her affidavit that she is a citizen by blood of the Choctaw Nation. If this is a fact you are kindly requested to state the time and place application was made for her enrollment, the name by which she was then known, also the names of the other members of the family to which she belongs, and any other information you may have which will enable the Commission to identify Mily Billy as a citizen by blood of the Choctaw Nation.

    Kindly give this matter prompt attention, returning your reply in the enclosed envelope which requires no postage.

                      Respectfully,
                      Tams Bixby

Env.   Chairman.

7-6594.

DEPARTMENT OF THE INTERIOR,
COMMISSION TO THE FIVE CIVILIZED TRIBES.
WISTER, IND. TER.   APRIL 18, 1905.

    In the matter of the application for the enrollment of Sidney Milton as a citizen by blood of the Choctaw Nation.

Mila Milton being duly sworn and examined through interpreter Robert Morris testifies as follows:

Applications for Enrollment of Choctaw Newborn
Act of 1905   Volume XV

EXAMINATION BY THE COMMISSION:

Q What is your name? A Mila Milton.
Q What is your age? A About thirty.
Q What is your post office address? A Wister.
Q You present here a letter from the Commission to the Five Civilized Tribes dates December 7, 1904 wherein they acknowledge receipt of the application for the enrollment of Sidney Billy as a citizen of the Choctaw Nation. In that affidavit you gave your name as Millie Billy is that your right name? A No it is Mila Milton.
Q Do your allotment certificate read Mila Milton? A Yes, sir.
Q Did you in June 1904 make application for the enrollment of your minor child Sidney Billy? A Yes, sir.
Q In that affidavit the father of the child was given as Thomas Quinn? A Yes, sir.
Q When was that boy born? A September 17, 1903.
Q Now is Thomas Quinn a citizen of the Choctaw Nation? A Yes, sir, citizen by blood of the Choctaw Nation.
Q Does his name appear upon the final roll of the Commission and has he filed? A Yes, sir, he filed in the Chickasaw Nation.
Q You were never married to Thomas Quinn? A No, sir.
Q In the former affidavit it is also states that Sidney Billy was born December 19, 1903 is that correct? A No, sir, that isn't correct, it is a mistake.
Q In the affidavit formerly made your name as Milly Billy, that is not the way your name appears upon the final roll is it? A No, sir, it appears as Mila Milton.
Q Milton is your maiden name? A Yes, sir.
Q And you married a Choctaw by the name of Billy? A Yes, sir.
Q Is Billy living now? A He is dead.

Witness excused.

Chas. T. Difendafer being first duly sworn states that the above and foregoing is a full, true and correct transcript of his stenographic notes taken in said cause on said date.

Chas.T. Difendafer

Subscribed and sworn to before me this 18th day of April 1905.

OL Johnson
Notary Public.

Applications for Enrollment of Choctaw Newborn
Act of 1905   Volume XV

Choc New Born 1095
    Nova Cleo Ward
    (Born Oct. 21, 1904)

NEW BORN AFFIDAVIT

No _____

CHOCTAW ENROLLING COMMISSION

IN THE MATTER OF THE APPLICATION FOR ENROLLMENT as a citizen of the Choctaw Nation, of Nova Cleo Ward born on the 21st day of October 190 4

Name of father Henry Ward a citizen of Choctaw Nation, final enrollment No. 12203

Name of mother ~~Willie Maud Ward~~ ~~a citizen of~~ ~~Choctaw~~ ~~Nation,~~ ~~final enrollment No.~~

Olney I.T. Postoffice.

AFFIDAVIT OF MOTHER

UNITED STATES OF AMERICA
    INDIAN TERRITORY
DISTRICT Central

I Willie Maud Ward , on oath state that I am 19 years of age ~~and a citizen by~~ ~~of the~~ ~~Nation, and as such have been placed upon the final roll of the~~ ~~Nation, by the Honorable Secretary of the Interior my final enrollment number being~~ that I am the lawful wife of Henry Ward , who is a citizen of the Choctaw Nation, and as such has been placed upon the final roll of said Nation by the Honorable Secretary of the Interior, his final enrollment number being 12203 and that a Female child was born to me on the 21st day of October 190 4; that said child has been named Nova Cleo Ward , and is now living.

WITNESSETH: Willie Maud Ward
  Must be two witnesses { J.M. Ward
  who are citizens   John S. Ward

Applications for Enrollment of Choctaw Newborn
Act of 1905   Volume XV

Subscribed and sworn to before me this, the 13th day of March, 190 5

Jno D Baldwin
Notary Public.

My Commission Expires: 4/6/08

Affidavit of Attending Physician or Midwife

UNITED STATES OF AMERICA,
INDIAN TERRITORY,
Central   DISTRICT

I, Cleo A McNeeley[sic] a Midwife on oath state that I attended on Mrs. Willie Maud Ward wife of Henry Ward on the 21st day of October, 190 4, that there was born to her on said date a Female child, that said child is now living, and is said to have been named Nova Cleo Ward

Cleo A McNeely   *Midwife*

Subscribed and sworn to before me this the 13th day of March 1905

Jno D Baldwin
Notary Public.

WITNESSETH:

Must be two witnesses who are citizens and know the child. { J.M. Ward
John S Ward

We hereby certify that we are well acquainted with Cleo A McNeely a Midwife and know her to be reputable and of good standing in the community.

Must be two citizen witnesses. { J.M. Ward
John S Ward

(Letter typed as given.)

APR 18 1905   4/17/05   Olney I.T.

Commission to the five civilized tribes
    Gentleman
Enclosed herewith is the certified copy of the marriage certificate and license. Also the affidavits. If there is any other evidence necessary notify me at once

Applications for Enrollment of Choctaw Newborn
Act of 1905 Volume XV

Very Respt

Henry Ward

No. 1652

Certificate of Record of Marriages.

UNITED STATES OF AMERICA,
INDIAN TERRITORY, } SCT:
Central DISTRICT.

I, E.J. Fannin , Clerk of the United States Court in the Indian Territory and District aforesaid, do hereby CERTIFY, that the License for and Certificate of the Marriage of

Mr. Henry Ward and

Miss W.M. McNeely was

filed in my office in said Territory and District the 28th day of Nov A.D., 190 2 and duly recorded in Book 2 of Marriage Record, Page 208 and the within is a certified copy of the same
WITNESS my hand and seal of said Court, at Atoka this 10 day of April A.D. 190 5

E.J. Fannin
Clerk.

By J.D. Catlin *Deputy.*

**Applications for Enrollment of Choctaw Newborn
Act of 1905   Volume XV**

No. 1652

MARRIAGE LICENSE

United States of America,   The Indian Territory,
                                                         Central   DISTRICT, SS.

To any Person Authorized by Law to Solemnize Marriage, Greeting:

You are hereby commanded to Solemnize the Rite and publish the Banns of Matrimony between Mr. Henry Ward
of Atoka   *in the Indian Territory, aged*   22   *years, and M* iss W.M. McNeely   *of*
in the Indian Territory., aged   17   *years, according to law, and do you officially sign and return this License to the parties therein named.*

                     WITNESS my hand and official seal, this   12   *day of*   Nov.   *A. D. 190* 2

                                                 E.J. Fannin
                                   Clerk of the United States Court.

                     J.D. Catlin   *Deputy*

                                    Certificate of Marriage.

United States of America,
   The Indian Territory,   } *ss.*
      Central   *District.*   *I,*   R.J. Hogue

a Minister of the Gospel   *, do hereby certify, that on the*   16   *day of* Nov.   *A. D. 190* 2 *, I did, duly and according to law, as commanded in the foregoing License, solemnize the Rite and publish the Banns of Matrimony between the parties therein named.*

            Witness my hand, this   16   *day of*   Nov   *A. D. 190* 2

My credentials are recorded in the office of the Clerk of   R.J. Hogue
   the United States Court in the Indian Territory,   }
     Central District, Book   A   *, Page*   49   *a*   Minister

---

      Note—This License and Certificate of Marriage must be returned to the Office of the Clerk of the United States Court of the Indian Territory, from whence it was issued, within sixty days from the date thereof, or the party to whom the License was issued will be liable in the amount of the One Hundred Dollars ($100.00)

Applications for Enrollment of Choctaw Newborn
Act of 1905   Volume XV

BIRTH AFFIDAVIT.

DEPARTMENT OF THE INTERIOR.
COMMISSION TO THE FIVE CIVILIZED TRIBES.

IN RE APPLICATION FOR ENROLLMENT, as a citizen of the Choctaw Nation, of Nova Cleo Ward, born on the 21st day of October, 1904

Name of Father: Henry Ward   a citizen of the Choctaw Nation.
Name of Mother: Willie Maud Ward   a citizen of the United States Nation.

Postoffice   Olney, I.T.

AFFIDAVIT OF MOTHER.

UNITED STATES OF AMERICA, Indian Territory,
Central DISTRICT.

I, Willie Maud Ward, on oath state that I am 20 *years of age and a citizen* ——— of the *United States* ~~Nation~~; that I am the lawful wife of Henry Ward, who is a citizen, by blood of the Choctaw Nation; that a female child was born to me on 21st day of October, 1904; that said child has been named Nova Cleo Ward, and was living March 4, 1905.

                                Willie Maud Ward

Witnesses To Mark:

Subscribed and sworn to before me this 8th day of April, 1905.

                                W.H. Angell
                                   Notary Public.

AFFIDAVIT OF ATTENDING PHYSICIAN OR MID-WIFE.

UNITED STATES OF AMERICA, Indian Territory,
Central DISTRICT.

I, Cleo A. McNeely, a midwife, on oath state that I attended on Mrs. Willie Maud Ward, wife of Henry Ward on the 21st day of October, 1904; that there was born to her on said date a .... child; that said child was living March 4, 1905, and is said to have been named Nova Cleo Ward

                                Cleo A McNeely

Applications for Enrollment of Choctaw Newborn
Act of 1905 Volume XV

Witnesses To Mark:
{

Subscribed and sworn to before me this 17th day of   April   , 1905

Jno D Baldwin
Notary Public.

Choc New Born 1096
Leroy H. Camden
(Born March 6, 1904)

BIRTH AFFIDAVIT.

DEPARTMENT OF THE INTERIOR.
COMMISSION TO THE FIVE CIVILIZED TRIBES.

IN RE APPLICATION FOR ENROLLMENT, as a citizen of the   Choctaw   Nation, of Leroy H. Camden   , born on the 6th day of March , 1904

Name of Father: A. B. Camden   a citizen of the Choctaw   Nation.
Name of Mother: Ida B. Camden   a citizen of the Choctaw   Nation.

Postoffice   Hugo, Ind. Ter.

AFFIDAVIT OF MOTHER.

UNITED STATES OF AMERICA, Indian Territory,
Central   DISTRICT.

I, Ida B. Camden , on oath state that I am 24   years of age and a citizen by   blood   , of the   Choctaw   Nation; that I am the lawful wife of   A. B. Camden   , who is a citizen, by marriage   of the   Choctaw   Nation; that a male   child was born to me on 6th day of March   , 1904; that said child has been named Leroy H. Camden   , and was living March 4, 1905.

Ida B. Camden

Witnesses To Mark:
{

Applications for Enrollment of Choctaw Newborn
Act of 1905   Volume XV

Subscribed and sworn to before me this 17th day of April, 1905

Wirt Franklin
Notary Public.

AFFIDAVIT OF ATTENDING PHYSICIAN OR MID-WIFE.

UNITED STATES OF AMERICA, Indian Territory,
Central DISTRICT.

I, J.S. Fulton, a physician, on oath state that I attended on Mrs. Ida B. Camden, wife of A. B. Camden on the 6th day of March, 1904; that there was born to her on said date a .... child; that said child was living March 4, 1905, and is said to have been named Leroy H. Camden

J.S. Fulton

Witnesses To Mark:

Subscribed and sworn to before me this 18th day of April, 1905

W.H. Angell
Notary Public.

Choc New Born 1097
Lonnie Burton Dills
(Born Feb. 3, 1903)

NEW-BORN AFFIDAVIT.

Number...............

Choctaw Enrolling Commission.

IN THE MATTER OF THE APPLICATION FOR ENROLLMENT, as a citizen of the Chocktaw[sic] Nation, of Lonnie Burton Dills

born on the 3 day of February 190 3

Name of father   Eugene Dills   a citizen of   United States
Nation final enrollment No...............

Applications for Enrollment of Choctaw Newborn
Act of 1905 Volume XV

Name of mother   Rosa Dills   a citizen of   Chocktaw
Nation final enrollment No   15722

Postoffice   Durant I.T.

AFFIDAVIT OF MOTHER.

UNITED STATES OF AMERICA,
INDIAN TERRITORY,
Central   DISTRICT

I   Rosa Dills   on oath state that I am 22 years of age and a citizen by Blood of the Chocktaw Nation, and as such have been placed upon the final roll of the Chocktaw Nation, by the Honorable Secretary of the Interior my final enrollment number being 15722 ; that I am the lawful wife of Eugene Dills , who is a citizen of the United States Nation, and as such has been placed upon the final roll of said Nation by the Honorable Secretary of the Interior, his final enrollment number being _____ and that a Male child was born to me on the 3 day of February 190 3 ; that said child has been named Lonnie Burton Dills , and is now living.

Rosa Dills

WITNESSETH:
Must be two Witnesses who are Citizens.
A B Beal
Albert Beal

Subscribed and sworn to before me this 20 day of Jan 190 5

F M Kizer
Notary Public.

My commission expires Mar 10 1907

Affidavit of Attending Physician or Midwife.

UNITED STATES OF AMERICA
INDIAN TERRITORY
Central   DISTRICT

I, Emily Hatinger a Mid wife on oath state that I attended on Mrs. Rosa Dills wife of Eugene Dills on the 3 day of Feb. , 190 3 , that there was born to her on said date a Male child, that said child is now living, and is said to have been named Lonnie Burton Dills

Emily Hatinger   *Midwife*

Applications for Enrollment of Choctaw Newborn
Act of 1905   Volume XV

Subscribed and sworn to before me this, the   20   day of   Jany   190 5

F M Kizer
Notary Public.

WITNESSETH:
Must be two witnesses
who are citizens and
know the child.   { A B Beal
                    Albert Beal

We hereby certify that we are well acquainted with   A.B. Beal
a   Albert Beal   and know   them   to be reputable and of good standing in the community.

{ George Beal
  Ada Bell Moore

BIRTH AFFIDAVIT.

DEPARTMENT OF THE INTERIOR.
COMMISSION TO THE FIVE CIVILIZED TRIBES.

IN RE APPLICATION FOR ENROLLMENT, as a citizen of the   Choctaw   Nation, of   Lonie[sic] Burton Dills   , born on the 3rd day of   February   , 1903

Name of Father: Eugene Dills   a citizen of the   Choctaw   Nation.
Name of Mother: Rosa Dills   a citizen of the   Choctaw   Nation.

Postoffice   Durant, I.T.

AFFIDAVIT OF MOTHER.

UNITED STATES OF AMERICA, Indian Territory, }
Central   DISTRICT.

I,   Rosa Dills   , on oath state that I am   23   years of age and a citizen by Blood   , of the   Chocktaw[sic]   Nation; that I am the lawful wife of   Eugene Dills   , who is a citizen, by United States   of the .... Nation; that a Male   child was born to me on   3   day of   Feb   , 1903; that said child has been named   Lonnie Burton Dills   , and was living March 4, 1905.

Rosa Dills

Witnesses To Mark:
{

Applications for Enrollment of Choctaw Newborn
Act of 1905 Volume XV

Subscribed and sworn to before me this 17 day of April , 1905

F M Kizer
Notary Public.

AFFIDAVIT OF ATTENDING PHYSICIAN OR MID-WIFE.

UNITED STATES OF AMERICA, Indian Territory,
Central DISTRICT.

I, Emily Hatinger , a Midwife , on oath state that I attended on Mrs. Rosa Dills , wife of Eugene Dills on the 3 day of Feb , 1903; that there was born to her on said date a male child; that said child was living March 4, 1905, and is said to have been named Lonnie Burton Dills

                                              her
Witnesses To Mark: Emily x Hatinger
  { J H Varnell   mark
  { R H Varnell

Subscribed and sworn to before me this 17 day of April , 1905

F M Kizer
Notary Public.

7-N.B. 1097.

Muskogee, Indian Territory, May 25, 1905.

Rosy Dills,
    Durant, Indian Territory.

Dear Madam:

    Receipt is hereby acknowledged of your letter of May 17, asking with reference to the enrollment of your child, Loney[sic] Burton Dills.

    In reply to your letter you are advised that the affidavits heretofore forwarded to the birth of your child, Lonnie Burton Dills, have been filed with our records in the matter of his enrollment, and in the event further evidence is necessary to enable us to determine his right to enrollment you will be duly notified.

                                       Respectfully,

                                                             Chairman.

Applications for Enrollment of Choctaw Newborn
Act of 1905 Volume XV

Choc New Born 1098
    Pearly McDonald
    (Born Nov. 12, 1904)

BIRTH AFFIDAVIT.

DEPARTMENT OF THE INTERIOR.
COMMISSION TO THE FIVE CIVILIZED TRIBES.

IN RE APPLICATION FOR ENROLLMENT, as a citizen of the Choctaw Nation, of Pearly McDonald, born on the 12 day of November, 1904

Name of Father: Author McDonald   a citizen of the United States Nation.
Name of Mother: Leeana Hudson   a citizen of the Choctaw Nation.

            Postoffice   Lukfata I.T.

AFFIDAVIT OF MOTHER.

UNITED STATES OF AMERICA, Indian Territory,
    Central   DISTRICT.

    I, Leeana Hudson, on oath state that I am 20 years of age and a citizen by blood, of the Choctaw Nation; that I am the lawful wife of Author McDonald, who is a citizen, ~~by~~ .... of the United States Nation; that a female child was born to me on 12th day of November, 1904; that said child has been named Pearly McDonald, and was living March 4, 1905.

                          her
                     Leeana x Hudson
Witnesses To Mark: mark
   { Carl Patterson
      J.O. Jones

    Subscribed and sworn to before me this 15 day of April, 1905

                    Carl Patterson
                        Notary Public.

AFFIDAVIT OF ATTENDING PHYSICIAN OR MID-WIFE.

UNITED STATES OF AMERICA, Indian Territory,
    Central   DISTRICT.

    I, Onie McDonald, a Mid-Wife, on oath state that I attended on Mrs. Leeana Hudson, wife of Author McDonald on the 12 day of

Applications for Enrollment of Choctaw Newborn
Act of 1905   Volume XV

November   , 1904; that there was born to her on said date a   female   child; that said child was living March 4, 1905, and is said to have been named Pearly McDonald

Onie McDonald

Witnesses To Mark:
{

Subscribed and sworn to before me this 15 day of April   , 1905

Carl Patterson
Notary Public.

BIRTH AFFIDAVIT.   7- nB 1098

DEPARTMENT OF THE INTERIOR.
COMMISSION TO THE FIVE CIVILIZED TRIBES.

IN RE APPLICATION FOR ENROLLMENT, as a citizen of the   Choctaw   Nation, of Pearly McDonald   , born on the 12 day of Nov , 1904

Name of Father: Author McDonald   a citizen of the   U.S.   ~~Nation~~.
Name of Mother: Leeana McDonald nee Hudson a citizen of the   Choctaw   Nation.

Postoffice   Lukfata I.T.

AFFIDAVIT OF MOTHER.

UNITED STATES OF AMERICA, Indian Territory, }
   Central   DISTRICT.

I, Leeana McDonald   , on oath state that I am 20   years of age and a citizen by   blood   , of the   Choctaw   Nation; that I am the lawful wife of   Author McDonald   , who is a citizen, by ———— of the   United States   Nation; that a   female   child was born to me on   12   day of   November   , 1904; that said child has been named   Pearly McDonald   , and was living March 4, 1905.

Leeana McDonald

Witnesses To Mark:
{

Subscribed and sworn to before me this 22 day of Aug   , 1905

J.L. Merry
Notary Public.

Applications for Enrollment of Choctaw Newborn
Act of 1905   Volume XV

AFFIDAVIT OF ATTENDING PHYSICIAN OR MID-WIFE.

UNITED STATES OF AMERICA, Indian Territory,
Central   DISTRICT.

I, Onie McDonald, a Midwife, on oath state that I attended on Mrs. Leeana McDonald, wife of Author McDonald on the 12 day of November, 1904; that there was born to her on said date a .... child; that said child was living March 4, 1905, and is said to have been named Pearly McDonald

Onie McDonald

Witnesses To Mark:

Subscribed and sworn to before me this 22 day of Aug, 1905

J.L. Merry
Notary Public.

7-NB-1098.

Muskogee, Indian Territory, June 9, 1905.

Commissioner in Charge,
    Choctaw Land Office,
        Atoka, Indian Territory.

Dear Sir:

There is enclosed herewith application for the enrollment of Pearly McDonald, which was executed before Carl Patterson, a Notary Public, and an employe[sic] in your office. The mother in her affidavit gives the date of the applicant's birth as November 12, 1904, while the midwife gives it as November 12, 1905. This latter date is apparently an error. You will please have it corrected and return the affidavits to this office.

Respectfully,

Chairman.

DeB--1/9.

Applications for Enrollment of Choctaw Newborn
Act of 1905   Volume XV

7-NB-1098

Muskogee, Indian Territory, July 25, 1905.

Leeana McDonald (Hudson),
    Lukfata, Indian Territory.

Dear Madam:

    There is inclosed you herewith for execution application for the enrollment of your infant child, Pearly McDonald, born November 12, 1904.

    In your affidavit of April 15, 1905, heretofore filed in this office you allege that you are the lawful wife of Authar[sic] McDonald, who is a citizen of the United States, that a female child was born to you on the 12th day of November, 1904, and that said child has been named Pealy[sic] McDonald, and was living March 4, 1905. Said affidavit is signed by you as "Leeana Hudson", in the inclosed application your name is given as "Leeana McDonald", and you should so sign the one inclosed.

    You are requested to have the affidavits properly executed and return to this office as early as possible, as no further action can be taken relative to the enrollment of your said child until the evidence requested is supplied.

                                    Respectfully,

LM 25/6.   Commissioner.

7-NB-1098

Muskogee, Indian Territory, August 26, 1905.

Leeanna[sic] McDonald,
    Lukfata, Indian Territory.

Dear Madam:

    Receipt is hereby acknowledged of the affidavits of Leeana McDonald and Onie McDonald to the birth of Pearly McDonald, daughter of Arthur[sic] and Leeana McDonald, November 12, 1904, and the same have been filed with the records in this case.

                                    Respectfully,

                                                                 Commissioner.

Applications for Enrollment of Choctaw Newborn
Act of 1905   Volume XV

7-NB-1098

Muskogee, Indian Territory, December 8, 1905.

Leeana McDonald,
    Glover, Indian Territory.

Dear Madam:

    Receipt is hereby acknowledged of your letter of December 3, 1905, asking if your baby Pearle[sic] McDonald has been approved.

    In reply to your letter you are advised that the name of your child Pearly McDonald has not yet been placed upon a schedule of new born citizens of the Choctaw Nation prepared for forwarding to the Secretary of the Interior, but you will be notified when her enrollment is approved by the Department.

                  Respectfully,

                          Acting Commissioner.

7-NB-1098

Muskogee, Indian Territory, April 13, 1906.

Authur[sic] McDonald,
    Glover, Indian Territory.

Dear Sir:

    Receipt is hereby acknowledged of your letter of April 9, 1906, asking the status of the application for the enrollment of your child Pearlie[sic] McDonald born November 12, 1904.

    In reply to your letter you are advised that on March 14, 1906, the Secretary of the Interior approved the enrollment of your child Pearlie McDonald as a new born citizen of the Choctaw Nation.

                    Respectfully,

                          Acting Commissioner.

Applications for Enrollment of Choctaw Newborn
Act of 1905   Volume XV

Choc New Born 1099
    Rebecca Willis
    (Born Feb. 22, 1904)

BIRTH AFFIDAVIT.

DEPARTMENT OF THE INTERIOR.
COMMISSION TO THE FIVE CIVILIZED TRIBES.

IN RE APPLICATION FOR ENROLLMENT, as a citizen of the Choctaw Nation, of Rebecca Willis, born on the 22nd day of Feb, 1904

Name of Father: Charley Hudson   a citizen of the Choctaw Nation.
Name of Mother: Elmira Willis   a citizen of the Choctaw Nation.

    Postoffice   Soper, Ind. Ter.

AFFIDAVIT OF MOTHER.

UNITED STATES OF AMERICA, Indian Territory, }
    Central   DISTRICT.

    I, Elmira Willis, on oath state that I am 36 years of age and a citizen by blood, of the Choctaw Nation; that I am the lawful wife of Charley Hudson, who is a citizen, by blood of the Choctaw Nation; that a female child was born to me on 22nd day of February, 1904; that said child has been named Rebecca Willis, and was living March 4, 1905.

                                     her
                            Elmira x Willis
Witnesses To Mark: mark
  { Robert Anderson
    Vester W Rose

    Subscribed and sworn to before me this 17th day of April, 1905

                         Wirt Franklin
                              Notary Public.

Applications for Enrollment of Choctaw Newborn
Act of 1905   Volume XV

AFFIDAVIT OF ATTENDING PHYSICIAN OR MID-WIFE.

UNITED STATES OF AMERICA, Indian Territory,
Central   DISTRICT.

I, W. M. Walace[sic] , a Physician , on oath state that I attended on Mrs. Elmira Willis , wife of .... on the 22 day of Feby , 1904; that there was born to her on said date a Female child; that said child was living March 4, 1905, and is said to have been named Rebecca Willis

W.M. Wallace, M.D.

Witnesses To Mark:

Subscribed and sworn to before me this 17 day of Apr , 1905

My commission expires
July 9th, 1908.

WE Larecy
Notary Public.

NEW-BORN AFFIDAVIT.

Number................

Choctaw Enrolling Commission.

IN THE MATTER OF THE APPLICATION FOR ENROLLMENT, as a citizen of the Choctaw   Nation, of   Rebeca[sic] Willis

born on the 22 day of February   1904

Name of father   Charley Hudson   a citizen of   Choctaw
Nation final enrollment No ....
Name of mother   Elmira Willis   a citizen of   Choctaw
Nation final enrollment No   4122

Postoffice   Soper I.T.

AFFIDAVIT OF MOTHER.

UNITED STATES OF AMERICA,
INDIAN TERRITORY,
Central   DISTRICT

I   Elmira Willis   on oath state that I am 36 years of age and a citizen by blood of the Choctaw Nation, and as such have been placed upon the final roll of the Choctaw Nation, by the Honorable Secretary of the Interior my final enrollment number being 4122 ; that I am ~~the lawful wife of~~ not married Charley Hudson , who is a citizen of the Choctaw

Applications for Enrollment of Choctaw Newborn
Act of 1905   Volume XV

Nation, and as such has been placed upon the final roll of said Nation by the Honorable Secretary of the Interior, his final enrollment number being .... and that a female child was born to me on the 22 day of February 190 4 ; that said child has been named Rebeca Willis , and is now living.

                                                    her

WITNESSETH: Elmira x Willis
Must be two Witnesses who are Citizens.   Tom Oakes Jr   mark
                  Joseph Cole

        Subscribed and sworn to before me this 24 day of Jan 190 5

                                WE Larecy
                                       Notary Public.

My commission expires July 9th 1908

Affidavit of Attending Physician or Midwife

UNITED STATES OF AMERICA,
    INDIAN TERRITORY,
    Central   DISTRICT

     I,   W.M. Hudson   a   Practicing Physician on oath state that I attended on Mrs. Elmira Willis ~~wife of~~ father of child Charley Hudson on the 22 day of February , 190 4, that there was born to her on said date a Female child, that said child is now living, and is said to have been named Rebecca Willis

                           W.M. Wallace   M. D.

        Subscribed and sworn to before me this the 24 day of Jan 1905

                              W.E. Larecy
                                   Notary Public.

WITNESSETH:
Must be two witnesses who are citizens and know the child.   Joseph Cole
                          TJ Oakes

     We hereby certify that we are well acquainted with W.M. Walace[sic] a Physician and know him to be reputable and of good standing in the community.

                           Must be two citizen witnesses.   R.C. Bills
                                                       Henry Williams

Applications for Enrollment of Choctaw Newborn
Act of 1905 Volume XV

Choc New Born 1100
    Sidney Hall
    (Born March 15, 1904)

NEW BORN AFFIDAVIT

No ....

CHOCTAW ENROLLING COMMISSION

IN THE MATTER OF THE APPLICATION FOR ENROLLMENT as a citizen of the Choctaw Nation, of Sidney Hall born on the 15th day of March 190 4

Name of father Joshua Hall a citizen of Choctaw Nation, final enrollment No. 1330
Name of mother Fannie Jefferson a citizen of Choctaw Nation, final enrollment No. 2070

Janis I.T. Postoffice.

AFFIDAVIT OF MOTHER

UNITED STATES OF AMERICA
    INDIAN TERRITORY
DISTRICT Central

I Fannie Jefferson , on oath state that I am 20 years of age and a citizen by blood of the Choctaw Nation, and as such have been placed upon the final roll of the Choctaw Nation, by the Honorable Secretary of the Interior my final enrollment number being 2070 ; that I am the lawful wife of Joshua Hall , who is a citizen of the Choctaw Nation, and as such has been placed upon the final roll of said Nation by the Honorable Secretary of the Interior, his final enrollment number being 1330 and that a Male child was born to me on the 15th day of March 190 4; that said child has been named Sidney Hall , and is now living.

                                                  her
WITNESSETH: Fannie x Jefferson
  Must be two witnesses Henry Alexander   mark
  who are citizens Eliza Trishka

Applications for Enrollment of Choctaw Newborn
Act of 1905   Volume XV

Subscribed and sworn to before me this, the   16   day of   Feb   , 190 5

W.A. Shoney
Notary Public.

My Commission Expires:
Jan 10, 1909

Affidavit of Attending Physician or Midwife

UNITED STATES OF AMERICA,
   INDIAN TERRITORY,
Central   DISTRICT

I,   Alice Hall   a   midwife   on oath state that I attended on Mrs.   Fannie Jefferson   wife of   Joshua Hall   on the   15th   day of   March   , 190 4, that there was born to her on said date a   male   child, that said child is now living, and is said to have been named   Sidney Hall

Alice Hall   M.D.

Subscribed and sworn to before me this the   16   day of   Feb   1905

W A Shoney
Notary Public.

WITNESSETH:

Must be two witnesses who are citizens and know the child. { Henry Alexander
Eliza Trishka

We hereby certify that we are well acquainted with   Alice Hall   a   midwife   and know   her   to be reputable and of good standing in the community.

Must be two citizen witnesses. { Henry Alexander
Eliza Trishka

BIRTH AFFIDAVIT.

DEPARTMENT OF THE INTERIOR.
COMMISSION TO THE FIVE CIVILIZED TRIBES.

IN RE APPLICATION FOR ENROLLMENT, as a citizen of the   Choctaw   Nation, of   Sidney Hall   , born on the   15   day of   March   , 1904

Name of Father: Joshua Hall   a citizen of the   Choctaw   Nation.
Name of Mother: Fannie Hall   a citizen of the   Choctaw   Nation.

Applications for Enrollment of Choctaw Newborn
Act of 1905   Volume XV

Postoffice   Janis, Ind Terr

AFFIDAVIT OF MOTHER.

UNITED STATES OF AMERICA, Indian Territory,
Central   DISTRICT.

I, Fannie Hall, on oath state that I am 20 years of age and a citizen by Blood, of the Choctaw Nation; that I am the lawful wife of Joshua Hall, who is a citizen, by Blood of the Choctaw Nation; that a Male child was born to me on 15 day of March, 1904; that said child has been named Sidney Hall, and was living March 4, 1905.

her
Fannie x Hall
mark

Witnesses To Mark:
{ Thompson Layon
  Ninnie Jefferson

Subscribed and sworn to before me this 17 day of April, 1905

J H Kirby
Notary Public.

AFFIDAVIT OF ATTENDING PHYSICIAN OR MID-WIFE.

UNITED STATES OF AMERICA, Indian Territory,
Central   DISTRICT.

I, Allice[sic] Jefferson, a mid wife, on oath state that I attended on Mrs. Fannie Hall, wife of Joshua Hall on the 15 day of March, 1904; that there was born to her on said date a male child; that said child was living March 4, 1905, and is said to have been named Sidney Hall

her
Allice x Jefferson
mark

Witnesses To Mark:
{ Thompson Layon
  Ninnie Jefferson

Subscribed and sworn to before me this 17 day of April, 1905

J H Kirby
Notary Public.

Applications for Enrollment of Choctaw Newborn
Act of 1905 Volume XV

7-NB-1100.

Muskogee, Indian Territory, June 2, 1905.

Joshua Hall,
    Janis, Indian Territory.

Dear Sir:

    There is returned herewith application for the enrollment of your infant child, Sidney Hall, born March 15, 1904, in which the Notary Public failed to affix his seal to the midwife's affidavit.

    Please have the Notary Public, J. H. Kirby, before whom this affidavit was executed, to affix his seal to the same and then return it to this office.

Respectfully,

VR 2-1.   [sic]

---

7 NB 1100

Muskogee, Indian Territory, June 17, 1905.

Joshua Hall,
    America, Indian Territory.

Dear Sir:

    Receipt is hereby acknowledged of the affidavits of Fannie Hall and Allice Jefferson to the birth of Sidney Hall, son of Joshua and Fannie Hall, March 15, 1904, and the same have been filed with our records in the matter of the enrollment of said child.

Respectfully,

Chairman.

Applications for Enrollment of Choctaw Newborn
Act of 1905   Volume XV

Choc New Born 1101
    Alice Bence[sic]
    (Born March 15, 1903)

BIRTH AFFIDAVIT.

DEPARTMENT OF THE INTERIOR.
COMMISSION TO THE FIVE CIVILIZED TRIBES.

IN RE APPLICATION FOR ENROLLMENT, as a citizen of the   Choctow[sic]   Nation, of   Alice Bench   , born on the   15   day of   March   , 1903

Name of Father: Sam Bench   a citizen of the   Choctow   Nation.
Name of Mother: Margarett Bench   a citizen of the   Choctow   Nation.

Postoffice   Boswell, Ind. Ter

AFFIDAVIT OF ~~MOTHER.~~ *Father*

UNITED STATES OF AMERICA, Indian Territory,
    Central Judicial   DISTRICT.

Bench, deceased

I, *Sam Bench, husband of Margarett* ^ , on oath state that I am   about 27   years of age and a citizen by   blood   , of the   Choctow Nation   Nation; that I ~~am~~ *was* the lawful ~~wife~~ *husband* of   Margarett Bench   , who ~~is~~ *was* a citizen, by blood   of the   Choctow   Nation; that a   female   child was born to ~~me~~ *her* on   15th   day of   March   , 1903; that said child has been named   Alice Bench   , and was living March 4, 1905.

                                  Sam Bench

Witnesses To Mark:
{

Subscribed and sworn to before me this   1st   day of   April   , 1905

                                  L.D. Horton
                                    Notary Public.

Applications for Enrollment of Choctaw Newborn
Act of 1905   Volume XV

AFFIDAVIT OF ATTENDING PHYSICIAN OR MID-WIFE.

UNITED STATES OF AMERICA, Indian Territory,
   Central Judicial   DISTRICT.

    I, J.L. Gentry M.D.   , a Physician , on oath state that I attended on Mrs. Margarett Bench , wife of Sam Bench on the 15th day of March , 1903; that there was born to her on said date a   female   child; that said child was living March 4, 1905, and is said to have been named Alice Bench

                                  J.L. Gentry, M.D.
Witnesses To Mark:

    Subscribed and sworn to before me this 1st day of April   , 1905

                                  L.D. Horton
                                  Notary Public.

(The affidavit below typed as given.)

Central Judicial District,
   Indian Territory.

    I, Sam Bench, after having been forst duly sworn state that I am about 27 years old and reside near Boswell, Indian Territory. That I was the lawful husband of Margaret Bench Deceased- That said Margaret died about November 1903-That she left surviving her Alice Bench a daughter born in March 1903- That The said Margaret was about 22 or 23 years old at the time of her death- That she was the daughter of Jimmie (or James) Belving and her mothers name was Lizie (or Eliza) Belvin and that they were choctaw indians by blood.

                                  Sam Bench

    Subscribed and sworn to before me this the 15th day of April 1905.

                                L.D. Horton
                                Notary Public.

Applications for Enrollment of Choctaw Newborn
Act of 1905 Volume XV

(The affidavit below typed as given.)

United States of America,
    Indian Territory,
Central Judicial District.

    We, Robert Crowder and Louisa Crowder, wife of the said Robert Crowder, after having been duly sworn, state that we are the ages of 62 and 57 and are citizens of the Choctaw Nation-and the said Robert Crowder is the guardian of Alice Bench a minor about two years old- We reside near Boswell, I.T.- We were acquainted with Mrs. Margarett Bench during her lifetime and she died in November 1903-She left surviving her the said Alice Bench whos is now living at our house and has so lived since the death of her said mother- We know the said Alice to be the daughter of the said Margarett and the said Margarett was the wife of Sam Bench who also makes a seperate affidavit on yes same paper-

    We know the said Margarett and the said Sam Bench to be citizens by blood of the Choctaw Nation.

                                       Louisa Crowder
Witness   Robert *his mark* Crowder
    L.D. Horton

Subscribed and sworn to before me this the 25th day of March 1905.

                                      L.D. Horton
                                      Notary Public.

United States of America,
    Indian Territory,
Central Judicial District.

    I, Sam Bench after being first duly sworn, state- I am about 27 years old and a citizen by blood of the Choctaw Nation- I am the father of Alice Bench, a minor about 2 years old for whose enrollment I am applying, I was the lawful husband of Margarett Bench deceased who died in the choctaw nation about Nov.1903 and she was a citizen by blood of the Choctaw Nation- And she was the mother of the said Alice-I was present and know that said baby was born to her and I know that she *the said Alice* is now living.

                                      Sam Bench

Subscribed and sworn to before me this the 25th day of March 1905.

                                      L.D. Horton
                                      Notary Public.

Applications for Enrollment of Choctaw Newborn
Act of 1905   Volume XV

Jackson County C. N.
October 21-1901

The man by the name Sam Binst (Bench) and the woman by the Makeslit Billvin (Margaret Belving) joined hand in marriage before me according to law.

So I give this marriage certificate this 21st day of October 1901.

A Preacher
Rev. J.D. Harrison
Atoka,
I.T.

Hon. Commission to the Five
Civilized Tribes,
Gentlemen:

Please address all communication to Robert Crowder, Guardian.
Boswell, I.T.

Very Truly
L.D. Horton

Muskogee, Indian Territory, April 7, 1905.

L. D. Horton,
Boswell, Indian Territory.

Dear Sir:

Receipt is hereby acknowledged of your letter of April 1, enclosing the affidavits of Louisa and Robert Crowder, Sam Bench and I. L. Gentry to the birth of Alice Bench, daughter of Sam and Margaret Bench, March 15, 1903.

It is stated that the mother, Margaret Bench, is a citizen by blood of the Choctaw Nation, and if this is correct you are requested to state under what name she was listed for enrollment, her age and the names of her parents in order that she may be identified upon our records as a citizen of the Choctaw Nation.

The birth certificate requested in your letter will be forwarded under a separate cover.

Respectfully,

Commissioner in Charge.

Applications for Enrollment of Choctaw Newborn
Act of 1905 Volume XV

7-3587

7 NB 285

Muskogee, Indian Territory, April 21, 1905.

L. D. Horton,
    Boswell, Indian Territory.

Dear Sir:

    Receipt is hereby acknowledged of your letter of April 15, 1905, enclosing affidavit of Sam Bench as to Margaret Bench, mother of Alice Bench, and the same has enabled the Commission to identify Margaret Bench as having been enrolled under the name of Margaret Belvin and the affidavits of Sam Bench, I. L. Gentry and joint affidavit of Louis[sic] Crowder and Robert Crowder heretofore forwarded have been filed with our records as an application for the enrollment of said child.

    Receipt is also acknowledged of a joint affidavit of J. J. Tompkins and H. Oshta to the birth of Sinie Carnes and the same has been filed with the record in the matter of the enrollment of said child.

    The matter of the application for the enrollment of Myrtle Lee Dowland will be made the subject of another communication.

    Respectfully,

    Chairman.

Choc New Born 1102
    Al Carey[sic]
    (Born March 8, 1904)

Applications for Enrollment of Choctaw Newborn
Act of 1905   Volume XV

BIRTH AFFIDAVIT.

DEPARTMENT OF THE INTERIOR.
COMMISSION TO THE FIVE CIVILIZED TRIBES.

IN RE APPLICATION FOR ENROLLMENT, as a citizen of the Choctaw Nation, of Al Carney, born on the 8 day of March, 1904

Name of Father: Allen Carney   a citizen of the Choctaw Nation.
Name of Mother: Ellar Carney   a citizen of the Choctaw Nation.

Postoffice   Quinton Ind. T.

AFFIDAVIT OF MOTHER.

UNITED STATES OF AMERICA, Indian Territory, }
Western   DISTRICT.

I, Ellar Carney, on oath state that I am 28 years of age and a citizen by Blood, of the Choctaw Nation; that I am the lawful wife of Allen Carney, who is a citizen, by Blood of the Choctaw Nation; that a Male child was born to me on 8 day of March, 1904; that said child has been named Al Carney, and was living March 4, 1905.

Ellar Carney

Witnesses To Mark:
{

Subscribed and sworn to before me this 4 day of April, 1905

J.M. White
Notary Public.

AFFIDAVIT OF ATTENDING PHYSICIAN OR MID-WIFE.

UNITED STATES OF AMERICA, Indian Territory, }
Western   DISTRICT.

I, Screna Carney, a Midwife, on oath state that I attended on Mrs. Ellar Carney, wife of Allen Carney on the 8 day of March, 1904; that there was born to her on said date a Male child; that said child was living March 4, 1905, and is said to have been named Al Carney

her
Screna x Carney
mark

Applications for Enrollment of Choctaw Newborn
Act of 1905   Volume XV

Witnesses To Mark:
{ *(Name Illegible)*
{ Clarence B. Burndage

Subscribed and sworn to before me this 4   day of   April   , 1905

J.M. White
Notary Public.

NEW-BORN AFFIDAVIT.

Number................

...Choctaw Enrolling Commission...

IN THE MATTER OF THE APPLICATION FOR ENROLLMENT, as a citizen of the Choctaw   Nation, of   Al Carney

born on the 8th day of ___March___ 190 4

Name of father Allen Carney   a citizen of   Choctaw
Nation final enrollment No. ....
Name of mother Ella[sic] Carney   a citizen of   Choctaw
Nation final enrollment No. 12461

Postoffice   Quinton

AFFIDAVIT OF MOTHER.

UNITED STATES OF AMERICA
INDIAN TERRITORY
  Western   DISTRICT

I   Ella Carney   , on oath state that I am 30   years of age and a citizen by blood   of the   Choctaw   Nation, and as such have been placed upon the final roll of the   Choctaw   Nation, by the Honorable Secretary of the Interior my final enrollment number being   12461 ; that I am the lawful wife of   Allen Carney   , who is a citizen of the   Choctaw   Nation, and as such has been placed upon the final roll of said Nation by the Honorable Secretary of the Interior, his final enrollment number being .... and that a   Male   child was born to me on the 8th day of   March   190 4; that said child has been named   Al Carney   , and is now living.

Ella Carney

Witnesseth.
  Must be two   } Joseph T Courts
  Witnesses who   }
  are Citizens.   F.R. Spann

Applications for Enrollment of Choctaw Newborn
Act of 1905   Volume XV

Subscribed and sworn to before me this 15th day of Feb 190 5

Guy A Curry
Notary Public.

My commission expires:
Apr 27-1907

AFFIDAVIT OF ATTENDING PHYSICIAN OR MIDWIFE

UNITED STATES OF AMERICA
INDIAN TERRITORY
   Western   DISTRICT

   I, Screna Carney a midwife on oath state that I attended on Mrs. Ella Carney wife of Allen Carney on the 8th day of March , 190 4 , that there was born to her on said date a Male child, that said child is now living, and is said to have been named Al Carney

her
Attest   Screna x Carney
Joseph T Courts   mark

Subscribed and sworn to before me this, the 15th day of February 190 5

Guy A Curry   Notary Public.

WITNESSETH:
Must be two witnesses
who are citizens
{ Joseph T Courts

   F.R. Spann

   We hereby certify that we are well acquainted with Screna Carney a midwife and know her to be reputable and of good standing in the community.

   Joseph T. Courts   _____

   F.R. Spann   _____

Muskogee, Indian Territory, April 7, 1905.

Allen Carney,
   Quinton, Indian Territory.

Dear Sir:

   Receipt is hereby acknowledged of the affidavits of Ellar Carney and Screna Carney to the birth of Al Carney, son of Allen and Ellar Carney, March 8, 1904.

Applications for Enrollment of Choctaw Newborn
Act of 1905 Volume XV

It is stated in the affidavit of the mother that she is a citizen by blood of the Choctaw Nation. If this is correct you are requested to state when, where and under what name she was enrolled, the names of her parents, and if she has selected an allotment, of the lands of the Choctaw and Chickasaw Nations please give her roll number as it appears on the certificate of allotment.

Respectfully,

Commissioner in Charge.

Choctaw 4491.

Muskogee, Indian Territory, April 21, 1905.

Allen Carney,
    Quinton, Indian Territory.

Dear Sir:

Receipt is hereby acknowledged of your letter of April 12, giving the roll number of your wife, Ella Carney, formerly Jones, also transmitting the affidavits of Ellar Carney and Screna Carney to the birth of your child, Al Carney, March 6, 1904, and the same have been filed with our records as an application for the enrollment of said child.

Respectfully,

Chairman.

Choc New Born 1103
    Bessie Jackson
    (Born Dec. 30, 1904)

Applications for Enrollment of Choctaw Newborn
Act of 1905 Volume XV

NEW-BORN AFFIDAVIT.

Number _____

...Choctaw Enrolling Commission...

IN THE MATTER OF THE APPLICATION FOR ENROLLMENT, as a citizen of the Choctaw Nation, of Bessie Jackson

born on the 30 day of ___Dec___ 190 4

Name of father   Ben Jackson   a citizen of   Choctaw
Nation final enrollment No. 7960
Name of mother   Lorena Jackson   a citizen of   Choctaw
Nation final enrollment No. 7640

Postoffice   Stigler I.T.

AFFIDAVIT OF MOTHER.

UNITED STATES OF AMERICA
INDIAN TERRITORY
   Central   DISTRICT

I   Lorena Jackson   , on oath state that I am 22 years of age and a citizen by Blood of the Choctaw Nation, and as such have been placed upon the final roll of the Choctaw Nation, by the Honorable Secretary of the Interior my final enrollment number being 7640 ; that I am the lawful wife of Ben Jackson , who is a citizen of the Choctaw Nation, and as such has been placed upon the final roll of said Nation by the Honorable Secretary of the Interior, his final enrollment number being 7960 and that a Female child was born to me on the 30 day of Dec 190 4; that said child has been named Bessie Jackson , and is now living.

Lorena Jackson

Witnesseth.

Must be two Witnesses who are Citizens.   }   Frank Wallace
                                              Joseph Folsom

Subscribed and sworn to before me this 28 day of Jan 190 5

R S Alexander
Notary Public.

My commission expires: Jan 20-1906

Applications for Enrollment of Choctaw Newborn
Act of 1905   Volume XV

AFFIDAVIT OF ATTENDING PHYSICIAN OR MIDWIFE

UNITED STATES OF AMERICA
INDIAN TERRITORY
Central   DISTRICT

I, Kizzie Martin a midwife on oath state that I attended on Mrs. Lorena Jackson wife of Ben Jackson on the 30 day of Dec, 190 4, that there was born to her on said date a Female child, that said child is now living, and is said to have been named Bessie Jackson

Kizzie Martin

Subscribed and sworn to before me this, the 28 day of Jan 190 5

WITNESSETH:
Must be two witnesses who are citizens { Frank Wallace
Joseph Folsom

R.S. Alexander   Notary Public.
My commission expires Jan. 20, 1908.

We hereby certify that we are well acquainted with Kizzie Martin a midwife and know her to be reputable and of good standing in the community.

Frank Wallace

Joseph Folsom

BIRTH AFFIDAVIT.

DEPARTMENT OF THE INTERIOR.
COMMISSION TO THE FIVE CIVILIZED TRIBES.

IN RE APPLICATION FOR ENROLLMENT, as a citizen of the Choctaw Nation, of Bessie Jackson, born on the 30 day of December, 1904

Name of Father: Ben Jackson   a citizen of the Choctaw Nation.
Name of Mother: Lorena Jackson   a citizen of the Choctaw Nation.

Postoffice   Stigler, I.T.

Applications for Enrollment of Choctaw Newborn
Act of 1905 Volume XV

AFFIDAVIT OF MOTHER.

UNITED STATES OF AMERICA, Indian Territory, }
Central   DISTRICT.

    I, Lorena Jackson, on oath state that I am 21 years of age and a citizen by blood, of the Choctaw Nation; that I am the lawful wife of Ben Jackson, who is a citizen, by blood of the Choctaw Nation; that a female child was born to me on 30th day of December, 1904; that said child has been named Bessie Jackson, and was living March 4, 1905.

                                      Lorena Jackson

Witnesses To Mark:
{

    Subscribed and sworn to before me this 4 day of April, 1905

                                      E.M. Dalton
                                      Notary Public.
                                      My commission expires Oct. 29 1908

AFFIDAVIT OF ATTENDING PHYSICIAN OR MID-WIFE.

UNITED STATES OF AMERICA, Indian Territory, }
Central   DISTRICT.

    I, Kizzie Martin, a mid-wife, on oath state that I attended on Mrs. Lorena Jackson, wife of Ben Jackson on the 30 day of December, 1904; that there was born to her on said date a female child; that said child was living March 4, 1905, and is said to have been named Bessie Jackson

                                        her
Witnesses To Mark: Kizzie x Martin
  { E.M. Dalton   mark
    William Martin

    Subscribed and sworn to before me this 4th day of April, 1905

                                      E.M. Dalton
                                      Notary Public.
                                    My commission expires Oct. 29 1908

Applications for Enrollment of Choctaw Newborn
Act of 1905   Volume XV

7-2628

Muskogee, Indian Territory, April 21, 1905

Foster & Dalton,
    Attorneys at Law,
        Stigler, Indian Territory.

Gentlemen:

    Receipt is hereby acknowledged of your letter of April 4, 1905, enclosing affidavits of Lorena Jackson and Kizzie Martin to the birth of Bessie Jackson daughter of Ben and Lorena Jackson, December 30, 1904, and the same have been filed with our records as an application for the enrollment of said child.

        Respectfully,

                Chairman.

Choc New Born 1104
    Thelma Anderson
    (Born March 26, 1904)

BIRTH AFFIDAVIT.

DEPARTMENT OF THE INTERIOR.
COMMISSION TO THE FIVE CIVILIZED TRIBES.

IN RE APPLICATION FOR ENROLLMENT, as a citizen of the Choctaw Nation, of Thelma Anderson, born on the 26 day of March, 1904

Name of Father: Wesley Anderson   a citizen of the Choc- Nation.
Name of Mother: Susan Anderson   a citizen of the Choc- Nation.

        Postoffice   Tuskahoma, I.T.

Applications for Enrollment of Choctaw Newborn
Act of 1905   Volume XV

AFFIDAVIT OF MOTHER.

UNITED STATES OF AMERICA, Indian Territory,
Central   DISTRICT.

I, Susan Anderson, on oath state that I am 37 years of age and a citizen by Blood, of the Choctaw Nation; that I am the lawful wife of Wesley Anderson, who is a citizen, by Blood of the Choctaw Nation; that a Female child was born to me on 26 day of March, 1904; that said child has been named Thelma Anderson, and was living March 4, 1905.

Susan Anderson

Witnesses To Mark:
{

Subscribed and sworn to before me this 10 day of April, 1905

My Commission Expires Feb. 24, 1906.   Peter W Hudson
                                             Notary Public.

AFFIDAVIT OF ATTENDING PHYSICIAN OR MID-WIFE.

UNITED STATES OF AMERICA, Indian Territory,
Central   DISTRICT.

I, J. C. McGinnis, a Physician, on oath state that I attended on Mrs. Susan Anderson, wife of Wesley Anderson on the 26 day of March, 1904; that there was born to her on said date a Female child; that said child was living March 4, 1905, and is said to have been named Thelma Anderson

J.C. McGinnis M.D.

Witnesses To Mark:
{

Subscribed and sworn to before me this 10 day of April, 1905

My Commission Expires Feb. 24, 1906.   Peter W Hudson
                                             Notary Public.

Applications for Enrollment of Choctaw Newborn
Act of 1905 Volume XV

Muskogee, Indian Territory, April 14, 1905.

Wesley Anderson,
    Tuskahoma, Indian Territory.

Dear Sir:

    Receipt is hereby acknowledged of the affidavits of Susan Anderson and J. C. McGinnis to the birth of Thelma Anderson, daughter of Wesley and Susan Anderson, March 26, 1904.

    It is stated in the affidavits of the mother that she is a citizen by blood of the Choctaw Nation. If this is correct you are requested to state the name under which she was enrolled, the names of her parents, and if she has selected an allotment of the lands of the Choctaw or Chickasaw Nations please give her roll number as it appears upon her allotment certificate.

                    Respectfully,

                      Commissioner in Charge.

(The letter below typed as given.)

Tuskahoma, I. T. April 17, 1905.

Commission to the Five Civilized Tribes,
    Muskogee, Indian Territory.

Sirs:

    Susan Anderson the mother of Thelma Anderson was enrolled under the Act of Congress approved March 3, 1905, as number name of Conser. Susan Conser. The names of her parents are Peter and Anie Conser she has selected an allotment of the Choctaw Nation roll No. 6605.

                    Wesley Anderson

Applications for Enrollment of Choctaw Newborn
Act of 1905   Volume XV

7-2280

Muskogee, Indian Territory, April 21, 1905.

Wesley Anderson,
  Tuskahoma, Indian Territory.

Dear Sir:

  Receipt is hereby acknowledged of your letter of April 17, 1905, stating that Susan Anderson, mother of Thelma Anderson is enrolled under the name of Susan Conser and the information contained therein has enabled us to identify her as an enrolled citizen by blood of the Choctaw Nation and the affidavits of Susan Anderson and J. C. McGinnis, to the birth of Thelma Anderson, daughter of Wesley and Susan Anderson, March 26, 1904, and the same have been filed with our records as an application for the enrollment of said child.

      Respectfully,

            Chairman.

Choc New Born 1105
  Ben Jacob
  (Born Sept. 1, 1904)

DEPARTMENT OF THE INTERIOR,
COMMISSIONER TO THE FIVE CIVILIZED TRIBES.

Valliant, Indian Territory, April 16, 1905.

  In the matter of the enrollment of Ben Jacob, Choctaw New Born, Card Number 1105.

  Testimony taken at Rufe, Indian Territory, April 11, 1906.

  HOUSTON B. JACOBS[sic], being first duly sworn, testified as follows:

      Through Interpreter Jacob Homer.

BY THE COMMISSIONER:

Q What is your name? A Houston B. Jacobs.
Q What is your post office? A Rufe, I. T.

Applications for Enrollment of Choctaw Newborn
Act of 1905   Volume XV

Q What is your age? A About 35 or 36, I do not know exactly.
Q Are you a citizen by blood of the Choctaw Nation?
A Yes.
Q Are you acquainted with Eastman Jacobs? A Yes, sir.

The father of the applicant here appears and is identified as Eastman Jacobs, a Choctaw by blood Roll Number 1238.

Q What is his wife's name? A Rhoda Jacobs.
Q What was her maiden name? A Rhoda Mishaia.
Q Have Eastman Jacobs and wife Rhoda any children?
A Yes.
Q What is the name of their youngest child?
A Ben.
Q Is the child Ben Jacobs a boy or girl? A Boy.
Q When was he born? A The first day of September 1904?
Q Is this child now living? A Yes, sir.
Q At the birth of Ben Jacobs, was the mother, Rhoda Mishaia, now Jacobs, attended by a physician or mid-wife? A No.
Q Are you related to this child, Ben Jacobs? A No.
Q Are you interested directly or indirectly in any estate the child may have by virtue of being a member of the tribe of Choctaw Indians? A No.

Witness Excused.

Testimony taken at Rufe, Indian Territory, April 11, 1906.

RHODA JACOBS, being first duly sworn, testified, through interpreter Jacob Homer, as follows:

BY THE COMMISSIONER:

Q What is your name? A Rhoda Jacobs.
Q What is your age? A About 40.
Q What is your post office address? A Rufe, I. T.
Q Are you a citizen by blood of the Choctaw Nation?
A Yes.
Q Who is your husband? A Houston B. Jacobs.
Q Are you acquainted with Ben Jacobs? A Yes.
Q Who is the mother of the child?
A Rhoda Mishaia, now Jacobs.
Q Who is the father of Ben Jacobs? A Eastman Jacobs.
Q When was Ben Jacobs born? A The 1st day of September?
Q What year?
A Year before last (1904).

Applications for Enrollment of Choctaw Newborn
Act of 1905   Volume XV

Q Is the child Ben Jacobs now living?
A Yes, sir, there he is (pointing to small child, apparently a full-blood, about a year old).
Q Do you live near the parents of Ben Jacobs?
A Yes, sir, I live right close.
Q Was the mother of this child attended by a physician or mid-wife at its birth? A No.
Q Are you in any way interested in the estate that this child, Ben Jacobs, may have by virtue of his enrollment as a citizen by blood of the Choctaw Nation? A No.

Witness Excused.

W. P. Covington, being first duly sworn, states that the above and foregoing is a full, true and correct transcript of his stenographic notes taken in said case on said date.

W.P. Covington

Subscribed and sworn to before me, this   16th   day of April, 1906.

Lacey P. Bobo
Notary Public.

BIRTH AFFIDAVIT.

DEPARTMENT OF THE INTERIOR.
COMMISSION TO THE FIVE CIVILIZED TRIBES.

IN RE APPLICATION FOR ENROLLMENT, as a citizen of the   Choctaw   Nation, of Ben Jacob   , born on the 1 day of Sept , 1904

Name of Father: Esman[sic] Jacob   a citizen of the Choctaw   Nation.
Name of Mother: Rhoda Mishaia   a citizen of the Choctaw   Nation.

Postoffice   Rufe
I T

AFFIDAVIT OF MOTHER.

UNITED STATES OF AMERICA, Indian Territory, }
    Central   DISTRICT. }

I,   Rhoda Mishaia   , on oath state that I am 24   years of age and a citizen by   Blood   , of the   Choctaw   Nation; that I am the lawful wife of   Esman Jacob   , who is a citizen, by Blood   of the   Choctaw   Nation; that a mail[sic]   child was born to me on 1   day of Sept   , 1904; that said child has been named   Ben Jacob   , and was living March 4, 1905.

135

Applications for Enrollment of Choctaw Newborn
Act of 1905 Volume XV

                        Rhoda Mishaia
Witnesses To Mark: x
{ Jonas Taylor   his mark
{ John Daniel

    Subscribed and sworn to before me this 15 day of   April   , 1905

                          H L Fowler
                          Notary Public.

AFFIDAVIT OF ATTENDING PHYSICIAN OR MID-WIFE.

UNITED STATES OF AMERICA, Indian Territory, }
  Central   DISTRICT. }

    I, Esman Jacob , a ...., on oath state that I attended on Mrs. Rhoda Mishaia , wife of Esman Jacob on the 1 day of Sept , 1904; that there was born to her on said date a male child; that said child was living March 4, 1905, and is said to have been named Ben Jacob

                        Esman Jacob
Witnesses To Mark: his x mark
{ Jonas Taylor
{ John Daniel

    Subscribed and sworn to before me this 15 day of   April   , 1905

                          H L Fowler
                          Notary Public.

(The testimony taken at Valliant, Indian Territory, April 16, 1905, above, given again.)

BIRTH AFFIDAVIT.   7- *nB* 1105
                    DEPARTMENT OF THE INTERIOR.
            COMMISSION TO THE FIVE CIVILIZED TRIBES.

      IN RE APPLICATION FOR ENROLLMENT, as a citizen of the   Choctaw   Nation, of Ben Jacob   , born on the 1 day of Sept , 1904

Name of Father: Eastman Jacob   a citizen of the Choctaw Nation.
Name of Mother: Rhoda Jacob   a citizen of the Choctaw Nation.

                      Postoffice   Rufe Ind Ter

Applications for Enrollment of Choctaw Newborn
Act of 1905   Volume XV

AFFIDAVIT OF MOTHER.

UNITED STATES OF AMERICA, Indian Territory, }
    Central   DISTRICT.

I, Rhoda Jacob, on oath state that I am 24 years of age and a citizen by blood, of the Choctaw Nation; that I am the lawful wife of Eastman Jacob, who is a citizen, by blood of the Choctaw Nation; that a male child was born to me on 1st day of September, 1904; that said child has been named Ben Jacob, and was living March 4, 1905.

                              Rhoda Mishaia Jacob
Witnesses To Mark:
 { L.E. Baken
   Edward Christie

Subscribed and sworn to before me this 22 day of Aug, 1905

                              H L Fowler
                                  Notary Public.

Witness
AFFIDAVIT OF ATTENDING ~~PHYSICIAN OR MID-WIFE.~~

UNITED STATES OF AMERICA, Indian Territory, }
    Central   DISTRICT.

                                                    are acquainted with
We, _____ and, ~~a~~ _____, on oath state that *we* ~~attended on~~ Mrs. Rhoda Jacob, wife of Eastman Jacob *and that* on *or about* the 1st day of Sept, 1904; that there was born to her on said date a male child; that said child was living March 4, 1905, and is said to have been named Ben Jacob *that we are not related to the applicant*

Witnesses To Mark:
 { L.E. Baken   Eastman Jacob
   Edward Christie

Subscribed and sworn to before me this 22 day of Aug, 1905

                              H L Fowler
                                  Notary Public.

Applications for Enrollment of Choctaw Newborn
Act of 1905   Volume XV

7--NB--1105

Muskogee, Indian Territory, June 2, 1905.

Eman[sic] Jacob,
    Rufe, Indian Territory.

Dear Sir:

    Referring to the application for the enrollment of your infant child, Ben Jacob, born September 1, 1904, it is noted from the affidavits heretofore filed in this office that you were the only one in attendance upon your wife at the time of the birth of the applicant.

    In this event it will be necessary that the affidavits of two persons, who are disinterested and not related to the applicant, who have actual knowledge of the facts that the child was born, the date of his birth; that he was living on March 4, 1905, and that Rhoda Jacob is his mother be filed in this office.

    This matter should receive your immediate attention as no further action can be taken relative to the enrollment of your child until the Commission is furnished these affidavits.

                    Respectfully,

[sic]

7-NB-1105.

Muskogee, Indian Territory, June 10, 1905.

Esmon Jacob,
    Rufe, Indian Territory.

Dear Sir:

    Referring to the application for the enrollment of your infant child, Ben Jacob, born September 1, 1904, it is noted in the affidavits heretofore filed in this office that you claim to be a citizen by blood of the Choctaw Nation.

    If this is correct you will please state when, where and under what name you were listed for enrollment, the names of your parents and other members of your family for whom application was made at the same time, and if you have selected an allotment of land, please give you roll number as the same appears upon your allotment certificate.

                    Respectfully,

                                Chairman.

Applications for Enrollment of Choctaw Newborn
Act of 1905   Volume XV

(The letter below typed as given.)

7/15-1905
Valliant I T

7-NB-1105
Muscogee I.

Dear Sir

Yours of the 7/10 Received Will Say I have been Enrolled Under the Name of Eastman Jacob And Have My filing papers as follows
E2   of SE4 of Sec 18 Town 53 Range 21 E- 80 Acres
NE4 " E2 SW2 of NW4 of Sec. 32 Town 4S Range 21 E 160 "
E2 SW2 of NW4 of Sec. 32 Town 4S Range 21 E 20
Mr Eastman is a full Blood Choctaw Indian and is All Right

Respectfully,
H. L. Fowler

7-NB-1105

Muskogee, Indian Territory, July 25, 1905.

Eastman Jacob,
Rufe, Indian Territory.

Dear Sir:

There is inclosed you herewith for execution application for the enrollment of your infant child, Ben Jacob, born September 1, 1904, it is noted in the affidavits of April 15, 1905, heretofore filed in this office, that your wife signed the mother's affidavit "Rhoda Mishaia" her former name, and that you were the only one in attendance upon your wife at the time of the birth of said child.

In the inclosed application the mother's affidavit should be signed "Rhoda Jacob" her present married name, and you should secure the affidavits of two persons who are disinterested and not related to the applicant who have actual knowledge of the facts, that the child was born, the date of his birth, that he was living March 4, 1905, and that Rhoda Jacob is his mother.

In having these affidavits executed care should be exercised to see that all names are written in full, as they appear in the body of the affidavit, and in the event that either of the persons signing the affidavit are unable to write, signatures by mark must be

Applications for Enrollment of Choctaw Newborn
Act of 1905   Volume XV

attested by two witnesses. Each affidavit must be executed before a Notary Public and the notarial seal and signature of the officer must be attached to each separate affidavit.

This matter should receive your immediate attention as no further action can be taken relative to the enrollment of your said child until the evidence requested is supplied.

Respectfully,

LM 25/7   Commissioner.

7-NB-1105

Muskogee, Indian Territory August 26, 1905.

Eastman Jacob,
    Rufe, Indian Territory.

Dear Sir:

Receipt is hereby acknowledged of the affidavits of Rhoda Meshaya[sic] Jacob and Eastman Jacob to the birth of Ben Jacob, son of Eastman and Rhoda Jacob, September 1, 1904, and the same have been filed with the records in this case.

Respectfully,

Commissioner.

7-NB-1105.

Muskogee, Indian Territory, September 27, 1905

Eastman Jacob,
    Rufe, Indian Territory.

Dear Sir:

In the matter of the application for the enrollment of your minor son, Ben Jacob, born September 1, 1904, it is noted that in the proof of birth, now on file with the records of this office, you executed the blank affidavit intended for the attending physician or midwife at the birth of said child.

If there was no attending physician or midwife at the birth of said child it will be necessary for you to furnish this office the affidavits of two disinterested witnesses relative thereto. Said affidavits must set forth said child's name, the names of his parents, the date of his birth and whether or not he was living on March 4, 1905.

Applications for Enrollment of Choctaw Newborn
Act of 1905   Volume XV

  This matter should have your immediate attention as until the affidavits of two disinterested persons, relative to the birth of said Ben Jacob have been filed with this office no further action can be taken in the matter of the enrollment of said child as a citizen by blood of the Choctaw Nation.

           Respectfully,

BC   Commissioner.
Env.

7-NB-1105.

          Muskogee, Indian Territory, January 27, 1906.

Eastman Jacob,
  Rufe, Indian Territory.

Dear Sir:

  Receipt is hereby acknowledged of your letter of January 13, 1906, in which you state that there was no one present at the birth of your child, Ben Jacob, September 21[sic], 1904, except yourself and you therefore ask what other proof would be required than the affidavits heretofore filed.

  In reply to your letter you are advised that if there was no other person present at the birth of your child, Ben Jacob, it will be necessary for you to forward the affidavits of two disinterested persons who know of the birth of said child, the date of his birth, the names of his parents, and that he was living on March 4, 1905. This matter should receive your immediate attention in order that disposition may be made of the application for the enrollment of Ben Jacob.

  The communication of this office of September 25, 1905, inclosed with your letter is herewith returned.

            Respectfully,

                       Acting Commissioner.

LBA 1/27.

Applications for Enrollment of Choctaw Newborn
Act of 1905   Volume XV

Choc New Born 1106
    Lillian B. Fowler
    (Born Sept. 4, 1903)

NEW-BORN AFFIDAVIT.

    Number............

...Choctaw Enrolling Commission...

    IN THE MATTER OF THE APPLICATION FOR ENROLLMENT, as a citizen of the Choctaw Nation, of Lillian Beatrice Fowler

born on the 4th day of September 190 3

Name of father Hosea L Fowler   a citizen of   Choctaw
Nation final enrollment No. 949
Name of mother Josephine Fowler   a citizen of   Choctaw
Nation final enrollment No. 15533

                                   Postoffice   Valliant, I.T.

AFFIDAVIT OF MOTHER.

UNITED STATES OF AMERICA
INDIAN TERRITORY
  Central   DISTRICT

         I   Josephine Fowler   , on oath state that I am 38 years of age and a citizen by blood of the Choctaw Nation, and as such have been placed upon the final roll of the Choctaw Nation, by the Honorable Secretary of the Interior my final enrollment number being 15533 ; that I am the lawful wife of Hosea L Fowler , who is a citizen of the Choctaw Nation, and as such has been placed upon the final roll of said Nation by the Honorable Secretary of the Interior, his final enrollment number being 949 and that a female child was born to me on the 4th day of September 190 3; that said child has been named Lillian Beatrice Fowler , and is now living.

                                       her
                             Josephine x Fowler
Witnesseth.   mark
   Must be two   }   William W Swink
   Witnesses who
   are Citizens.   Edmond Gardner

Applications for Enrollment of Choctaw Newborn
Act of 1905   Volume XV

Subscribed and sworn to before me this   22   day of   Feb   190 5

W A Shoney
Notary Public.

My commission expires:

AFFIDAVIT OF ATTENDING PHYSICIAN OR MIDWIFE

UNITED STATES OF AMERICA
INDIAN TERRITORY
Central   DISTRICT

I,   M M Cooper   a   midwife on oath state that I attended on Mrs.   Josephine Fowler   wife of   Hosea L Fowler on the 4th day of September , 190 3, that there was born to her on said date a   female child, that said child is now living, and is said to have been named   Lillian Beatrice Fowler

M M Cooper   ~~M.D.~~

WITNESSETH:
Must be two witnesses who are citizens and know the child.
{ William W Swink
  Edmond Gardner

Subscribed and sworn to before me this, the   22nd day of   Feb   190 5

W A Shoney   Notary Public.

We hereby certify that we are well acquainted with   M M Cooper   a   midwife   and know   her   to be reputable and of good standing in the community.

{ William W Swink
  Edmond Gardner

BIRTH AFFIDAVIT.

DEPARTMENT OF THE INTERIOR.
COMMISSION TO THE FIVE CIVILIZED TRIBES.

IN RE APPLICATION FOR ENROLLMENT, as a citizen of the   Choctaw   Nation, of   Lillian B. Fowler   , born on the 4th day of Sept , 1903

Name of Father: Hosea L Fowler   a citizen of the   Choctaw   Nation.
Name of Mother: Josephine Fowler   a citizen of the   Choctaw   Nation.

Applications for Enrollment of Choctaw Newborn
Act of 1905   Volume XV

Postoffice   Valliant Ind. Ter.

AFFIDAVIT OF MOTHER.

UNITED STATES OF AMERICA, Indian Territory, } DISTRICT.

I, Josephine Fowler, on oath state that I am 38 years of age and a citizen by blood, of the Choctaw Nation; that I am the lawful wife of Hosea L Fowler, who is a citizen, by Intermarriage of the Choctaw Nation; that a female child was born to me on 4th day of Sept, 1903; that said child has been named Lillian B. Fowler, and was living March 4, 1905.

Josephine Fowler

Witnesses To Mark:

Subscribed and sworn to before me this 15 day of April, 1905

D. O. Spencer
Notary Public.

AFFIDAVIT OF ATTENDING PHYSICIAN OR MID-WIFE.

UNITED STATES OF AMERICA, Indian Territory, } DISTRICT.

I, _____, a _____, on oath state that I attended on Mrs. Josephine Fowler wife of Hosea L. Fowler on the 4th day of September, 1903; that there was born to her on said date a female child; that said child was living March 4, 1905, and is said to have been named Lillian B. Fowler

Anna Williams

Witnesses To Mark:

Subscribed and sworn to before me this 15 day of April, 1905

D. O. Spencer
Notary Public.

Applications for Enrollment of Choctaw Newborn
Act of 1905 Volume XV

7-5651

Muskogee, Indian Territory, April 21, 1905.

Hosea L. Fowler,
    Valliant, Indian Territory.

Dear Sir:

    Receipt is hereby acknowledged of your letter of April 15, 1905, enclosing affidavits of Josephine Fowler and Anna Williams to the birth of Lillian B. Fowler, daughter of Hosea L. and Josephine Fowler, September 4, 1903, and the same have been filed with our records as an application for the enrollment of said child.

    Respectfully,

Chairman.

Choc New Born 1107
    Earl Lee Labor
    (Born Oct. 18, 1903)

NEW-BORN AFFIDAVIT.

Number................

Choctaw Enrolling Commission.

IN THE MATTER OF THE APPLICATION FOR ENROLLMENT, as a citizen of the Choctaw Nation, of Earl Lee Labor

born on the 18th day of October 190 3

Name of father Alexander Labor   a citizen of Choctaw
Nation final enrollment No 3067
Name of mother Eria Labor   a citizen of Choctaw
Nation final enrollment No ....

    Postoffice   Bennington I.T.

Applications for Enrollment of Choctaw Newborn
Act of 1905   Volume XV

AFFIDAVIT OF MOTHER.

UNITED STATES OF AMERICA,
 INDIAN TERRITORY,
 Cent   DISTRICT

I   Eria Labor   on oath state that I am   17   years of age and a citizen by   Marriage   of the   Choctaw   Nation, and as such have **not** been placed upon the final roll of the   Choctaw   Nation, by the Honorable Secretary of the Interior my final enrollment number being .... ; that I am the lawful wife of   Alexander Labor   , who is a citizen of the   Choctaw   Nation, and as such has been placed upon the final roll of said Nation by the Honorable Secretary of the Interior, his final enrollment number being   3067   and that a   male   child was born to me on the   18th day of   October   190 3 ; that said child has been named   Earl Lee Labor   , and is now living.

WITNESSETH: Eria Labor
 Must be two Witnesses who are Citizens.   M S Smith
   Moses Armstrong

Subscribed and sworn to before me this   20th day of   Jan   190 5

B.W. Williams
Notary Public.

My commission expires   16th Oct 1907

Affidavit of Attending Physician or Midwife.

UNITED STATES OF AMERICA
INDIAN TERRITORY
 Cent   DISTRICT

I,   B C Rutherford   a   Practicing Physician   on oath state that I attended on Mrs.   Eria Labor   wife of   Alexander Labor   on the   18th day of   October   , 190 3 , that there was born to her on said date a   Male   child, that said child is now living, and is said to have been named   Earl Lee Labor

B C Rutherford   M.D.

Subscribed and sworn to before me this, the   20 day of   Jan   190 5

B.W. Williams
Notary Public.

WITNESSETH:
 Must be two witnesses who are citizens and know the child.

Applications for Enrollment of Choctaw Newborn
Act of 1905   Volume XV

We hereby certify that we are well acquainted with   B.C. Rutherford a Physician   and know   him   to be reputable and of good standing in the community.

M S Smith

Moses Armstrong

(The affidavit below typed as given.)

C. D. Bransford
President & Gen'l Mg'r

G. D. Duncan
Vice President

J. T. Yeager
Sec'y & Treas.

Boswell Mercantile Company,
General Merchandise,

*Boswell Ind. Ter.*_____*190__*

Jackson County Choctaw Nation

This is to certify that I E. T. Dwight County and Probate Judge of Jackson County Choctaw Nation, on the 14th day of Jan - 1903, Joined together in Holey Bonds of Matrimoney Mr Alexander Labor and Miss Eria Ranolds.

E.T. Dwight
Ex Co. & Pro. Judge

J C En.

BIRTH AFFIDAVIT.

DEPARTMENT OF THE INTERIOR.
COMMISSION TO THE FIVE CIVILIZED TRIBES.

IN RE APPLICATION FOR ENROLLMENT, as a citizen of the   Choctaw   Nation, of Earl Lee Labor   , born on the   18th   day of   October   , 1903

Name of Father: Alexander Labor   a citizen of the Choctaw   Nation.
Name of Mother: Erie[sic] Labor   a citizen of the   ——   Nation.

Postoffice   Bennington Ind Ter

Applications for Enrollment of Choctaw Newborn
Act of 1905   Volume XV

AFFIDAVIT OF MOTHER.

UNITED STATES OF AMERICA, Indian Territory, }
Central   DISTRICT.

I, Erie Labor, on oath state that I am 17 years of age and a citizen by ...., of the .... Nation; that I am the lawful wife of Alexander Labor, who is a citizen, by blood of the Choctaw Nation; that a male child was born to me on 18th day of October, 1903; that said child has been named Earl Lee Labor, and was living March 4, 1905.

                              Mrs Erie Labor

Witnesses To Mark:
{

Subscribed and sworn to before me this 15th day of April, 1905

                              (Name Illegible)
                              Notary Public.

AFFIDAVIT OF ATTENDING PHYSICIAN OR MID-WIFE.

UNITED STATES OF AMERICA, Indian Territory, }
Central   DISTRICT.

I, B.C. Rutherford, a physician, on oath state that I attended on Mrs. Erie Labor, wife of Alexander Labor on the 18th day of October, 1903; that there was born to her on said date a male child; that said child was living March 4, 1905, and is said to have been named Earl Lee Labor

                              B.C. Rutherford M.D.

Witnesses To Mark:
{

Subscribed and sworn to before me this 15th day of April, 1905

                              (Name Illegible)
                              Notary Public.

Applications for Enrollment of Choctaw Newborn
Act of 1905 Volume XV

7-NB-1107

Muskogee, Indian Territory, June 1, 1905.

Alexander Labor,
    Bennington, Indian Territory.

Dear Sir:

    Referring to your application for the enrollment of your infant child, Earl Lee Labor, born October 18, 1903, it is noted from the affidavits heretofore filed in this office that the applicant claims through you.

    In this event it will be necessary that you file in this office, either the original or a certified copy of the license and certificate of your marriage to the applicant's mother, Eria Labor.

                        Respectfully,

                               Chairman.

7-NB-1107

Muskogee, Indian Territory, July 12, 1905.

Alexander Labor,
    Bennington, Indian Territory.

Dear Sir:

    Receipt is hereby acknowledged of your letter of July 3, 1905, addressed to the United States Indian Agent which has been by him referred to this office for appropriate action. Therein you enclos[sic] a marriage certificate between yourself and Eria Ranolds which you offer in support of the application for the enrollment of your child Earl Lee Labor as a citizen by blood of the Choctaw Nation and the same has been filed with the record in the matter of the enrollment of said child. this case.

                        Respectfully,

                               Commissioner.

Applications for Enrollment of Choctaw Newborn
Act of 1905 Volume XV

Choc New Born 1108
    Pearley Ann Stidham
    (Born April 9, 1903)

BIRTH AFFIDAVIT.

DEPARTMENT OF THE INTERIOR.
COMMISSION TO THE FIVE CIVILIZED TRIBES.

IN RE APPLICATION FOR ENROLLMENT, as a citizen of the Choctaw Nation, of Pearley Ann Stidham, born on the 9th day of April, 1903

Name of Father: Frank R. Stidham   a citizen of the Choctaw Nation.
Name of Mother: Susie Ann Stidham   a citizen of the —— (U.S.) ~~Nation~~.

Postoffice   Berwyn, Ind Ter

AFFIDAVIT OF MOTHER.

UNITED STATES OF AMERICA, Indian Territory,
Southern DISTRICT.

I, Susie Ann Stidham, on oath state that I am .... years of age and a citizen by — — —, of the (U.S.) ~~Nation~~; that I am the lawful wife of Frank R. Stidham, who is a citizen, by blood of the Choctaw Nation; that a female child was born to me on 9th day of April, 1903; that said child has been named Pearley Ann Stidham, and was living March 4, 1905.

                                         her
                                Susie Ann x Stidham
Witnesses To Mark: mark
    { A.W. Gaines
      A.S. Gilliam

Subscribed and sworn to before me this 17 day of April, 1905

                        T.J. Carson
                            Notary Public.

Applications for Enrollment of Choctaw Newborn
Act of 1905   Volume XV

AFFIDAVIT OF ATTENDING PHYSICIAN OR MID-WIFE.

UNITED STATES OF AMERICA, Indian Territory, }
Southern   DISTRICT.

I,   R H Alvis   , a Physician   , on oath state that I attended on Mrs.   Susie Ann Stidham   , wife of   Frank R. Stidham   on the 9th   day of April , 1903; that there was born to her on said date a   female   child; that said child was living March 4, 1905, and is said to have been named Pearley Ann Stidham

R H Alvis M.D.

Witnesses To Mark:
{

Subscribed and sworn to before me this 17   day of   Aprl   , 1905

(Name Illegible)
Notary Public.

Marriage License.

United States of America,   (
)
    Indian Territory,   (SS.
)
         Southern District. (

To Any Person Authorized by Law to Solemnize Marriage--Greeting:

YOU ARE HEREBY COMMANDED to solemnize the Rite and publish the Banns of Matrimony between Mr. F.R. Stidham of Fox in the Indian Territory, aged 29 years, and Susie Huffman, of Fox in the Indian Territory, aged 30 years, according to law, and do you officially sign and return this License to the parties therein named.

WITNESS my hand and official seal, this 25th day of April, A.D. 1902.

C.M. Campbell,

Clerk of the U.S. Court.

_____Deputy.

##

Applications for Enrollment of Choctaw Newborn
Act of 1905 Volume XV

CERTIFICATE OF MARRIAGE.

United States of America, (
    Indian Territory,) SS.   I, J.F. Young, a minister,
        Southern District.(do hereby certify, that on the 25th, day of April, A.D. 1902, I did duly and according to law as commanded in the foregoing License, solemnize the Rite and publish the Banns of Matrimony between the parties therein named.

    Witness my hand, this 25th, day of April, A.D. 1902.

    My credentials are recorded in the office of the Clerk of the United States Court, Indian Territory, Southern District, at Ardmore, Book A, Page ____.

        J.F. Young,
        A Minister.

CERTIFICATE OF RECORD OF MARRIAGE.

UNITED STATES OF AMERICA, (
    INDIAN TERRITORY,) Set.
    SOUTHERN DISTRICT. (
    I, C.M. Campbell, Clerk of the United States court[sic] in the Indian Territory and District aforesaid, do hereby certify that the License for, and Certificate of Marriage of

    Mr. F.R. Stidham

and

    Miss Susie Huffmann[sic]

were filed in my office in said Territory and District the 25th day of April, A.D. 1902, and duly recorded in Book F. of Marriage Record, page 325.

    Witness my hand and seal od[sic] said Court at Ardmore, this the 20th, day of May, 1902.

        C.M. Campbell,
        Clerk.

Ardmore, Indian Territory,
    Southern District.
    I, Ola Holloway, a Notary Public in and for the Southern District of the Indian Territory, do hereby certify that the above and foregoing is a true and correct copy of the Marriage License and Marriage Certificate No. 533 of F.R. Stidham and Susie Huffman as appears of record in the United States Clerk's Office at Ardmore, Indian Territory, filed May 20th, 1902.

Applications for Enrollment of Choctaw Newborn
Act of 1905 Volume XV

Witness my [sic] and official seal on this the 20th, day of April, 1905.

Ola Holloway
Notary Public.

My Commission expires Jan. 17th, 1909.

Choctaw N.B. 1108.

Muskogee, Indian Territory, May 1, 1905.

F. R. Stidham,
    Berwyn, Indian Territory.

Dear Sir:

Receipt is hereby acknowledged of your letter of April 26, enclosing a certified copy of the marriage license and certificate between F. R. Stidham and Susie Hoffman which you offer in support of the application for the enrollment of Pearly[sic] Ann Stidham and the same has been filed with the records in this case.

Respectfully,

Chairman.

Choc New Born *(1109)*
    Arena Whistler
    (Born May 26, 1903)

BIRTH AFFIDAVIT.

DEPARTMENT OF THE INTERIOR.
COMMISSION TO THE FIVE CIVILIZED TRIBES.

IN RE APPLICATION FOR ENROLLMENT, as a citizen of the Chocktaw[sic] Nation, of Arena Whistler, born on the 26 day of May, 1903.

Name of Father: Robinson Whistler   a citizen of the Chocktaw Nation.
Name of Mother: Dora Whistler   a citizen of the Chocktaw Nation.

Postoffice   Pontotoc, Ind. Ter

Applications for Enrollment of Choctaw Newborn
Act of 1905 Volume XV

AFFIDAVIT OF MOTHER.

UNITED STATES OF AMERICA, Indian Territory, }
Southern DISTRICT.

I, Dora Whistler, on oath state that I am 24 years of age and a citizen by Blood, of the Chocktaw Nation; that I am the lawful wife of Robinson Whistler, who is a citizen, by Blood of the Chocktaw Nation; that a female child was born to me on 26 day of May, 1903; that said child has been named Arena Whistler, and was living March 4, 1905.

Dora Whistler

Witnesses To Mark:

Subscribed and sworn to before me this 11th day of April, 1905

M.S. Bradford
Notary Public.

AFFIDAVIT OF ATTENDING PHYSICIAN OR MID-WIFE.

UNITED STATES OF AMERICA, Indian Territory, }
Southern DISTRICT.

I, Alsi Anderson, a mid wife, on oath state that I attended on Mrs. Dora Whistler, wife of Robinson Whistler on the 26 day of May, 1903; that there was born to her on said date a female child; that said child was living March 4, 1905, and is said to have been named Arena Whistler

her
Alsi x Anderson
mark

Witnesses To Mark:
J L Boatright
F.M. Stamps

Subscribed and sworn to before me this 11th day of April, 1905

M.S. Bradford
Notary Public.

Applications for Enrollment of Choctaw Newborn
Act of 1905   Volume XV

Choc New Born 1110
    Willie Jewell Burns
    (Born Aug. 19, 1903)

BIRTH AFFIDAVIT.

DEPARTMENT OF THE INTERIOR.
COMMISSION TO THE FIVE CIVILIZED TRIBES.

IN RE APPLICATION FOR ENROLLMENT, as a citizen of the Choctaw Nation, of Willie Jewell Burns, born on the 19th day of August, 1903

Name of Father: Joseph Burns-roll #7485   a citizen of the Choctaw Nation.
                                                                                    By I.M.
Name of Mother: Alice Burns   a citizen of the Choctaw Pend App. Nation.

                        Postoffice   McCurtain Ind Ter

AFFIDAVIT OF MOTHER.

UNITED STATES OF AMERICA, Indian Territory, }
    Central   DISTRICT. }

    I, Alice Burns, on oath state that I am 32 years of age and a citizen by intermarriage, of the Choctaw - Pend App'l. Nation; that I am the lawful wife of Joseph Burns, who is a citizen, by blood of the Choctaw Nation; that a female child was born to me on 19th day of August, 1903; that said child has been named Willie Jewell Burns, and was living March 4, 1905.

                                                                            Alice Burns
Witnesses To Mark:
  {

    Subscribed and sworn to before me this 12th day of April, 1905

                                                     Lacey P Bobo
                                                     Notary Public.

Applications for Enrollment of Choctaw Newborn
Act of 1905 Volume XV

AFFIDAVIT OF ATTENDING PHYSICIAN OR MID-WIFE.

UNITED STATES OF AMERICA, Indian Territory,
Central DISTRICT.

I, W.H. Holbrooks, a Midwife[sic], on oath state that I attended on Mrs. Alice Burns, wife of Joseph Burns on the 19th day of August, 1903; that there was born to her on said date a Female child; that said child was living March 4, 1905, and is said to have been named Willie Jewell Burns

W.H. Holbrook[sic]

Witnesses To Mark:

Subscribed and sworn to before me this 17 day of April, 1905

Chas. W. Self
Notary Public.

AFFIDAVIT OF ATTENDING PHYSICIAN OR MIDWIFE

UNITED STATES OF AMERICA
INDIAN TERRITORY
Central DISTRICT

I, W.H. Holbrooks[sic] a physician on oath state that I attended on Mrs. Alice Burns wife of Joseph Burns on the 19 day of August, 1903, that there was born to her on said date a girl child, that said child is now living, and is said to have been named Willie Jewell Burns

W.H. Holbrook M.D.

Subscribed and sworn to before me this, the 3 day of March 1905

Jas. L. Lewis   Notary Public.

WITNESSETH:
Must be two witnesses who are citizens
J.W. Leflore
(Name Illegible)

We hereby certify that we are well acquainted with W.H. Holbrooks a physician and know him to be reputable and of good standing in the community.

J.W. Leflore   Milton I.T.

(Name Illegible)   "   "

Applications for Enrollment of Choctaw Newborn
Act of 1905   Volume XV

NEW-BORN AFFIDAVIT.

Number..............

...Choctaw Enrolling Commission...

IN THE MATTER OF THE APPLICATION FOR ENROLLMENT, as a citizen of the Choctaw   Nation, of   Willie Jewell Burns

born on the .... day of ____August____ 190 4[sic]

Name of father   Joseph Burns   a citizen of   Choctaw
Nation final enrollment No.   7485
Name of mother   Alice Burns   a citizen of   Choctaw
Nation final enrollment No.   ——

                                                Postoffice   Milton, I.T.

AFFIDAVIT OF MOTHER.

UNITED STATES OF AMERICA
INDIAN TERRITORY
   Central   DISTRICT

        I   Alice Burns   , on oath state that I am   32   years of age and a citizen by   marriage   of the   Choctaw   Nation, and as such have been placed upon the final roll of the   Choctaw   Nation, by the Honorable Secretary of the Interior my final enrollment number being   ——; that I am the lawful wife of   Joseph Burns   , who is a citizen of the   Choctaw   Nation, and as such has been placed upon the final roll of said Nation by the Honorable Secretary of the Interior, his final enrollment number being   7485   and that a   girl   child was born to me on the   19   day of   Aug   190 3; that said child has been named   Willie Jewell Burns   , and is now living.

                                                             Alice Burns

Witnesseth.
  Must be two   ⎫   J.W. Leflore
  Witnesses who ⎬
  are Citizens. ⎭   *(Name Illegible)*

Subscribed and sworn to before me this   3   day of   Mch   190 5

                                              J.L. Lewis
                                                        Notary Public.

My commission expires:
   My commission expires Mar. 15, 1905

Applications for Enrollment of Choctaw Newborn
Act of 1905 Volume XV

Choctaw 2578.

Muskogee, Indian Territory, April 22, 1905.

Joseph Burns,
McCurtain, Indian Territory.

Dear Sir:

Receipt is hereby acknowledged of the affidavits of Alice Burns and W. H. Holbrook to the birth of Willie Jewell Burns, daughter of Joseph and Alice Burns, August 19, 1903, and the same have been filed with our records in the matter of the enrollment of said child.

Respectfully,

Chairman.

Choc New Born 1111
    Mary Throhbe[sic]
    (Born Nov. 20, 1903)

BIRTH AFFIDAVIT.

DEPARTMENT OF THE INTERIOR.
COMMISSION TO THE FIVE CIVILIZED TRIBES.

IN RE APPLICATION FOR ENROLLMENT, as a citizen of the Choctaw Nation, of Mary Trohbe, born on the 20th day of November, 1903

Name of Father: Charles Trohbe   a citizen ~~of the~~ United States ~~Nation~~.
Name of Mother: M.L. Elizabeth Trohbe   a citizen of the Choctaw Nation.

Postoffice   McAlester I.T.

AFFIDAVIT OF MOTHER.

UNITED STATES OF AMERICA, Indian Territory,
    Central District   DISTRICT.

I, M.L. Elizabeth Trohbe, on oath state that I am 20 years of age and a citizen by blood, of the Choctaw Nation; that I am the lawful wife of Charles Trohbe, who is a citizen, ~~by~~ .... of the United States

Applications for Enrollment of Choctaw Newborn
Act of 1905   Volume XV

~~Nation~~; that a   female   child was born to me on   20th   day of November   , 1903; that said child has been named Mary Trohbe   , and was living March 4, 1905.

                              M.L. Elizabeth Trohbe
                                      her x mark

Witnesses To Mark:
  { W B McAlester
    R A Bendley

    Subscribed and sworn to before me this 17th   day of   April   , 1905

                              DW Hopkins
                                  Notary Public.

AFFIDAVIT OF ATTENDING PHYSICIAN OR MID-WIFE.

UNITED STATES OF AMERICA, Indian Territory, }
  Central   DISTRICT. }

    I,   Gertrude Steinsieppe   , a Midwife   , on oath state that I attended on Mrs. M.L. Elizabeth Trohbe   , wife of Charles Trohbe   on the 20th day of November   , 1903; that there was born to her on said date a   female   child; that said child was living March 4, 1905, and is said to have been named Mary Trohbe

                            Gertrude Steinsieppe
Witnesses To Mark: her x mark
  { W B McAlester
    R A Bendley

    Subscribed and sworn to before me this 17th   day of   April   , 1905

                              DW Hopkins
                                  Notary Public.

NEW-BORN AFFIDAVIT.

          Number..................

...Choctaw Enrolling Commission...

    IN THE MATTER OF THE APPLICATION FOR ENROLLMENT, as a citizen of the Choctaw   Nation, of   Mary Traube[sic]

born on the   20th   day of____November_____190 3

Applications for Enrollment of Choctaw Newborn
Act of 1905 Volume XV

Name of father Charley Traube — ~~a~~ not a citizen ~~of~~ ~~Nation final enrollment No...~~

Name of mother Elizabeth Traube — a citizen of Choctaw
Nation final enrollment No. 13298

Postoffice McAlester I.T.

AFFIDAVIT OF MOTHER.

UNITED STATES OF AMERICA
INDIAN TERRITORY
Central DISTRICT

I Elizabeth Traube, on oath state that I am 20 years of age and a citizen by blood of the Choctaw Nation, and as such have been placed upon the final roll of the Choctaw Nation, by the Honorable Secretary of the Interior my final enrollment number being 13298; that I am the lawful wife of Charley Traube, who is not a citizen ~~of the~~ ~~Nation~~, and as such has ~~been placed upon the final roll of said Nation by the Honorable Secretary of the Interior, his final enrollment number being~~ and that a Female child was born to me on the 20th day of November 190 3; that said child has been named Mary Traube, and is now living.

Elizabeth Traube
her x mark

Witnesseth.
Must be two Witnesses who are Citizens. J P Wright
Nancy Cartlidge
her x mark

Subscribed and sworn to before me this 23 day of Jany 190 5

Witness to mark
James N Reed
A Watson

DW Hopkins
Notary Public.

My commission expires: Dec 15" 1905

AFFIDAVIT OF ATTENDING PHYSICIAN OR MIDWIFE

UNITED STATES OF AMERICA
INDIAN TERRITORY
Central DISTRICT

I, Gertrude Steinsipe[sic] a Midwife on oath state that I attended on Mrs. Mrs Elizabeth Traube wife of Charley Traube on the 20th day of November, 190 3, that there was born to her on said date a Female child, that said child is now living, and is said to have been named Mary Traube

Witness to mark
(Name Illegible)
James N Reed

Gertrude Steinsipe Midwife
her x mark

Applications for Enrollment of Choctaw Newborn
Act of 1905 Volume XV

Subscribed and sworn to before me this, the 23ᵈ day of January 190 5

WITNESSETH: DW Hopkins   Notary Public.

Must be two witnesses who are citizens { J P Wright

James N Reed

We hereby certify that we are well acquainted with Elizabeth Traube a*nd* Charley Traube and know them to be reputable and of good standing in the community.

        J.P. Wright   James N Reed

Choc New Born 1112
       Florence Glenn McFarland
       (Born Dec. 20, 1903)

BIRTH AFFIDAVIT.

DEPARTMENT OF THE INTERIOR.
COMMISSION TO THE FIVE CIVILIZED TRIBES.

IN RE APPLICATION FOR ENROLLMENT, as a citizen of the Choctaw Nation, of Florence Glenn McFarland , born on the 20 day of Dec , 1903

Name of Father: J.B. McFarland   a citizen of the Choctaw Nation.
Name of Mother: Abbie L. McFarland   a citizen of the Choctaw Nation.

                   Postoffice   Harris, Ind. Ter.

AFFIDAVIT OF MOTHER.

UNITED STATES OF AMERICA, Indian Territory, }
     Central   DISTRICT. }

     I, Abbie L. McFarland , on oath state that I am 33 years of age and a citizen by Blood , of the Choctaw Nation; that I am the lawful wife of J B McFarland , who is a citizen, by Marriage of the Choctaw Nation;

Applications for Enrollment of Choctaw Newborn
Act of 1905   Volume XV

that a   Female   child was born to me on   20   day of   Dec   , 1903; that said child has been named   Florence Glenn McFarland   , and was living March 4, 1905.

Abbie L McFarland

Witnesses To Mark:
{

Subscribed and sworn to before me this   15   day of   April   , 1905

N.P. Hutchinson
Notary Public.

AFFIDAVIT OF ATTENDING PHYSICIAN OR MID-WIFE.

UNITED STATES OF AMERICA, Indian Territory, }
Central   DISTRICT.

I,   Laura Smith   , a   Midwife   , on oath state that I attended on Mrs.   Abbie L. McFarland   , wife of   J.B. McFarland   on the   20   day of   Dec , 1903; that there was born to her on said date a   Female   child; that said child was living March 4, 1905, and is said to have been named   Florence Glenn McFarland

Laura x Smith

Witnesses To Mark:
{ S.F. Scott
  E.H. Williams

Subscribed and sworn to before me this   15   day of   April   , 1905

N.P. Hutchinson
Notary Public.

NEW-BORN AFFIDAVIT.

Number............

...Choctaw Enrolling Commission...

IN THE MATTER OF THE APPLICATION FOR ENROLLMENT, as a citizen of the Choctaw   Nation, of   Florence Glenn McFarland

born on the   20th   day of   December   190 3

Applications for Enrollment of Choctaw Newborn
Act of 1905   Volume XV

Name of father   J.B. McFarland   a citizen of   Choctaw
Nation final enrollment No. 69
Name of mother   Abbie L McFarland   a citizen of   Choctaw
Nation final enrollment No. 3638

                          Postoffice   Harris I.T.

AFFIDAVIT OF MOTHER.

UNITED STATES OF AMERICA
INDIAN TERRITORY
  Central   DISTRICT

        I   Abbie L. McFarland   , on oath state that I am   33   years of age and a citizen by   blood   of the   Choctaw   Nation, and as such have been placed upon the final roll of the   Choctaw   Nation, by the Honorable Secretary of the Interior my final enrollment number being   3638 ; that I am the lawful wife of   J.B. McFarland   , who is a citizen of the   Choctaw   Nation, and as such has been placed upon the final roll of said Nation by the Honorable Secretary of the Interior, his final enrollment number being _____ and that a   female   child was born to me on the   20th day of   Dec   190 3; that said child has been named   Florence Glenn McFarland   , and is now living.

                                        Abbie L McFarland

Witnesseth.
   Must be two ⎫   S E Morris
   Witnesses who ⎬
   are Citizens. ⎭   Lou Anna Coleman

    Subscribed and sworn to before me this   21   day of   Jan   190 5

                              W.A. Shoney
                                       Notary Public.
My commission expires: Jan 10, 1909

AFFIDAVIT OF ATTENDING PHYSICIAN OR MIDWIFE

UNITED STATES OF AMERICA
INDIAN TERRITORY
  Central   DISTRICT

      I,   Laura Smith   a   midwife   on oath state that I attended on Mrs. Abbie L McFarland   wife of   J B McFarland   on the   20th day of   Dec , 190 3 , that there was born to her on said date a   female   child, that said child is now living, and is said to have been named   Florence Glenn McFarland   her
                                    Laura Smith x
                                        mark

Applications for Enrollment of Choctaw Newborn
Act of 1905 Volume XV

Subscribed and sworn to before me this, the 21 day of Jan 1905

WITNESSETH: W.A. Shoney Notary Public.
Must be two witnesses who are citizens { S.E. Morris
Lou Anna Coleman

We hereby certify that we are well acquainted with Laura Smith a midwife and know her to be reputable and of good standing in the community.

S.E. Morris

Lou Anna Coleman

Roll No.
Abbie McFarland 3638

Wife of J.B. McFarland
his Roll No 69

Choc New Born 1113
Guy Self
(Born May 17, 1903)

BIRTH AFFIDAVIT.
DEPARTMENT OF THE INTERIOR.
COMMISSION TO THE FIVE CIVILIZED TRIBES.

IN RE APPLICATION FOR ENROLLMENT, as a citizen of the Choctaw Nation, of Guy Self , born on the 17 day of May , 1903

Name of Father: Joseph M Self a citizen of the Choctaw Nation.
Name of Mother: Lillian O Self a citizen of the Choctaw Nation.

Postoffice Lehigh I T

Applications for Enrollment of Choctaw Newborn
Act of 1905 Volume XV

AFFIDAVIT OF MOTHER.

UNITED STATES OF AMERICA, Indian Territory, }
Central   DISTRICT.

I, Lillian O Self   , on oath state that I am 25   years of age and a citizen by blood   , of the   Choctaw   Nation; that I am the lawful wife of   Joseph M Self , who is a citizen, by intermarried   of the   Choctaw   Nation; that a   male child was born to me on   17th day of   May   , 1903; that said child has been named Guy Self   , and was living March 4, 1905.

Lillian O. Self

Witnesses To Mark:
{

Subscribed and sworn to before me this 17 day of   April   , 1905

AT West
Notary Public.

AFFIDAVIT OF ATTENDING PHYSICIAN OR MID-WIFE.

UNITED STATES OF AMERICA, Indian Territory, }
Central   DISTRICT.

I,   Annie E Burchfiel[sic]   , a   Midwife   , on oath state that I attended on Mrs.   Lillian O Self   , wife of   Joseph M Self   on the 17th day of   May , 1903; that there was born to her on said date a   male   child; that said child was living March 4, 1905, and is said to have been named Guy Self

Annie Burchfiel

Witnesses To Mark:
{

Subscribed and sworn to before me this 17th day of   April   , 1905

AT West
Notary Public.

Applications for Enrollment of Choctaw Newborn
Act of 1905 Volume XV

Choctaw 4378.

Muskogee, Indian Territory, April 21, 1905.

Joseph M. Self,
    Lehigh, Indian Territory.

Dear Sir:

    Receipt is hereby acknowledged of the affidavits of Lillian O. Self and Annie Burchfiel to the birth of Guy Self, son of Joseph M. and Lillian O. Self, May 17, 1903, and the same have been filed with our records as an application for the enrollment of said child.

Respectfully,

Chairman.

Choc New Born 1114
    Iler May King
    (Born Aug. 19, 1903)

NEW-BORN AFFIDAVIT.

Number............

...Choctaw Enrolling Commission...

    IN THE MATTER OF THE APPLICATION FOR ENROLLMENT, as a citizen of the Chocktaw[sic]   Nation, of   Ida[sic] May King

born on the 19th day of ___Aug___ 190 3

Name of father   William S King   a citizen of   Chocktaw
Nation final enrollment No. 12885
Name of mother   Sarah Jane King   a citizen of   Chocktaw
Nation final enrollment No. 769

                        Postoffice   Interprise I.T.

Applications for Enrollment of Choctaw Newborn
Act of 1905 Volume XV

AFFIDAVIT OF MOTHER.

UNITED STATES OF AMERICA
INDIAN TERRITORY
Western DISTRICT

I Sarah Jane King , on oath state that I am 30 years of age and a citizen by marriage of the Chocktaw Nation, and as such have been placed upon the final roll of the Chocktaw Nation, by the Honorable Secretary of the Interior my final enrollment number being 769 ; that I am the lawful wife of William S King , who is a citizen of the Chocktaw Nation, and as such has been placed upon the final roll of said Nation by the Honorable Secretary of the Interior, his final enrollment number being 12885 and that a Female child was born to me on the 19th day of August 190 3; that said child has been named Ida May King , and is now living. his[sic]

Sarah Jane x King
Witnesseth. mark
Must be two ⎫ T.J. Halls
Witnesses who ⎬
are Citizens. ⎭ James Fizer

Subscribed and sworn to before me this 6 day of Jan 190 5

James Lan
Notary Public.
My commission expires: 9-10-1907

AFFIDAVIT OF ATTENDING PHYSICIAN OR MIDWIFE

UNITED STATES OF AMERICA
INDIAN TERRITORY
Western DISTRICT

I, (Name Illegible) a Physician on oath state that I attended on Mrs. Sarah Jane King wife of William S King on the 19th day of August , 190 3 , that there was born to her on said date a Female child, that said child is now living, and is said to have been named Ida[sic] May King

Subscribed and sworn to before me this, the 6 day of Jan 190 5

WITNESSETH: James Lan Notary Public.
Must be two witnesses ⎰ T.J. Halls
who are citizens ⎱
James Fizer

Applications for Enrollment of Choctaw Newborn
Act of 1905   Volume XV

We hereby certify that we are well acquainted with   *(Name Illegible)* a   Physician   and know................ to be reputable and of good standing in the community.

_____   *(Name Illegible)*

_____   Lizzy Arnett

_____

BIRTH AFFIDAVIT.

DEPARTMENT OF THE INTERIOR.
COMMISSION TO THE FIVE CIVILIZED TRIBES.

_____

IN RE APPLICATION FOR ENROLLMENT, as a citizen of the   Choctaw   Nation, of Iler May King   , born on the   19   day of   August   , 1903

Name of Father: William S. King   a citizen of the   Choctaw   Nation.
Name of Mother: Sarah J. King   a citizen of the   Chotaw[sic] Nation.

Postoffice   Quinton, Ind. T.

_____

AFFIDAVIT OF MOTHER.

UNITED STATES OF AMERICA, Indian Territory, }
    Western   DISTRICT.

I,   Sarah J. King   , on oath state that I am   30   years of age and a citizen by In=termarriage[sic]   , of the   Choctaw   Nation; that I am the lawful wife of William S. King   , who is a citizen, by Blood   of the   Choctaw   Nation; that a   Female   child was born to me on   19   day of   August   , 1903; that said child has been named   Iler May King   , and was living March 4, 1905.

Sarah J King

Witnesses To Mark:
{

Subscribed and sworn to before me this   17   day of   April   , 1905

J.M. White
Notary Public.

_____

168

Applications for Enrollment of Choctaw Newborn
Act of 1905 Volume XV

AFFIDAVIT OF ATTENDING PHYSICIAN OR MID-WIFE.

UNITED STATES OF AMERICA, Indian Territory, }
Western DISTRICT.

I, Lizzie Arnett, a Midwife, on oath state that I attended on Mrs. Sarah J. King, wife of William S. King on the 19 day of August, 1903; that there was born to her on said date a Female child; that said child was living March 4, 1905, and is said to have been named Iler May King.

Leizy Arnett

Witnesses To Mark:
{

Subscribed and sworn to before me this 17 day of April, 1905

J.M. White
Notary Public.

Choctaw 2199.

Muskogee, Indian Territory, April 21, 1905.

William S. King,
Quinton, Indian Territory.

Dear Sir:

Receipt is hereby acknowledged of the affidavits of Sarah King and Leizy Arnett to the birth of Iler May King, daughter of William S. and Sarah J. King, August 19, 1903, and the same have been filed with our records as an application for the enrollment of said child.

Respectfully,

Chairman.

Choc New Born 1115
Lynn Rabon
(Born Oct. 28, 1904)

Applications for Enrollment of Choctaw Newborn
Act of 1905 Volume XV

NEW-BORN AFFIDAVIT.

Number..........

...Choctaw Enrolling Commission...

IN THE MATTER OF THE APPLICATION FOR ENROLLMENT, as a citizen of the Choctaw Nation, of Lynn Rabon

born on the 28th day of ___October___ 190 4

Name of father   Rufus Rabon   a citizen of   Choctaw Nation final enrollment No. 130
Name of mother   Ethel M Rabon   a citizen of   Choctaw Nation final enrollment No. 8278

Postoffice   Kinta IT

AFFIDAVIT OF MOTHER.

UNITED STATES OF AMERICA
INDIAN TERRITORY
Western   DISTRICT

I   Ethel M Rabon   , on oath state that I am 28 years of age and a citizen by blood of the Choctaw Nation, and as such have been placed upon the final roll of the Choctaw Nation, by the Honorable Secretary of the Interior my final enrollment number being 8278 ; that I am the lawful wife of Rufus Rabon , who is a citizen of the Choctaw Nation, and as such has been placed upon the final roll of said Nation by the Honorable Secretary of the Interior, his final enrollment number being 130 and that a female child was born to me on the 28th day of October 190 4; that said child has been named Lynn Rabon , and is now living.

Ethel M. Rabon

Witnesseth.
Must be two Witnesses who are Citizens.   } H.M. Moore
                                              JW Rabon

Subscribed and sworn to before me this   6 day of   Jan   190 5

L.C. Tuey
Notary Public.

My commission expires: Jan 17-1907

Applications for Enrollment of Choctaw Newborn
Act of 1905 Volume XV

AFFIDAVIT OF ATTENDING PHYSICIAN OR MIDWIFE

UNITED STATES OF AMERICA
INDIAN TERRITORY
Western DISTRICT

I, E Johnson a Practicing Physician on oath state that I attended on Mrs. Ethel M Rabon wife of Rufus Rabon on the 28th day of October , 190 4 , that there was born to her on said date a female child, that said child is now living, and is said to have been named Lynn Rabon

E. Johnson MD *M.D.*

Subscribed and sworn to before me this, the 6- day of Jan 190 5

WITNESSETH: L.C. Tuey Notary Public.
Must be two witnesses who are citizens
{ HM Moore
  JW Rabon

We hereby certify that we are well acquainted with E. Johnson a practicing physician and know him to be reputable and of good standing in the community.

Tobias Brashears

HM Moore

BIRTH AFFIDAVIT.

DEPARTMENT OF THE INTERIOR.
COMMISSION TO THE FIVE CIVILIZED TRIBES.

IN RE APPLICATION FOR ENROLLMENT, as a citizen of the Choctaw Nation, of Lynn Rabon , born on the 28 day of October , 1904

by intermarriage

Name of Father: Rufus Rabon   a citizen of the Choctaw Nation.
Name of Mother: Ethel M Rabon   a citizen of the Choctaw Nation.

Postoffice Madill, Ind. Ter.

Applications for Enrollment of Choctaw Newborn
Act of 1905 Volume XV

AFFIDAVIT OF MOTHER.

UNITED STATES OF AMERICA, Indian Territory,
~~Western~~ Central DISTRICT.

I, Ethel M. Rabon, on oath state that I am 29 years of age and a citizen by blood, of the Choctaw Nation; that I am the lawful wife of Rufus Rabon, who is a citizen, by intermarriage of the Choctaw Nation; that a female child was born to me on 28th day of October, 1904; that said child has been named Lynn Rabon, and was living March 4, 1905.

Ethel M. Rabon

Witnesses To Mark: No. 8278

Subscribed and sworn to before me this 3rd day of April, 1905

OL Johnson
Notary Public.

AFFIDAVIT OF ATTENDING PHYSICIAN OR MID-WIFE.

UNITED STATES OF AMERICA, Indian Territory,
Western DISTRICT.

I, Dr E Johnson, a Physician, on oath state that I attended on Mrs. Ethel M Rabon, wife of Rufus Rabon on the 28th day of October, 1904; that there was born to her on said date a female child; that said child was living March 4, 1905, and is said to have been named Lynn Rabon

E. Johnson MD

Witnesses To Mark:

Subscribed and sworn to before me this 12 day of April, 1905

LD Allen
Notary Public.

Applications for Enrollment of Choctaw Newborn
Act of 1905   Volume XV

Choctaw 2818.

Muskogee, Indian Territory, April 21, 1905.

Rufus Rabon,
    Madill, Indian Territory.

Dear Sir:

    Receipt is hereby acknowledged of the affidavits of Ethel M. Rabon and E. Johnson to the birth of Lynn Rabon, daughter of Rufus and Ethel M. Rabon, October 28, 1904, and the same have been filed with our records as an application for the enrollment of said child.

Respectfully,

Chairman.

Choc New Born 1116
    Rose James
    (Born Jan. 6, 1904)

BIRTH AFFIDAVIT.

DEPARTMENT OF THE INTERIOR.
COMMISSION TO THE FIVE CIVILIZED TRIBES.

IN RE APPLICATION FOR ENROLLMENT, as a citizen of the   Choctaw   Nation, of Rose James   , born on the 6th day of January , 1904

Name of Father: Jackson James   a citizen of the Choctaw Nation.
Name of Mother: Wicey James   a citizen of the Choctaw Nation.

Postoffice   Wilburton, I.T.

AFFIDAVIT OF MOTHER.

UNITED STATES OF AMERICA, Indian Territory,
    Central   **DISTRICT.**

    I, Wicey James , on oath state that I am 33 years of age and a citizen by blood , of the Choctaw Nation; that I am the lawful wife of Jackson James , who is a citizen, by blood of the   Choctaw   Nation; that a Female

Applications for Enrollment of Choctaw Newborn
Act of 1905 Volume XV

child was born to me on 6th day of January , 1905; that said child has been named Rose James , and was living March 4, 1905.

             her
            Wicey x James
Witnesses To Mark: mark
 { Louise McKinney
  Joseph Jackson

  Subscribed and sworn to before me this 17th day of April , 1905

           L. Jake Collins
            Notary Public.

AFFIDAVIT OF ATTENDING PHYSICIAN OR MID-WIFE.

UNITED STATES OF AMERICA, Indian Territory,
 Central   **DISTRICT.**

  I, Gincy[sic] James , a midwife , on oath state that I attended on Mrs. Wicey James , wife of Jackson James on the 6th day of January , 1904; that there was born to her on said date a Female child; that said child was living March 4, 1905, and is said to have been named Rose James

             her
           Jensie x James
Witnesses To Mark: mark
 { Louise McKinney
  Joseph Jackson

  Subscribed and sworn to before me this 17th day of April , 1905

           L. Jake Collins
            Notary Public.

               Choctaw 3180.

      Muskogee, Indian Territory, April 21, 1905.

Jackson James,
  Wilburton, Indian Territory.

Dear Sir:

  Receipt is hereby acknowledged of the affidavits of Wicey and Jensie James to the birth of Rose James, daughter of Jackson and Wicey James, January 6, 1904, and the same have been filed with our records as an application for the enrollment of said child.

Applications for Enrollment of Choctaw Newborn
Act of 1905 Volume XV

Respectfully,

Chairman.

Choc New Born 1117
    Ed G. W. Murphy
    (Born Nov. 29, 1903)

BIRTH AFFIDAVIT.

DEPARTMENT OF THE INTERIOR.
COMMISSION TO THE FIVE CIVILIZED TRIBES.

IN RE APPLICATION FOR ENROLLMENT, as a citizen of the Choctaw Nation, of Ed G. W. Murphy, born on the 29th day of November, 1903

Name of Father: Robinson Murphy   a citizen of the Choctaw Nation.
Name of Mother: Elizabeth Murphy nee Billy   a citizen of the Choctaw Nation.

Postoffice   Herbert, I.T.

AFFIDAVIT OF MOTHER.

UNITED STATES OF AMERICA, Indian Territory,
  Central   DISTRICT.

    I, Elizabeth Murphy, on oath state that I am 22 years of age and a citizen by blood, of the Choctaw Nation; that I am the lawful wife of Robinson Murphy, who is a citizen, by blood of the Choctaw Nation; that a male child was born to me on 29th day of November, 1903; that said child has been named Ed G.W. Murphy, and was living March 4, 1905.

                                            Elizabeth Murphy
Witnesses To Mark:

    Subscribed and sworn to before me this 19th day of April, 1905

                                        W.H. Angell
                                            Notary Public.

Applications for Enrollment of Choctaw Newborn
Act of 1905   Volume XV

AFFIDAVIT OF ATTENDING PHYSICIAN OR MID-WIFE.

UNITED STATES OF AMERICA, Indian Territory, }
Central   DISTRICT.

    I,   Rebecca Billy   , a   midwife   , on oath state that I attended on Mrs.   Elizabeth Murphy   , wife of   Robinson Murphy   on the 29th day of November , 1903; that there was born to her on said date a   male   child; that said child was living March 4, 1905, and is said to have been named Ed G. W. Murphy

                                   Rebecca Billy

Witnesses To Mark:
{

    Subscribed and sworn to before me this 19th day of   April   , 1905

                                  W.H. Angell
                                     Notary Public.

Choc New Born 1118
    Benjamin Thomas Scott
    (Born April 22, 1903)

BIRTH AFFIDAVIT.

    IN RE-APPLICATION FOR ENROLLMENT, as a citizen of the   Choctaw   Nation, of Benjamin Thomas Scott , born on the   22   day of   April , 190 3

Name of Father: John P. Scott   a citizen of the   Chickasaw   Nation.
Name of Mother: Phoebe Scott   a citizen of the   Choctaw   Nation.

                    Postoffice   Roff, Ind Ter

AFFIDAVIT OF MOTHER.

UNITED STATES OF AMERICA, INDIAN TERRITORY, }
Southern   District.

    I,   Phoebe Scott   , on oath state that I am   31   years of age and a citizen by blood , of the   Choctaw   Nation; that I am the lawful wife of   John P. Scott   , who is a citizen, by   intermarriage   of the   Chickasaw   Nation; that a   male   child was

Applications for Enrollment of Choctaw Newborn
Act of 1905   Volume XV

born to me on   22   day of   April   , 190 3, that said child has been named   Benjamin Thomas Scott   , and ~~is now~~ was living March 4, 1905.

Phoebe Scott

Witnesses To Mark:
{ Silina Wilton
  J M Sanders

Subscribed and sworn to before me this   18   day of   April   , 1905.
My Commission Expires Jan. 30, 1907.

J.C. Little
Notary Public.

AFFIDAVIT OF ATTENDING PHYSICIAN OR MID-WIFE.

UNITED STATES OF AMERICA, INDIAN TERRITORY, }
Southern   District.

I,   J.M. Settle   , a   practicing physician   , on oath state that I attended on Mrs.   Phoebe Scott   , wife of   John P Scott   on the   22   day of   April   , 190 3; that there was born to her on said date a   male   child; that said child ~~is now~~ was living March 4, 1905 and is said to have been named   Benjamin Thomas Scott

Dr J M Settle

Witnesses To Mark:
{ Marvin J Burris
  George F Byrd

Subscribed and sworn to before me this   10   day of   April   , 1905.

Minnie Lillard
Notary Public.

Choctaw 5446.

Muskogee, Indian Territory, April 22, 1905.

J. C. Little,
    Attorney at Law,
        Roff, Indian Territory.

Dear Sir:

   Receipt is hereby acknowledged of your letter of April 18, transmitting the affidavits of Phoebe Scott and Dr. J. M. Settle to the birth of Benjamin Thomas Scott, son

Applications for Enrollment of Choctaw Newborn
Act of 1905   Volume XV

of John P. and Phoebe Scott, April 22, 1903, and the same have been filed with our records as an application for the enrollment of said child.

          Respectfully,

                              Chairman.

Choc New Born 1119
    Sylvan G. Moore
    (Born Dec. 4, 1903)

BIRTH AFFIDAVIT.
DEPARTMENT OF THE INTERIOR.
COMMISSION TO THE FIVE CIVILIZED TRIBES.

IN RE APPLICATION FOR ENROLLMENT, as a citizen of the   Choctaw   Nation, of Sylvan G. Moore   , born on the 4th day of Dec , 1903

Name of Father: Robert M Moore   a citizen of the   Choctaw   Nation.
Name of Mother: Olive M Moore   a citizen of the   Choctaw   Nation.

                Postoffice   Atoka, Ind Terr.

AFFIDAVIT OF MOTHER.

UNITED STATES OF AMERICA, Indian Territory, }
    Central   **DISTRICT.** }

I,   Olive M. Moore   , on oath state that I am   29   years of age and a citizen by   blood   , of the   Choctaw   Nation; that I am the lawful wife of   Robert M Moore   , who is a citizen, by marriage   of the   Choctaw   Nation; that a male   child was born to me on   the 4th day of   December   , 1903; that said child has been named   Sylvan G Moore   , and was living March 4, 1905.

                        Olive M Moore
Witnesses To Mark:
{

Applications for Enrollment of Choctaw Newborn
Act of 1905   Volume XV

Subscribed and sworn to before me this 18th day of April , 1905

Fred H Ayers
Notary Public.

My commission expires June 29th 1908.

AFFIDAVIT OF ATTENDING PHYSICIAN OR MID-WIFE.

UNITED STATES OF AMERICA, Indian Territory, }
  Central   DISTRICT. }

I, Thomas J Long , a physician , on oath state that I attended on Mrs. Olive M Moore , wife of Robert M Moore on the 4th day of December , 1903; that there was born to her on said date a male child; that said child was living March 4, 1905, and is said to have been named Sylvan G Moore

Thomas J Long

Witnesses To Mark:
{

Subscribed and sworn to before me this 18th day of April , 1905

Fred H Ayers
Notary Public.

My commission expires June 29th 1908.

Choctaw 4440.

Muskogee, Indian Territory, April 22, 1905.

Robert M. Moore,
  Atoka, Indian Territory.

Dear Sir:

Receipt is hereby acknowledged of the affidavits of Olive M. Moore and Thomas J. Long to the birth of Sylvan G. Moore, son of Thomas[sic] M. and Olive M. Moore, December 4, 1903, and the same have been filed with our records as an application for the enrollment of said child.

Respectfully,

Chairman.

Applications for Enrollment of Choctaw Newborn
Act of 1905   Volume XV

7 NB 1119

Muskogee, Indian Territory, April 27, 1905.

R. M. Moore,
    Atoka, Indian Territory.

Dear Sir:

    Receipt is hereby acknowledged of your letter of April 23, 1905, in which you state that Sylvan G. Moore is the son of Robert Moore, instead of Thomas M. Moore and ask to be advised if affidavits forwarded by you do not show this fact.

    In reply to your letter you are informed that it appears from our records that Sylvan G. Moore is the son of Robert Moore and Olive M. Moore.

                  Respectfully,

                            Chairman.

Choc New Born 1120
    Dora Frances Hays
    (Born Jan. 5, 1903)

BIRTH AFFIDAVIT.

DEPARTMENT OF THE INTERIOR.
COMMISSION TO THE FIVE CIVILIZED TRIBES.

    IN RE APPLICATION FOR ENROLLMENT, as a citizen of the   Choctaw   Nation, of Dora Frances Hays   , born on the 5th day of January , 1903

Name of Father: Thomas Hays   a citizen of the Choctaw Nation.
Name of Mother: Rosa Hays   a citizen of the Choctaw Nation.

                    Postoffice   Daugherty I.T.

Applications for Enrollment of Choctaw Newborn
Act of 1905   Volume XV

AFFIDAVIT OF MOTHER.

UNITED STATES OF AMERICA, Indian Territory, }
Southern   DISTRICT.

    I, Rosa Hays, on oath state that I am 28 years of age and a citizen by marriage, of the Choctaw Nation; that I am the lawful wife of Thomas Hays, who is a citizen, by blood of the Choctaw Nation; that a female child was born to me on the 5th day of January, 1903; that said child has been named Dora Frances Hays, and was living March 4, 1905.

                                  Rosa Hays

Witnesses To Mark:
{

    Subscribed and sworn to before me this 17 day of April, 1905

                        (Name Illegible)
                        Notary Public.

AFFIDAVIT OF ATTENDING PHYSICIAN OR MID-WIFE.

UNITED STATES OF AMERICA, Indian Territory, }
Southern   DISTRICT.

    I,......................................., a physician, on oath state that I attended on Mrs. Rosa Hays, wife of Thomas Hays on the 5th day of January, 1903; that there was born to her on said date a female child; that said child was living March 4, 1905, and is said to have been named Dora Frances Hays

                                I.W. Hooper M.D.

Witnesses To Mark:
{

    Subscribed and sworn to before me this 17 day of April, 1905

                        (Name Illegible)
                        Notary Public.

Applications for Enrollment of Choctaw Newborn
Act of 1905   Volume XV

1120
Choctaw ~~5458~~.

Muskogee, Indian Territory, April 22, 1905.

Thomas Hayes[sic],
Dougherty, Indian Territory.

Dear Sir:

Receipt is hereby acknowledged of the affidavits of Rosa Hayes and I. W. Hooper to the birth of Dora Frances Hayes[sic], daughter of Thomas and Rosa Hayes, January 5, 1903, and the same have been filed with our records as an application for the enrollment of said child.

Respectfully,

Chairman.

Choc New Born 1121
   Dollie M. Nail
   (Born May 28, 1903)

BIRTH AFFIDAVIT.

DEPARTMENT OF THE INTERIOR.
COMMISSION TO THE FIVE CIVILIZED TRIBES.

IN RE APPLICATION FOR ENROLLMENT, as a citizen of the   Choctaw   Nation, of Dollie M. Nail, born on the 28 day of May, 1903

Name of Father: Joe Nail   a citizen of the   Choctaw   Nation.
Name of Mother: Paralee Nail   a citizen of the   Choctaw   Nation.

Postoffice   Soper Ind Terr.

Applications for Enrollment of Choctaw Newborn
Act of 1905   Volume XV

AFFIDAVIT OF MOTHER.

UNITED STATES OF AMERICA, Indian Territory, }
Central   DISTRICT. }

 I, Paralee Nail , on oath state that I am 35 years of age and a citizen by Intermarriage , of the Choctaw Nation; that I am the lawful wife of Joe Nail , who is a citizen, by Blood of the Choctaw Nation; that a Female child was born to me on 28th day of May , 1903; that said child has been named Dollie M. Nail , and was living March 4, 1905.

              her
            Paralee x Nail
Witnesses To Mark: mark
{ S.S. Markham
{ Harley Hughes

 Subscribed and sworn to before me this 17th day of April , 1905

My Com expires July 9th 1908   W.E. Larecy
              Notary Public.

AFFIDAVIT OF ATTENDING PHYSICIAN OR MID-WIFE.

UNITED STATES OF AMERICA, Indian Territory, }
Central   DISTRICT. }

 I, W.M. Walace[sic] , a   , on oath state that I attended on Mrs. Paralee Nail , wife of Joe Nail on the 28 day of May , 1903; that there was born to her on said date a Female child; that said child was living March 4, 1905, and is said to have been named Dollie M. Nail

            W.M. Wallace, M.D.
Witnesses To Mark:

{

 Subscribed and sworn to before me this 17th day of April , 1905

My commission expires
July 9th, 1908.   W.E. Larecy
            Notary Public.

Applications for Enrollment of Choctaw Newborn
Act of 1905   Volume XV

NEW BORN AFFIDAVIT

No ....

CHOCTAW ENROLLING COMMISSION

IN THE MATTER OF THE APPLICATION FOR ENROLLMENT as a citizen of the Choctaw Nation, of   Dollie M. Nail   born on the 28th day of   May   190 3

Name of father   Joe Nail   a citizen of   Choctaw   Nation, final enrollment No.   4266

Name of mother   Parley[sic] Nail   a citizen of   Choctaw   Nation, final enrollment No.   706

Soper I.T.   Postoffice.

AFFIDAVIT OF MOTHER

UNITED STATES OF AMERICA
INDIAN TERRITORY
DISTRICT   Central

I   Parley Nail   , on oath state that I am   35   years of age and a citizen by   Ind. M   of the   Choctaw   Nation, and as such have been placed upon the final roll of the   Choctaw   Nation, by the Honorable Secretary of the Interior my final enrollment number being   706   ; that I am the lawful wife of   Joe Nail   , who is a citizen of the   Choctaw   Nation, and as such has been placed upon the final roll of said Nation by the Honorable Secretary of the Interior, his final enrollment number being   4266   and that a   Female   child was born to me on the 28th day of   May   190 3; that said child has been named   Dollie M Nail   , and is now living.

WITNESSETH:
Must be two witnesses { Linn Folsom
who are citizens   { Robert Sanders

Parley x Nail
her   mark

Subscribed and sworn to before me this, the 27th day of   Feby   , 190 5

W.E. Larecy
Notary Public.

My Commission Expires: July 9th 1908

Applications for Enrollment of Choctaw Newborn
Act of 1905 Volume XV

Affidavit of Attending Physician or Midwife

UNITED STATES OF AMERICA,
   INDIAN TERRITORY,
Central   DISTRICT

I, W M Walace[sic] a Practicing Physician on oath state that I attended on Mrs. Parley Nail wife of Joe Nail on the 28th day of May, 190 3, that there was born to her on said date a Female child, that said child is now living, and is said to have been named Dollie M Nail

W.M. Wallace   M. D.

Subscribed and sworn to before me this the 27th day of Feby 1905

My commission expires
July 9th, 1908.   W.E. Larecy
                    Notary Public.

WITNESSETH:

Must be two witnesses who are citizens and know the child.
{ Tom Oakes
  J.U. Parsons

We hereby certify that we are well acquainted with a Practicing Physician and know him W.M. Walace[sic] to be reputable and of good standing in the community.

Must be two citizen witnesses.
{ Thompson Coleman
  Linn Folsom

Choc New Born 1122
    Susie May Colbert
    (Born Feb. 25, 1905)
    Eliza Colbert
    (Born Feb. 25, 1905)[sic]

Applications for Enrollment of Choctaw Newborn
Act of 1905   Volume XV

BIRTH AFFIDAVIT.

DEPARTMENT OF THE INTERIOR.
COMMISSION TO THE FIVE CIVILIZED TRIBES.

IN RE APPLICATION FOR ENROLLMENT, as a citizen of the Choctaw Nation, of Susie May Colbert, born on the 25 day of February, 1905

Name of Father: Alexander Colbert   a citizen of the Choctaw Nation.
Name of Mother: Martha Colbert   a citizen of the Choctaw Nation.

Postoffice   Tuskahoma I.T.

AFFIDAVIT OF MOTHER.

UNITED STATES OF AMERICA, Indian Territory,
Central   DISTRICT.

I, Martha Colbert, on oath state that I am 28 years of age and a citizen by blood, of the Choctaw Nation; that I am the lawful wife of Alexander Colbert, who is a citizen, by blood of the Choctaw Nation; that a female child was born to me on 25 day of February, 1905; that said child has been named Susie May Colbert, and was living March 4, 1905.

Witnesses To Mark:
{ Chas T. Difendafer
{ OL Johnson

her
Martha x Colbert
mark

Subscribed and sworn to before me this 10 day of April, 1905

OL Johnson
Notary Public.

BIRTH AFFIDAVIT.

DEPARTMENT OF THE INTERIOR.
COMMISSION TO THE FIVE CIVILIZED TRIBES.

IN RE APPLICATION FOR ENROLLMENT, as a citizen of the Choctaw Nation, of Eliza Colbert, born on the 21 day of September, 1903

Name of Father: Alexander Colbert   a citizen of the Choctaw Nation.
Name of Mother: Martha Colbert   a citizen of the Choctaw Nation.

Postoffice   Tuskahoma I.T.

Applications for Enrollment of Choctaw Newborn
Act of 1905 Volume XV

AFFIDAVIT OF MOTHER.

UNITED STATES OF AMERICA, Indian Territory, ⎫
Central   DISTRICT.   ⎬

I, Martha Colbert , on oath state that I am 28 years of age and a citizen by blood , of the Choctaw Nation; that I am the lawful wife of Alexander Colbert , who is a citizen, by blood of the Choctaw Nation; that a female child was born to me on 21 day of September , 1903; that said child has been named Eliza Colbert , and was living March 4, 1905.

                                                her
                                    Martha x Colbert

Witnesses To Mark: mark
⎰ Chas T. Difendafer
⎱ OL Johnson

Subscribed and sworn to before me this 10 day of April , 1905

                                    OL Johnson
                                    Notary Public.

DEPARTMENT OF THE INTERIOR,
COMMISSION TO THE FIVE CIVILIZED TRIBES.
TUSKAHOMA, IND. TER.,   APRIL 10, 1905.

In the matter of the application for the enrollment of Eliza Colbert and Susie May Colbert as citizens by blood of the Choctaw Nation.

Martha Colbert being first duly sworn testifies as follows:

EXAMINATION BY THE COMMISSION:

Q What is your name? A Martha Colbert.
Q What is your age? A Twenty-eight.
Q What is your post office address? A Tuskahoma.
Q You are a citizen by blood of the Choctaw Nation? A Yes, sir.
Q You have this day made application for the enrollment of your two children Eliza Colbert and Susie May Colbert as citizens by blood of the Choctaw Nation; when was Eliza Colbert born? A 21st day of September, 1903.
Q When was Susie May Colbert born? A 25th of February, 1905.
Q These children were both living on March 4, 1905? A Yes, sir.
Q Who attented[sic] you when these children were born? A No one.

                                Witness excused.

Applications for Enrollment of Choctaw Newborn
Act of 1905   Volume XV

Alexander Colbert being first duly sworn testified as follows:

EXAMINATION BY THE COMMISSION:

Q What is your name? A Alexander Colbert.
Q What is your age? A Twenty-eight.
Q What is your post office address? A Tuskahoma.
Q Your wife Martha Colbert has this day made application for the enrollment of your two children Eliza and Susie May Colbert as citizens of the Choctaw Nation; when was Eliza Colbert born? A 21st September, 1903.
Q When was Susie May born? A 25th February 1905.
Q They were both living on March 4, 1905? A Yes, sir.
Q Who attended your wife when these children were born? A No one.

Witness excused.

Tandy Walls being first duly sworn testifies as follows:

EXAMINATION BY THE COMMISSION:

Q What is your name? A Tandy Walls.
Q What is your age? A Twenty-four.
Q What is your post office address? A Tuskahoma.
Q Are you a citizen by blood of the Choctaw Nation? A Yes, sir.
Q Are you acquainted with Alexander Colbert and Martha Colbert? A Yes, sir.
Q How far from them do you reside? A About a mile.
[sic] Martha Colbert has this day made application for the enrollment of her two children Eliza Colbert and Susie May Colbert as citizens of the Choctaw Nation; do you know when Eliza was born - about when? A I don't remember what day.
Q What month? A September 1903.
Q Do you remember when Susie May Colbert was born; what month? A February 1905.
Q Both of these children were living on March 4, 1905? A Yes, sir.

Witness excused.

Chas. T. Difendafer being first duly sworn states that the above and foregoing is a full, true and correct transcript of his stenographic notes taken in said cause on said date.

Chas T. Difendafer

Subscribed and sworn to before me this sworn to before me this 10th day of April, 1905

OL Johnson
Notary Public.

Applications for Enrollment of Choctaw Newborn
Act of 1905   Volume XV

(The above testimony given again.)

Muskogee, Indian Territory, April 14, 1905.

Alexander Colbert,
    Tuskahoma, Indian Territory.

Dear Sir:

    Receipt is hereby acknowledged of the affidavits of Martha Colbert to the birth of Susie May Colbert, daughter of Alexander and Martha Colbert, February 25, 1905.

    It is stated in her affidavit that she is a citizen by blood of the Choctaw Nation. If this is correct you are requested to state the name under which she was enrolled, the names of her parents, and if she has selected an allotment of the lands of the Choctaw or Chickasaw Nation please give her roll number as it appears upon her allotment certificate.

                   Respectfully,

Roll No. of Martha Colbert is 13979.
  "   " Alexander Colbert "   761.
Please let me know when we can file on the land for the new
enrolled. (Signed Alexander Colbert)
                                     Commissioner in Charge.

7--NB--1122

Muskogee, Indian Territory, June 2, 1905.

Alexander Colbert,
    Tuskahoma, Indian Territory.

Dear Sir:

    Referring to the applications for the enrollment of your two infant children, Eliza Colbert, born September 21, 1903, and Susie May Colbert, born February 25, 1905, it is noted that your wife was not attended by a physician or midwife at the time of the birth of these applicants.

    In this case it will be necessary that the affidavits of two persons, who are disinterested and not related to the applicants, who have actual knowledge of the facts of their being born; the dates of their birth; that they were living on March 4, 1905, and that Martha Colbert is their mother be filed with this office.

Applications for Enrollment of Choctaw Newborn
Act of 1905   Volume XV

The testimony of Tandy Walls to these facts has been filed. It will, therefore, be necessary for you to secure the affidavit of another person to the birth of these children and that they were living on March 4, 1905.

This matter should receive your immediate attention as no further action can be taken relative to the enrollment of these applicants until the Commission has been furnished these affidavits.

        Respectfully,

            [sic]

7-NB-1122.

Muskogee, Indian Territory, June 22, 1905.

Alexander Colbert,
  Tuskahoma, Indian Territory.

Dear Sir:

Receipt is hereby acknowledged of the joint affidavit of Isom Allen and Green Bohanan to the birth of Eliza and Susie May Colbert. These affidavits should have been executed separately, and it will be necessary before any further action can be taken in these two cases that separate affidavits be filed in regard to the birth of each one of the applicants.

These affidavits should be made by persons who are disinterested and not related to the applicants, who know that the child was born, the date of its birth, that it was living on March 4, 1905, and that Martha Colbert was its mother.

        Respectfully,

           Chairman.

(The affidavit below typed as given.)

U. S. America
  Central Dist
    Ind. Ter.

We David Allen and Rufus Allen. Both citizen by blood of the Choctaw Nation on oath states that they are personally acquainted with Susie May Colbert, and that she was born Feby. 25-1905 and her Mother is Martha Colbert and that she was living March 4-1905. Signed this the 17 day July-1905.

           David Allen

Applications for Enrollment of Choctaw Newborn
Act of 1905 Volume XV

Rufus Allen

Subscribed & sworn to before me this 17 day of July-1905.

PW Hudson
Notary

My Com expires 2/24/06

(The affidavit below typed as given.)

U.S. of A.
Ind Ter
Central District

We. Isom Allen and Green Bohanan, Both citizen by blood of the Choc. Nation, on oath stated that they are personally acquinted with Eliza Colbert and that she was born Sept 21-1903, and Susie May Colbert was born Feby 25th 1905, and were both living March 4-1905 and their mother is Martha Colbert.

Isom Allen
Green Bohanan

Subscribed & sworn to before me this 17th day of June-1905.

My Com Expires 2/24/06

P W Hudson
Notary Public

Choc New Born 1123
    Charles Shotuby
    (Born Sept. 3, 1905)

AFFIDAVIT OF ATTENDING PHYSICIAN OR MIDWIFE

UNITED STATES OF AMERICA
INDIAN TERRITORY
  Central   DISTRICT

I, Dickson Shotube[sic] a attendant on oath state that I attended on Mrs. Jane Shotube *my* wife of .... on the 3rd day of Sept, 190 3, that there was born to her on said date a male child, that said child is now living, and is said to have been named Charles Shotube

Applications for Enrollment of Choctaw Newborn
Act of 1905   Volume XV

                         Dickson Shotube   ~~M.D.~~

WITNESSETH:
Must be two witnesses who are citizens and know the child.
{ Jesse Christy
   H B Jacob

         Subscribed and sworn to before me this, the   23rd day of
Feb   190 5

                          W A Shoney   Notary Public.

    We hereby certify that we are well acquainted with   Dickson Shotube
a   attendant   and know   him   to be reputable and of good standing in the community.

                     { Jesse Christy
                       H B Jacob

BIRTH AFFIDAVIT.

DEPARTMENT OF THE INTERIOR.
COMMISSION TO THE FIVE CIVILIZED TRIBES.

    IN RE APPLICATION FOR ENROLLMENT, as a citizen of the   Choctaw   Nation, of Charles Shotuby   , born on the   3   day of   Sept   , 1903

Name of Father: Dickson Shotuby   a citizen of the   Choctaw   Nation.
Name of Mother: Jane Shotuby   a citizen of the   Choctaw   Nation.

                     Postoffice   Valliant I T

AFFIDAVIT OF MOTHER.

UNITED STATES OF AMERICA, Indian Territory, }
    Central   **DISTRICT.** }

    I,   Jane Shotuby   , on oath state that I am   3?   years of age and a citizen by Blood   , of the   Choctaw   Nation; that I am the lawful wife of   Dickson Shotuby   , who is a citizen, by Blood   of the   Choctaw   Nation; that a   mail[sic] child was born to me on   3   day of   Sept   , 1903; that said child has been named Charles Shotuby   , and was living March 4, 1905.

                             her
                      Jane x Shotuby
Witnesses To Mark: mark
   { Lillian Wallace
     (Name Illegible)

Applications for Enrollment of Choctaw Newborn
Act of 1905 Volume XV

Subscribed and sworn to before me this 10 day of April , 1905

H L Fowler
Notary Public.

AFFIDAVIT OF ATTENDING PHYSICIAN OR MID-WIFE.

UNITED STATES OF AMERICA, Indian Territory, }
  Central   DISTRICT.

I, Emma Bond , a................., on oath state that I attended on Mrs. Jane Shotuby , wife of Dickson Shotuby on the 3 day of Sept , 1903; that there was born to her on said date a mail child; that said child was living March 4, 1905, and is said to have been named Charles Shotuby

                                      her
                               Emma x Bond
Witnesses To Mark: mark
  { Lillian Wallace
    (Name Illegible)

Subscribed and sworn to before me this 10 day of April , 1905

H L Fowler
Notary Public.

NEW-BORN AFFIDAVIT.

Number...........

...Choctaw Enrolling Commission...

IN THE MATTER OF THE APPLICATION FOR ENROLLMENT, as a citizen of the Choctaw Nation, of Charles Shotube

born on the 3rd day of __September__ 190 3

Name of father Dickson Shotube   a citizen of Choctaw
Nation final enrollment No. 1650
Name of mother Jane Shotube   a citizen of Choctaw
Nation final enrollment No. 1651

                                          Postoffice Valliant I T

Applications for Enrollment of Choctaw Newborn
Act of 1905   Volume XV

AFFIDAVIT OF MOTHER.

UNITED STATES OF AMERICA
INDIAN TERRITORY
Central   DISTRICT

I   Jane Shotube   , on oath state that I am   36   years of age and a citizen by   blood   of the   Choctaw   Nation, and as such have been placed upon the final roll of the   Choctaw   Nation, by the Honorable Secretary of the Interior my final enrollment number being   1651 ; that I am the lawful wife of   Dickson Shotube   , who is a citizen of the   Choctaw   Nation, and as such has been placed upon the final roll of said Nation by the Honorable Secretary of the Interior, his final enrollment number being   1650   and that a   Male   child was born to me on the   3rd day of   September   190 3; that said child has been named   Charles Shotube   , and is now living.

her
Jane x Shotube
mark

Witnesseth.

Must be two
Witnesses who
are Citizens.   } Jesse Christy

H B Jacob

Subscribed and sworn to before me this   23rd day of   Feb   190 5

W A Shoney
Notary Public.

My commission expires: Jan 10, 1909

Choctaw 685.

Muskogee, Indian Territory, April 22, 1905.

Hosea L. Fowler,
   Valliant, Indian Territory.

Dear Sir:

Receipt is hereby acknowledged of your letter without date, transmitting the affidavits of Jane Shotuby and Emma Bond to the birth of Charles Shotuby, son of Dickson and Jane Shotuby, September 3, 1903, and the same have been filed in the matter of the enrollment of said child.

The other affidavits enclosed in your letter have been made the subject of a separate communication.

Respectfully,

Chairman.

Applications for Enrollment of Choctaw Newborn
Act of 1905   Volume XV

Choc New Born 1124
    Leo Garland
    (Born Nov. 9, 1903)

NEW-BORN AFFIDAVIT.

Number..............

...Choctaw Enrolling Commission...

IN THE MATTER OF THE APPLICATION FOR ENROLLMENT, as a citizen of the Choctaw Nation, of Leo Garland

born on the 9 day of ___November___ 190 3

Name of father Columbus Garland   a citizen of Choctaw
Nation final enrollment No. 7073
Name of mother Lettie Garland   ~~a citizen of~~ white
Nation final enrollment No...............

                Postoffice

AFFIDAVIT OF MOTHER.

UNITED STATES OF AMERICA
INDIAN TERRITORY
Western   DISTRICT

    I Lettie Garland   , on oath state that I am 19 years of age and a citizen by marriage of the ——— Nation, and as such have been placed upon the final roll of the ——— Nation, by the Honorable Secretary of the Interior my final enrollment number being .... ; that I am the lawful wife of Columbus Garland , who is a citizen of the Choctaw Nation, and as such has been placed upon the final roll of said Nation by the Honorable Secretary of the Interior, his final enrollment number being 7073 and that a Male child was born to me on the 9th day of November 190 3; that said child has been named Leo Garland , and is now living.

                              Lettie Garland

Witnesseth.
   Must be two } Bennie Donald
   Witnesses who
   are Citizens. Ward Garland Jr.

    Subscribed and sworn to before me this 10 day of Feb 190 5

                         C C Jones
                               Notary Public.

My commission expires:

Applications for Enrollment of Choctaw Newborn
Act of 1905 Volume XV

AFFIDAVIT OF ATTENDING PHYSICIAN OR MIDWIFE

UNITED STATES OF AMERICA
INDIAN TERRITORY
Western DISTRICT

I, C.C. Jones a Practicing Physician on oath state that I attended on Mrs. Lettie Garland wife of Columbus Garland on the 9th day of November , 190 3 , that there was born to her on said date a male child, that said child is now living, and is said to have been named Leo Garland

C C Jones *M.D.*

Subscribed and sworn to before me this, the 10 day of Feb 190 5

WITNESSETH: J N Jones Notary Public.

Must be two witnesses who are citizens { Bennie Donald
Ward Garland Jr

We hereby certify that we are well acquainted with Dr C C Jones a Practicing Physician and know him to be reputable and of good standing in the community.

Bennie Donald _____

Ward Garland, Jr _____

BIRTH AFFIDAVIT.

DEPARTMENT OF THE INTERIOR.
COMMISSION TO THE FIVE CIVILIZED TRIBES.

IN RE APPLICATION FOR ENROLLMENT, as a citizen of the Choctaw Nation, of Leo Garland , born on the 9th day of November , 1902[sic]

Name of Father: Columbus Garland   a citizen of the Choctaw Nation.
Name of Mother: Lettie Garland   a citizen of the White Nation.

Postoffice Garland I.T.

Applications for Enrollment of Choctaw Newborn
Act of 1905   Volume XV

AFFIDAVIT OF MOTHER.

UNITED STATES OF AMERICA, Indian Territory, }
Central   DISTRICT.

I, Lettie Garland, on oath state that I am 19 years of age and a citizen by Intermarriage, of the Choctaw Nation; that I am the lawful wife of Columbus Garland, who is a citizen, by Blood of the Choctaw Nation; that a male child was born to me on 9th day of November, 1902; that said child has been named Leo Garland, and was living March 4, 1905.

Lettie Garland

Witnesses To Mark:
{

Subscribed and sworn to before me this 18 day of April, 1905

C.C. Jones
Notary Public.

AFFIDAVIT OF ATTENDING PHYSICIAN OR MID-WIFE.

UNITED STATES OF AMERICA, Indian Territory, }
Central   DISTRICT.

I, C. C. Jones, a Physician, on oath state that I attended on Mrs. Lettie Garland, wife of Columbus Garland on the 9th day of November, 1902; that there was born to her on said date a male child; that said child was living March 4, 1905, and is said to have been named Leo Garland

C C Jones

Witnesses To Mark:
{

Subscribed and sworn to before me this 18 day of April, 1905

J N Jones
Notary Public.

Applications for Enrollment of Choctaw Newborn
Act of 1905 Volume XV

BIRTH AFFIDAVIT.

DEPARTMENT OF THE INTERIOR.
COMMISSION TO THE FIVE CIVILIZED TRIBES.

IN RE APPLICATION FOR ENROLLMENT, as a citizen of the Choctaw Nation, of Leo Garland, born on the 9 day of November, 1903

Name of Father: Columbus Garland a citizen of the Choctaw Nation.
Name of Mother: Lettie Garland a citizen of the White Nation.

Postoffice Garland I.T.

AFFIDAVIT OF MOTHER.

UNITED STATES OF AMERICA, Indian Territory, }
Central DISTRICT.

I, Lettie Garland, on oath state that I am 19 years of age and a citizen by intermarriage, of the Choctaw Nation; that I am the lawful wife of Columbus Garland, who is a citizen, by blood of the Choctaw Nation; that a male child was born to me on 9 day of November, 1903; that said child has been named Leo Garland, and was living March 4, 1905.

Lettie Garland

Witnesses To Mark:

Subscribed and sworn to before me this 14 day of June, 1905

C.C. Jones
Notary Public.

AFFIDAVIT OF ATTENDING PHYSICIAN OR MID-WIFE.

UNITED STATES OF AMERICA, Indian Territory, }
Central DISTRICT.

I, C. C. Jones, a Physician, on oath state that I attended on Mrs. Lettie Garland, wife of Columbus Garland on the 9 day of November, 1903; that there was born to her on said date a male child; that said child was living March 4, 1905, and is said to have been named Leo Garland

C C Jones

Witnesses To Mark:

Applications for Enrollment of Choctaw Newborn
Act of 1905   Volume XV

Subscribed and sworn to before me this   14   day of   June   , 1905

J N Jones
Notary Public.

7-2442

Muskogee, Indian Territory, April 25, 1905.

Columbus Garland,
Garland, Indian Territory.

Dear Sir:

Receipt is hereby acknowledged of the affidavits of Lettie Garland and C. C. Jones to the birth of Leo Garland, son of Columbus and Lettie Garland, November 9, 1902[sic], and the same have been filed with our records as an application for the enrollment of said child.

Respectfully,

Chairman.

7-NB-1124.

Muskogee, Indian Territory, Jun 10, 1905.

Columbus Garland,
Garland, Indian Territory.

Dear Sir:

There is enclosed herewith for execution application for the enrollment of your infant child, Leo Garland.

In the affidavits of February 10, 1905 heretofore filed in this office, the date of the applicant's birth was given as November 9, 1903, while in the affidavits of April 18, 1905, this date is given as November 9, 1902. Please insert the correct date and when the affidavits are properly executed return them to this office.

In having these affidavits executed care should be exercised to see that all names are written in full, as they appear in the body of the affidavit, and in the event either of the persons signing the affidavit are unable to write, signatures by mark must be attested by two witnesses. Each affidavit must be executed before a Notary Public and the notarial seal and signature of the officer must be attached to each separate affidavit.

Applications for Enrollment of Choctaw Newborn
Act of 1905   Volume XV

DeB--3/10

Respectfully,

Chairman.

7 NB 1124

Muskogee, Indian Territory, June 19, 1905.

Columbus Garland,
    Garland, Indian Territory.

Dear Sir:

    Receipt is hereby acknowledged of the affidavits of Lettie Garland and C. C. Jones to the birth of Leo Garland, son of Columbus and Lettie Garland, November 9, 1903, and the same have been filed with our records in the matter of the enrollment of said child.

Respectfully,

Chairman.

Choc New Born 1125
    Jessie Airington
    (Born June 20, 1903)
    Make Airington
    (Born Feb. 26, 1905)

BIRTH AFFIDAVIT.

DEPARTMENT OF THE INTERIOR.
COMMISSION TO THE FIVE CIVILIZED TRIBES.

IN RE APPLICATION FOR ENROLLMENT, as a citizen of the   Choctaw   Nation, of Make Arrington[sic]   , born on the   26   day of   February   , 1905

Name of Father: Benjamin F Arrington   a citizen of the   Choctaw   Nation.
Name of Mother: Willie Arrington   a citizen of the   Choctaw   Nation.
    Postoffice   Ireton I.T.

Applications for Enrollment of Choctaw Newborn
Act of 1905   Volume XV

AFFIDAVIT OF MOTHER.

UNITED STATES OF AMERICA, Indian Territory, }
Southern   DISTRICT.

I, Willie Airington, on oath state that I am Thirty-Three years of age and a citizen by Intermarried, of the Choctaw Nation; that I am the lawful wife of Benjamin F. Airington, who is a citizen, by Blood of the Choctaw Nation; that a Male child was born to me on 26th day of February, 1905; that said child has been named Make Airington, and was living March 4, 1905.

                                                            her
                                              Willie x Airington
Witnesses To Mark: mark
{ O J Breeding
  J W Folk

Subscribed and sworn to before me this 20th day of April, 1905

                                  James M Gordon
                                      Notary Public.
        My commission expires March 1907

AFFIDAVIT OF ATTENDING PHYSICIAN OR MID-WIFE.
State of Texas
UNITED STATES OF AMERICA, ~~Indian Territory~~, }
Tarrant County   ~~DISTRICT~~.

I, J. Bennett McBride, a Physician, on oath state that I attended on Mrs. Willie Arrington, wife of Benjamin F Arrington on the 26 day of February, 1905; that there was born to her on said date a male child; that said child was living March 4, 1905, and is said to have been named Make Arrington

                                  J Bennett McBride M.D.
Witnesses To Mark:
{

Subscribed and sworn to before me this 14 day of April, 1905

                                    John Kaiser
                                      Notary Public.
                          Notary Public, Tarrant County, Texas.

Applications for Enrollment of Choctaw Newborn
Act of 1905 Volume XV

BIRTH AFFIDAVIT.

DEPARTMENT OF THE INTERIOR.
COMMISSION TO THE FIVE CIVILIZED TRIBES.

IN RE APPLICATION FOR ENROLLMENT, as a citizen of the Choctaw Nation, of Jesse Airington , born on the 20 day of June , 1903

Name of Father: Benjamin F Airington   a citizen of the Choctaw Nation.
Name of Mother: Willie Airington   a citizen of the Intermarried Nation.

Postoffice Ireton
I.T.

AFFIDAVIT OF MOTHER.

UNITED STATES OF AMERICA, Indian Territory, }
   Southern   DISTRICT.

I, Willie Airington , on oath state that I am Thirty-Three years of age and a citizen by Intermarried , of the Choctaw Nation; that I am the lawful wife of Benjamin F. Airington , who is a citizen, by Blood of the Choctaw Nation; that a Male child was born to me on 20 day of June , 1903; that said child has been named Jesse Airington , and was living March 4, 1905.

                                                 her
                                    Willie x Airington
Witnesses To Mark: mark
 { (Name Illegible)
 { Charlie H Horstman

Subscribed and sworn to before me this 11th day of April , 1905

                                    James M Gordon
                                       Notary Public.

AFFIDAVIT OF ATTENDING PHYSICIAN OR MID-WIFE.

UNITED STATES OF AMERICA, Indian Territory, }
   Southern   DISTRICT.

I, John H Howard , a M.D. , on oath state that I attended on Mrs. Willie Arrington , wife of Benjamin F Arrington on the 20 day of June , 1903; that there was born to her on said date a male child; that said child was living March 4, 1905, and is said to have been named Jesse Arrington

                                    John H Howard M.D.

Applications for Enrollment of Choctaw Newborn
Act of 1905   Volume XV

Witnesses To Mark:

Subscribed and sworn to before me this 11 day of   April   , 1905

James M Gordon
Notary Public.
My term of office expires Mch 1907

7-3522.

Muskogee, Indian Territory, April 27, 1905.

Benjamin F. Airington,
   Ireton, Indian Territory.

Dear Sir:

Receipt is hereby acknowledged of the affidavits of Willie Airington and J. Bennett McBride, to the birth of Make Airington, child of Benjamin F. and Willie Airington, February 26, 1905, and the same have been filed with our records as an application for the enrollment of said child.

Respectfully,

Chairman.

Choc New Born 1126
   Myrtle Grace Oakes
   (Born Oct. 17, 1904)
   Edward Oakes
   (Born May 31, 1903)

Applications for Enrollment of Choctaw Newborn
Act of 1905   Volume XV

NEW-BORN AFFIDAVIT.

Number..............

Choctaw Enrolling Commission.

IN THE MATTER OF THE APPLICATION FOR ENROLLMENT, as a citizen of the Choctaw Nation, of Myrtle Grace Oakes

born on the 17 day of   October   190 4

Name of father   David F. Oakes   a citizen of   Choctaw Nation
Nation final enrollment No   4246
Name of mother   Elsie Jane Oakes   a citizen of   white
Nation final enrollment No..............

Postoffice   Hugo IT

AFFIDAVIT OF MOTHER.

UNITED STATES OF AMERICA, }
  INDIAN TERRITORY,   }
  Central   DISTRICT   }

I   Elsie Jane Oakes   on oath state that I am 18 years of age and a citizen by ———— of the ———— Nation, and as such have been ~~placed upon the final roll of~~ the ———— Nation, ~~by the Honorable Secretary of the~~ Interior ~~my final enrollment number being~~ ————; that I am the lawful wife of   David F Oakes, who is a citizen of the   Choctaw   Nation, and as such has been placed upon the final roll of said Nation by the Honorable Secretary of the Interior, his final enrollment number being 4246 and that a   female   child was born to me on the 17 day of   October   190 4; that said child has been named   Myrtle Grace Oakes , and is now living.

WITNESSETH: Elsie Jane Oakes
  Must be two   } Martin B Crowder
  Witnesses who }
  are Citizens. } W.M. Griggs

Subscribed and sworn to before me this   17   day of   Jany   190 5

                              W.T. Glenn
                                    Notary Public.
My commission expires   1907

Applications for Enrollment of Choctaw Newborn
Act of 1905 Volume XV

Affidavit of Attending Physician or Midwife

UNITED STATES OF AMERICA,
INDIAN TERRITORY,
Central DISTRICT

I, Perry Fling a Practicing Physician on oath state that I attended on Mrs. Elsie Jane Oakes wife of David F Oakes on the 17 day of October, 190 4, that there was born to her on said date a female child, that said child is now living, and is said to have been named Myrtle Grace Oakes

Perry Fling M. D.

Subscribed and sworn to before me this the 17 day of Jany 1905

WT Glenn
Notary Public.

WITNESSETH:
Must be two witnesses who are citizens and know the child.
{ (Name Illegible)
John McIntosh }

We hereby certify that we are well acquainted with Perry Fling a Physicn[sic] and know him to be reputable and of good standing in the community.

Must be two citizen witnesses.
{ (Name Illegible)
John McIntosh }

BIRTH AFFIDAVIT.

DEPARTMENT OF THE INTERIOR.
COMMISSION TO THE FIVE CIVILIZED TRIBES.

IN RE APPLICATION FOR ENROLLMENT, as a citizen of the Choctaw Nation, of Myrtle Grace Oakes, born on the 17th day of October, 1904

Name of Father: David F. Oakes   a citizen of the Choctaw Nation.
Name of Mother: Elsie Jane Oakes   a citizen of the United States Nation.

Postoffice Hugo, Ind. Ter.

Applications for Enrollment of Choctaw Newborn
Act of 1905   Volume XV

AFFIDAVIT OF MOTHER.

UNITED STATES OF AMERICA, Indian Territory, }
Central   DISTRICT.

I,   Elsie Jane Oakes   , on oath state that I am   18   years of age and a citizen ~~by~~ .... , of the   United States   ~~Nation~~; that I am the lawful wife of David F. Oakes   , who is a citizen, by blood   of the   Choctaw   Nation; that a   female   child was born to me on   17th   day of   October   , 1904; that said child has been named   Myrtle Grace Oakes   , and was living March 4, 1905.

Elsie J Oakes

Witnesses To Mark:
{

Subscribed and sworn to before me this   19th   day of   April   , 1905

Wirt Franklin
Notary Public.

AFFIDAVIT OF ATTENDING PHYSICIAN OR MID-WIFE.

UNITED STATES OF AMERICA, Indian Territory, }
Central   DISTRICT.

I,   Perry E. A. Fling   , a   physician   , on oath state that I attended on Mrs.   Elsie Jane Oakes   , wife of   David F. Oakes   on the   17th   day of   October   , 1904; that there was born to her on said date a   female   child; that said child was living March 4, 1905, and is said to have been named Myrtle Grace Oakes

Perry E.A. Fling

Witnesses To Mark:
{

Subscribed and sworn to before me this   19th   day of   April   , 1905

Wirt Franklin
Notary Public.

Applications for Enrollment of Choctaw Newborn
Act of 1905 Volume XV

E.M. EVERIDGE, Judge.
P.C. HARRIS, District Attorney.
WILL EVERIDGE, Clerk.

CIRCUIT COURT THIRD DISTRICT
CHOCTAW NATION
WILL EVERIDGE, Clerk

TERMS OF COURT:
FIRST MONDAY FEBRUARY AND
SECOND MONDAY IN AUGUST.

GRANT, I. T.   Sept 14   190 2

    This to certify that I have this day Joined together in the Holy Bonds of Matrimony Mr David Oakes to Miss Elsiea Evins

                        Given under my hand and official signature this the 16 day Sept 1902

Recorded in the office
of County Clerk of
Tciamichi County
Choctaw Nation Sept 17th 1902.

                        EM Everidge
                        Circuit Judge 3rd
                        Judicial District

      G.W. Oasces
Clerk Tciamichi County
      Choctaw Nation

                                  Choctaw Nation

                                  7-NB-1126.

                Muskogee, Indian Territory, June 10, 1905.

David F. Oakes,
    Hugo, Indian Territory.

Dear Sir:

    In the matter of the application for the enrollment of your infant child, Edward Oakes, born May 31, 1903, it appears from the records of the Commission that said child died prior to March 4, 1905.

    For the purpose of make his death a matter of record there is inclosed herewith a blank for proof of death which you are requested to have filled out, properly executed and return to this office.

    Please give this matter your immediate attention.

                        Respectfully,

                                    Chairman.

D C
Env.

Applications for Enrollment of Choctaw Newborn
Act of 1905   Volume XV

7 NB 1126

Muskogee, Indian Territory, June 20, 1905.

D. F. Oakes,
    Hugo, Indian Territory.

Dear Sir:

    Receipt is hereby acknowledged of your letter of June 14, 1905, relative to the enrollment of Edward Oakes in which you state that this child died prior to March 4, 1905.

    For the purpose of making the date of the death of this child a matter of record there is inclosed you herewith blank form for proof of death which please have executed and return to this office as early as practicable. In having the same executed be careful to see that all blanks are properly filled, all names written in full, and that the Notary Public before whom the affidavits are acknowledged affixes his name and seal to each affidavit. Signatures by mark must be attested by two disinterested witnesses.

                        Respectfully,

                                Chairman.

DEPARTMENT OF THE INTERIOR,
COMMISSIONER TO THE FIVE CIVILIZED TRIBES.

    In the matter of the application for the enrollment as a citizen by blood of the Choctaw Nation . . . .

                  EDWARD OAKES..........................7-NB-1126.

Applications for Enrollment of Choctaw Newborn
Act of 1905   Volume XV

DEPARTMENT OF THE INTERIOR,
COMMISSIONER TO THE FIVE CIVILIZED TRIBES.
CHOCTAW-CHICKASAW DIVISION.
Hugo, Indian Territory, March 10, 1906.

In the matter of the enrollment of Edward Oakes, Choctaw New Born, Card Number 1126.

Testimony taken at Hugo, Indian Territory, March 5, 1906.

DAVID F. OAKES, being first duly sworn, testified as follows:

BY THE COMMISSIONER:

Q What is your name? A David F. Oakes.
Q How old are you? A 23.
Q Are you a citizen by blood of the Choctaw Nation?
A Yes.
Q What is your post office? A Hugo, I. T.
Q Are you a married man? A Yes, sir.
Q What is your wife's name? A Elsie Jane Oakes.
Q Is she a citizen or non-citizen of the Choctaw Nation?
A Non-citizen.
Q Have you children; if so, name them?
A One living named Myrtle Grace Oakes and one dead named Edward Oakes.
Q When was Edward Oakes born?
A May 31, 1903.
Q When did Edward Oakes die?
A The same day, about four hours after he was born.

Witness Excused.

Testimony taken in Hugo, Indian Territory, March 9, 1906:

ELSIE JANE OAKES, being first duly sworn, testified as follows:

BY THE COMMISSIONER:

Q What is your name? A Elsie Jane Oakes.
Q What is your age? A 19.
Q What is your post office address? A Hugo, I. T.
Q Are you a citizen of the Choctaw Nation?
A Non-citizen.
Q Are you the wife of David F. Oakes, a citizen by blood of the Choctaw Nation?
A Yes, sir.
Q Did you give birth to a child named Edward Oakes? A Yes, sir.

Applications for Enrollment of Choctaw Newborn
Act of 1905 Volume XV

Q When was Edward born? A The 31st of May, 1903.
Q Is Edward Oakes now living? A No, sir.
Q When did he die? A He lived only 3 or 4 hours.
Q And died the 31st of May, 1903? A Yes, sir.

Witness Excused

W. P. Covington, being first duly sworn, states that the above and foregoing is a full, true and correct transcript of his stenographic notes taken in said case on said date.

W.P. Covington

Subscribed and sworn to before me, this 10th day of March 1906.

Lacey P Bobo
Notary Public.

7-NB-1367
COPY
Muskogee, Indian Territory, June 1, 1905.

David F. Oakes,
Jugo[sic], Indian Territory.

Dear Sir:

There is enclosed you herewith for execution application for the enrollment of your infant child, Edward Oakes, born May 31, 1903.

The affidavits heretofore filed with the Commission show the child was living on January 17, 1905. It is necessary, for the child to be enrolled, that she was living on March 4, 1905. child to be enrolled, that he wa living on March 4, 1905.

In having these affidavits executed care should be exercised to see that all names are written in full, as they appear in the body of the affidavit, and in the event that either of the persons signing the affidavit are unable to write, signatures by mark must be attested by two witnesses. Each affidavit must be executed before a Notary Public and the notarial seal and signature of the officer must be attached to each separate affidavit.

Respectfully,

SIGNED *Tams Bixby*
Chairman.

Enc. FVK-2

Applications for Enrollment of Choctaw Newborn
Act of 1905 Volume XV

NEW-BORN AFFIDAVIT.

Number...........

Choctaw Enrolling Commission.

IN THE MATTER OF THE APPLICATION FOR ENROLLMENT, as a citizen of the Choctaw Nation, of Edward Oakes

born on the 31 day of May 190 3

Name of father David F Oakes   a citizen of Choctaw Nation
Nation final enrollment No 4246
Name of mother Elsie Jane Oakes   a citizen of white
Nation final enrollment No...........

Postoffice   Hugo I T

AFFIDAVIT OF MOTHER.

UNITED STATES OF AMERICA, ⎫
    INDIAN TERRITORY,   ⎬
    Central   DISTRICT   ⎭

I   Elsie Jane Oakes   on oath state that I am 18 years of age and a citizen by ——— of the ——— Nation, and as such have been placed upon the final roll of the ——— Nation, by the Honorable Secretary of the Interior my final enrollment number being ——— ; that I am the lawful wife of David F Oakes , who is a citizen of the Choctaw   Nation, and as such has been placed upon the final roll of said Nation by the Honorable Secretary of the Interior, his final enrollment number being 4246   and that a male   child was born to me on the 31 day of May 1903 ; that said child has been named Edward Oakes , and is now living.

Witnesseth: Elsie Jane Oakes

Must be two ⎫ J.O. Kirkpatrick
Witnesses who ⎬
are Citizens. ⎭ Martin B Crowder

Subscribed and sworn to before me this 17 day of Jany 190 5

W T Glenn
Notary Public.

My commission expires 1907

Applications for Enrollment of Choctaw Newborn
Act of 1905 Volume XV

Affidavit of Attending Physician or Midwife

UNITED STATES OF AMERICA, }
   INDIAN TERRITORY, }
Central   DISTRICT }

I, Aurilla Oakes a mid wife on oath state that I attended on Mrs. Elsie Jane Oakes wife of David F Oakes on the 31 day of May, 190 3, that there was born to her on said date a male child, that said child is now living, and is said to have been named Edward Oakes

                           Aurilla Oakes   M. D.

Subscribed and sworn to before me this the 17 day of Jany 1905

                           Notary Public.

WITNESSETH:
Must be two witnesses { J O Kirkpatrick
who are citizens and {
know the child. { Chas H Gooding

We hereby certify that we are well acquainted with Aurilla Oakes a mid wife and know her to be reputable and of good standing in the community.

                 Must be two citizen { J O Kirkpatrick
                 witnesses. { Chas H Gooding

7-NB-1126.
OLJ

DEPARTMENT OF THE INTERIOR,
COMMISSIONER TO THE FIVE CIVILIZED TRIBES.

In the matter of the application for the enrollment of Edward Oakes as a citizen by blood of the Choctaw Nation.

D E C I S I O N.

It appears from the record in this case that on April 25, 1905, there was filed with the Commission to the Five Civilized Tribes an application for the enrollment of Edward Oakes as a citizen by blood of the Choctaw Nation.

It further appears from the record herein and from the records of the Commission to the Five Civilized Tribes that the application was born May 31, 1903, and is a son of David F. Oakes, a recognized and enrolled citizen by blood of the Choctaw Nation, whose name appears as number 4246 upon the final roll of citizens by blood of the

Applications for Enrollment of Choctaw Newborn
Act of 1905   Volume XV

Choctaw Nation approved by the Secretary of the Interior December 12, 1902, and Elsie Jane Oakes, a non-citizen white woman; and that said applicant died May 31, 1903.
The Act of Congress approved March 3, 1905 (33 Stats., 1070) provides:

> "That the Commission to the Five Civilized Tribes is authorized for sixty days after the date of the approval of this act to receive and consider applications for enrollment of children born subsequent to September twenty-fifth, nineteen hundred and two, and prior to March fourth, nineteen hundred and five, and who were living on said latter date, to citizens by blood of the Choctaw and Chickasaw tribes of Indians whose enrollment has been approved by the Secretary of the Interior prior to the date of the approval of this act; and to enroll and make allotments to such children."

It is therefore ordered that the application for the enrollment of Edward Oakes as a citizen by blood of the Choctaw Nation be, and the same is hereby dismissed.

Tams Bixby   Commissioner.

Muskogee, Indian Territory.
APR 28 1906

7-NB-1126

COPY

Muskogee, Indian Territory, April 28, 1906.

David F. Oakes,
   Hugo, Indian Territory.

Dear Sir:

Inclosed herewith you will find a copy of the decision of the Commissioner to the Five Civilized Tribes, rendered April 28, 1906, dismissing the application for the enrollment of your minor child, Edward Oakes as a citizen by blood of the Choctaw Nation.

Respectfully,

SIGNED   *Tams Bixby*
Chairman.

Registered.
Incl. 7-NB-1126

Applications for Enrollment of Choctaw Newborn
Act of 1905   Volume XV

7-NB-1126   **COPY**

Muskogee, Indian Territory, April 28, 1906.

Mansfield, McMurray & Cornish,
    Attorneys for Choctaw and Chickasaw Nations,
        South McAlester, Indian Territory.

Gentlemen:

    Inclosed herewith you will find a copy of the decision of the Commissioner to the Five Civilized Tribes, rendered April 28, 1906, dismissing the application for the enrollment of Edward Oakes as a citizen by blood of the Choctaw Nation.

        Respectfully,

        SIGNED *Tams Bixby*
Incl. 7-NB-1126   Chairman.

Choc New Born 1127
    Minnie Lee Roebuck
    (Born Feb. 22, 1904)

BIRTH AFFIDAVIT.

DEPARTMENT OF THE INTERIOR.
COMMISSION TO THE FIVE CIVILIZED TRIBES.

    IN RE APPLICATION FOR ENROLLMENT, as a citizen of the Choctaw Nation, of Minnie Lee Roebuck, born on the 22 day of February, 1904

Name of Father: Edward Roebuck   a citizen of the Choctaw Nation.
Name of Mother: Betsie Roebuck   a citizen of the Choctaw Nation.

    Postoffice   Hugo, Ind. Ter

Applications for Enrollment of Choctaw Newborn
Act of 1905   Volume XV

AFFIDAVIT OF MOTHER.

UNITED STATES OF AMERICA, Indian Territory, }
Central   DISTRICT.

I,   Betsie Roebuck   , on oath state that I am   26   years of age and a citizen by   blood   , of the   Choctaw   Nation; that I am the lawful wife of   Edward Roebuck   , who is a citizen, by   blood   of the   Choctaw   Nation; that a   female   child was born to me on   22nd   day of   February   , 1904; that said child has been named   Minnie Lee Roebuck   , and was living March 4, 1905.

                                    Betsie Robuck[sic]
Witnesses To Mark:
{

    Subscribed and sworn to before me this 19th   day of   April   , 1905

                                    Wirt Franklin
                                    Notary Public.

AFFIDAVIT OF ATTENDING PHYSICIAN OR MID-WIFE.

UNITED STATES OF AMERICA, Indian Territory, }
Central   DISTRICT.

I,   H. C. Heathcock   , a   mid-wife   , on oath state that I attended on Mrs.   Betsie Roebuck   , wife of   Edward Roebuck   on the   22nd   day of   February   , 1904; that there was born to her on said date a   female   child; that said child was living March 4, 1905, and is said to have been named   Minnie Lee Roebuck

                                    H.C. Heathcock
Witnesses To Mark:
{

    Subscribed and sworn to before me this 19th   day of   April   , 1905

                                    Wirt Franklin
                                    Notary Public.

Applications for Enrollment of Choctaw Newborn
Act of 1905   Volume XV

Choc New Born 1128
    Noel J. Wilson
    (Born Nov. 17, 1904)

NEW-BORN AFFIDAVIT.

        Number............

Choctaw Enrolling Commission.

    IN THE MATTER OF THE APPLICATION FOR ENROLLMENT, as a citizen of the Choctaw   Nation, of   Noah[sic] J. Wilson

born on the   17th   day of   November   190 4

Name of father   Silas W. Wilson   a citizen of   ————
Nation final enrollment No ————
Name of mother   Narsissa Wilson   a citizen of   Choctaw
Nation final enrollment No   11413

                Postoffice   Atoka I.T.

            AFFIDAVIT OF MOTHER.

UNITED STATES OF AMERICA,
    INDIAN TERRITORY,
    Central   DISTRICT

    I   Narsissa Wilson   on oath state that I am   20   years of age and a citizen by   blood   of the   Choctaw   Nation, and as such have been placed upon the final roll of the   Choctaw   Nation, by the Honorable Secretary of the Interior my final enrollment number being   11413   ; that I am the lawful wife of   Silas W. Wilson   , who is a citizen of the   ————   Nation, and as such has been placed upon the final roll of said Nation by the Honorable Secretary of the Interior, his final enrollment number being ———— and that a   male   child was born to me on the   17th   day of   November   190 4 ; that said child has been named   Noah J. Wilson   , and is now living.

                                    her
                      Narsissa x Wilson
                          mark

WITNESSETH:
    Must be two   Lou Anderson
    Witnesses who
    are Citizens.   Wilson Gibson

Applications for Enrollment of Choctaw Newborn
Act of 1905 Volume XV

Subscribed and sworn to before me this 23" day of February 190 5

A.E. Folsom
Notary Public.

My commission expires
Jan 9-1909

Affidavit of Attending Physician or Midwife.

UNITED STATES OF AMERICA ⎫
INDIAN TERRITORY ⎬
  Central   DISTRICT ⎭

I, Susan R. Wilson a Mid Wife on oath state that I attended on Mrs. Narsissa Wilson wife of Silas W Wilson on the 17th day of November , 190 4 , that there was born to her on said date a Male child, that said child is now living, and is said to have been named Noah[sic] J Wilson

Susan E[sic] Willson[sic] M.D.

Subscribed and sworn to before me this, the 23" day of February 190 5

A E Folsom
Notary Public.

WITNESSETH:
Must be two witnesses who are citizens and know the child.
{ Lou Anderson
  Wilson Gibson

We hereby certify that we are well acquainted with Susan W[sic] Wilson a Mid Wife and know her to be reputable and of good standing in the community.

{ Lou Anderson
  Wilson Gibson

BIRTH AFFIDAVIT.

DEPARTMENT OF THE INTERIOR.
COMMISSION TO THE FIVE CIVILIZED TRIBES.

IN RE APPLICATION FOR ENROLLMENT, as a citizen of the Choctaw Nation, of Noel J Wilson , born on the 17th day of October[sic] , 1904

Name of Father: S.W. Wilson   a citizen of the Choctaw Nation.
Name of Mother: Narcissa[sic] Wilson   a citizen of the Choctaw Nation.

Applications for Enrollment of Choctaw Newborn
Act of 1905 Volume XV

Postoffice   Atoka, I.T.

AFFIDAVIT OF MOTHER.

UNITED STATES OF AMERICA, Indian Territory, }
Central   DISTRICT.

I, Narcissa Wilson , on oath state that I am 21 years of age and a citizen by blood , of the Choctaw Nation; that I am the lawful wife of S.W. Wilson , who is a citizen, ~~by~~ — of the United States ~~Nation~~; that a male child was born to me on 17th day of October[sic] , 1904; that said child has been named Noel J Wilson , and was living March 4, 1905.

                her
        Narcissa x Wilson
Witnesses To Mark: mark
{ Richard Shanafelt
{ W^m H Cunningham

Subscribed and sworn to before me this 20th day of April , 1905

        W.H. Angell
          Notary Public.

AFFIDAVIT OF ATTENDING PHYSICIAN OR MID-WIFE.

UNITED STATES OF AMERICA, Indian Territory, }
Central   DISTRICT.

I, Susan Wilson , a midwife , on oath state that I attended on Mrs. Narcissa Wilson , wife of S.W. Wilson on the 17th day of October , 1904; that there was born to her on said date a male child; that said child was living March 4, 1905, and is said to have been named Noel J Wilson

        her
    Susan x Wilson
Witnesses To Mark: mark
{ Richard Shanafelt
{ W^m H Cunningham

Subscribed and sworn to before me this 20th day of April , 1905

      W.H. Angell
        Notary Public.

Applications for Enrollment of Choctaw Newborn
Act of 1905   Volume XV

BIRTH AFFIDAVIT.

DEPARTMENT OF THE INTERIOR.
COMMISSION TO THE FIVE CIVILIZED TRIBES.

IN RE APPLICATION FOR ENROLLMENT, as a citizen of the   Choctaw   Nation, of Noel J Wilson   , born on the 17th day of November , 1904

Name of Father: S.W. Wilson   a citizen of the   non citizen Nation.
Name of Mother: Narcissa[sic] Wilson Roll 11413   a citizen of the   Choctaw   Nation.

   Postoffice   Atoka, I.T.

AFFIDAVIT OF MOTHER.

UNITED STATES OF AMERICA, Indian Territory, }
    Central   DISTRICT.   }

I, Narcissa Wilson , on oath state that I am 20 years of age and a citizen by blood , of the Choctaw Nation; that I am the lawful wife of S.W. Wilson, a non citizen , ~~who is a citizen, by of the Nation~~; that a male child was born to me on 17th day of November , 1904; that said child has been named Noel J Wilson , and was living March 4, 1905.

                                          her
                                Narcissa x Wilson
Witnesses To Mark: mark
 { WH Martin
 { Richard Shanafelt

Subscribed and sworn to before me this 10th day of June , 1905

                        W.H. Angell
                         Notary Public.

AFFIDAVIT OF ATTENDING PHYSICIAN OR MID-WIFE.

UNITED STATES OF AMERICA, Indian Territory, }
    Central   DISTRICT.   }

I, Susan Wilson , a midwife , on oath state that I attended on Mrs. Narcissa Wilson , wife of S.W. Wilson on the 17th day of November , 1904; that there was born to her on said date a male child; that said child was living March 4, 1905, and is said to have been named Noel J Wilson

                              her
                         Susan x Wilson
                              mark

Applications for Enrollment of Choctaw Newborn
Act of 1905   Volume XV

Witnesses To Mark:
{ WH Martin
{ Richard Shanafelt

Subscribed and sworn to before me this 10th day of June, 1905

W.H. Angell
Notary Public.

$W^m O.B.$

COMMISSIONERS:
TAMS BIXBY,
THOMAS B. NEEDLES,
C.R. BRECKINBRIDGE.

WM. O. BEALL
Secretary

DEPARTMENT OF THE INTERIOR,
COMMISSIONER TO THE FIVE CIVILIZED TRIBES.

REFER IN REPLY TO THE FOLLOWING:

7-NB-1128.

ADDRESS ONLY THE
COMMISSION TO THE FIVE CIVILIZED TRIBES.

Muskogee, Indian Territory, June 2, 1905.

S. W. Wilson,
   Atoka, Indian Territory.

Dear Sir:

    There is enclosed you herewith for execution application for the enrollment of your infant child.

    In the affidavits of February 23, 1905, heretofore filed in this office, the name of the applicant appears to be ~~Noel J.~~ Wilson and the date of his birth as November 17, 1904, while in the affidavits of April 20, 1905, the name appears as Noel J. Wilson and the date of birth as October 17, 1904. In the enclosed application the applicant's name and date of birth are left blank. Please insert the correct name and date of birth and, when the affidavits are properly executed, return them to this office.

    In having these affidavits executed care should be exercised to see that all names are written in full, as they appear in the body of the affidavit, and in the event that either of the persons signing the affidavit are unable to write, signatures by mark must be attested by two witnesses. Each affidavit must be executed before a Notary Public and the notarial seal and signature of the officer must be attached to each separate affidavit.

Respectfully,
T.B. Needles
Commissioner in Charge.

VR 2-6.

Applications for Enrollment of Choctaw Newborn
Act of 1905   Volume XV

7 NB 1128

Muskogee, Indian Territory, June 14, 1905.

S. W. Wilson,
    Atoka, Indian Territory.

Dear Sir:

    Receipt is hereby acknowledged of the affidavits of Narcissa Wilson and Susan Wilson to the birth of Noel J. Wilson, son of S. W. and Narcissa Wilson, November 17, 1904, and the same have been filed in the matter of the enrollment of said child.

        Respectfully,

                Chairman.

Choc New Born 1129
    Nellie Fobb
    (Born May 16, 1903)

BIRTH AFFIDAVIT.

DEPARTMENT OF THE INTERIOR.
COMMISSION TO THE FIVE CIVILIZED TRIBES.

IN RE APPLICATION FOR ENROLLMENT, as a citizen of the   Choctaw   Nation, of Nellis[sic] Fobb   , born on the   16th   day of   May   , 1903

Name of Father: Simon Fobb   a citizen of the   Choctaw   Nation.
Name of Mother: Adeline Fobb   a citizen of the   Choctaw   Nation.

        Postoffice   Eagletown, Ind. Ter.

AFFIDAVIT OF MOTHER.

UNITED STATES OF AMERICA, Indian Territory,
    Central   DISTRICT.

    I,   Simon Fobb   , on oath state that I am   40   years of age and a citizen by blood   , of the   Choctaw   Nation; that I am the lawful ~~wife~~ *husband* of   Adeline Fobb   , who is a citizen, by   blood   of the   Choctaw   Nation; that a

Applications for Enrollment of Choctaw Newborn
Act of 1905   Volume XV

female   child was born to ~~me~~ us on   16th   day of   May   , 1903; that said child has been named   Nellis Fobb   , and was living March 4, 1905.

                                      his
                            Simon x Fobb

Witnesses To Mark: mark
{ Robert Anderson
{ Vester W Rose

    Subscribed and sworn to before me this   18th day of   April   , 1905

                                  Wirt Franklin
                                      Notary Public.

BIRTH AFFIDAVIT.

DEPARTMENT OF THE INTERIOR.
COMMISSION TO THE FIVE CIVILIZED TRIBES.

    IN RE APPLICATION FOR ENROLLMENT, as a citizen of the   Choctaw   Nation, of Nellis[sic] Fobb   , born on the   16th   day of   May   , 1903

Name of Father: Simon Fobb   a citizen of the   Choctaw   Nation.
Name of Mother: Adeline Fobb   a citizen of the   Choctaw   Nation.

                        Postoffice   Eagletown, Ind. Ter.

                        AFFIDAVIT OF MOTHER.

UNITED STATES OF AMERICA, Indian Territory, }
    Central   DISTRICT. }

    I,   Adeline Fobb   , on oath state that I am   27   years of age and a citizen by blood   , of the   Choctaw   Nation; that I am the lawful wife of   Simon Fobb   , who is a citizen, by blood   of the   Choctaw   Nation; that a   female   child was born to me on   16th   day of   May   , 1903; that said child has been named Nellis Fobb   , and was living March 4, 1905.

                                    her
                            Adline[sic] x Fobb

Witnesses To Mark: mark
{ J M Campbell
{ W.H. Beale

Applications for Enrollment of Choctaw Newborn
Act of 1905   Volume XV

Subscribed and sworn to before me this 28 day of April, 1905

My commission
expires 23rd Dec 1905

Jeff Gardner
Notary Public.

AFFIDAVIT OF ATTENDING PHYSICIAN OR MID-WIFE.

UNITED STATES OF AMERICA, Indian Territory,
Central   DISTRICT.

I, Simon Fobb, a midwife, on oath state that I attended on Mrs. Adeline Fobb *my*, wife of .... on the 16th day of May, 1903; that there was born to her on said date a Female child; that said child was living March 4, 1905, and is said to have been named Nellis Fobb

                                  his
                            Simon x Fobb

Witnesses To Mark: mark
{ J M Campbell
{ W.H. Beale

Subscribed and sworn to before me this 28th day of April, 1905

My commission
expires 23rd Dec 1905

Jeff Gardner
Notary Public.

AFFIDAVIT OF ~~ATTENDING PHYSICIAN OR MID-WIFE.~~
Disinterested Witness.

UNITED STATES OF AMERICA, Indian Territory,
Central   DISTRICT.

                                                am acquainted with

I, William Bowman, a *disinterested witness*, on oath state that I ~~attended on~~ Mrs. Adeline Fobb, wife of Simon Fobb on the 16 day of May, 1903; that there was born to her on said date a Female child; that said child was living March 4, 1905, and is said to have been named Nellie Fobb

                                   William Bowman

Witnesses To Mark:
{

Subscribed and sworn to before me this 17 day of May, 1906

                               Lacey P Bobo
                                  Notary Public.

Applications for Enrollment of Choctaw Newborn
Act of 1905 Volume XV

BIRTH AFFIDAVIT.

DEPARTMENT OF THE INTERIOR,
COMMISSIONER TO THE FIVE CIVILIZED TRIBES.

ENROLLMENT OF MINORS. ACT OF CONGRESS, APPROVED APRIL 26, 1906.

IN RE APPLICATION FOR ENROLLMENT, as a citizen of the Choctaw Nation, of Nellie Fobb , born on the 16th day of May , 1903

Name of Father: Simon Fobb   a citizen of the Choctaw Nation.
Name of Mother: Adeline Fobb   a citizen of the Choctaw Nation.

Tribal enrollment of father .... Tribal enrollment of mother ....

Postoffice   Eagletown, Ind. Ter.

AFFIDAVIT OF MOTHER.

UNITED STATES OF AMERICA, Indian Territory, }
Central   District.

I, Adeline Fobb , on oath state that I am 38± years of age and a citizen by blood , of the Choctaw Nation; that I am the lawful wife of Simon Fobb , who is a citizen, by blood of the Choctaw Nation; that a female child was born to me on 16th day of May , 1903 , that said child has been named Nellie Fobb , and was living March 4, 1906. *that no one attended me at said child's birth.*

                           Her
                     Adeline x Fobb
WITNESSES TO MARK: mark
{ Jacob Homer
   W.P. Covington

Subscribed and sworn to before me this 17th day of May , 1906.

                           Lacey P Bobo
                             Notary Public.

AFFIDAVIT OF ATTENDING PHYSICIAN OR MID-WIFE.

UNITED STATES OF AMERICA, Indian Territory, }
Central   District.

                                                     am acquainted with

I, Benjamin Bohanan , a *disinterested witness* , on oath state that I ~~attended on~~ Adeline Fobb , wife of Simon Fobb on the 16th day of May , 1903; that there was born to her on said date a Female child; that said child was living March 4, 1906, and is said to have been named Nellis Fobb

Applications for Enrollment of Choctaw Newborn
Act of 1905   Volume XV

WITNESSES TO MARK:
{ JW Homer
{ WP Covington

Benjamin x Bohanan
his   mark

Subscribed and sworn to before me this 19th day of May , 1906.

Lacey P Bobo
Notary Public.

The child appeared
(Initials illegible)

Birth affidavit.

DEPARTMENT OF THE INTERIOR,
COMMISSIONER TO THE FIVE CIVILIZED TRIBES.

In re application for enrollment as a citizen of the Choctaw Nation, of Nellie Fobb , born May 16. 1903

Name of father   Simon Fobb   a citizen of   Choctaw Nation
Name of mother   Adeline Fobb   a citizen of   Choctaw Nation, Indian Territory

Postoffice   Eagletown, Ind. Ter.

AFFIDAVIT OF MOTHER.

State of Arkansas
UNITED STATES OF AMERICA, Indian Territory,)
County of Sevier   )
_____ District.)

I, Adeline Fobb , on oath state that I am 29 years of age and a citizen by blood of the Choctaw Nation; that I am the lawful wife of Simon Fobb , who is a citizen by blood of the Choctaw Nation; that a female child was born to me on the 16th day of May 1903,1__ that said child has been named Nellie Fobb and is now living.

Witnesses to mark:
    James Dyer Jr
    Laura Dyer

Adeline x Fobb
her   mark

Applications for Enrollment of Choctaw Newborn
Act of 1905 Volume XV

Subscribed and sworn to before me this 23 day of April ,1906.

R.P. Mitchell
Com Ex 9/8/07   Notary Public.

AFFIDAVIT OF ATTENDING PHYSICIAN, OR MIDWIFE.

State of Arkansas
UNITED STATES OF AMERICA, Indian Territory,)
County of Sevier   )
_____ District.)

    I, Simon Fobb, an Indian Doctor, a _____, on oath state that I attended on Mrs. Adeline Fobb , wife of Simon Fobb on the 16 day of May 1906[sic] , 1___ ; that there was born to her on said date a female child; that said child is now living and is said to have been named Nellie Fobb .

                                       his
                               Simon x Fobb
Witnesses to mark: mark
    James Dyer Jr
    Laura Dyer   Subscribed and sworn to before me this
                              16th day of April 1906 , 1906.

                              R.P. Mitchell
Com Ex 9/8/07   Notary Public.

                                                                  7-550.

                           Muskogee, Indian Territory, May 4, 1905.

Simon Fobb,
    Eagletown, Indian Territory.

Dear Sir:

    Receipt is hereby acknowledged of the affidavits of Adline[sic] Fobb and Simon Fobb to the birth of Nellie Fobb, daughter of Adline and Simon Fobb, May 16, 1903, and the same have been filed with our records in the matter of the enrollment of said child.

                              Respectfully,

                                        Chairman.

Applications for Enrollment of Choctaw Newborn
Act of 1905   Volume XV

Choctaw N B 1129

Muskogee, Indian Territory, October 11, 1905.

Simeon[sic] Fobb,
    Eagletown, Indian Territory.

Dear Sir:

    Receipt is hereby acknowledged of the affidavit of Tennessee Colbert to the birth of your child, Nellie Fobb, May 16, 1903, and the same has been filed with the record in the matter of the enrollment of said child.

Respectfully,

Commissioner.

7-NB-1129
7--------550

Muskogee, Indian Territory, May 9, 1906.

J. H. Jackson,
    DeQueen, Arkansas.

Dear Sir:

    Receipt is hereby acknowledged of your letter of May 7, 1906, inclosing the affidavits of Adeline Fobb and Simon Fobb to the birth of Philliston Fobb, child of Simon and Adeline Fobb, April 6, 1905, and the same have been filed with the records of this office as an application for the enrollment of said child.

    Receipt is also acknowledged of the affidavits of Adeline Fobb and Simon Fobb to the birth of Nellie Fobb, child of Simon and Adeline Fobb May 16, 1903.

    You are advised that Nellie Fobb, born May 16, 1903, who is the child of Simon and Adeline Fobb was enrolled as a new born citizen of the Choctaw Nation, under the act of Congress approved March 3, 1905, and her enrollment approved by the Secretary of the Interior March 14, 1906. It is believed that this is the same child referred to as Nellie Fobb.

Respectfully,

Acting Commissioner.

Applications for Enrollment of Choctaw Newborn
Act of 1905 Volume XV

7-NB-1129

Muskogee, Indian Territory, June 25, 1906.

J. H. Jackson,
    Attorney at Law,
        DeQueen, Arkansas.

Dear Sir:-

    Receipt is hereby acknowledged of your letter of June 14, 1906, in which you state that Nellis Fobb and Nellie Fobb are one and the same person, and that this is the child of Simon and Adeline Fobb, and you now desire to know whether an allotment may be selected for this person.

    In reply you are advised that on March 14, 1906, the Secretary of the Interior approved the enrollment of Nellis Fobb as a new born citizen of the Choctaw Nation, and selection in allotment may now be made in her behalf in accordance with the rules and regulations governing selection of allotments and designation of homesteads in the Choctaw and Chickasaw Nations.

        Respectfully,

                Commissioner.

7--NB--1129

Muskogee, Indian Territory, June 2, 1905.

Simon Fobb,
    Eagletown, Indian Territory.

Dear Sir:

    Referring to the application for the enrollment of your infant child, Nellis Fobb, born May 16, 1903, it is noted from the affidavits heretofore filed in this office that you were the only one in attendance upon your wife at the time of the birth of the applicant.

    In this event it will be necessary that the affidavits of two persons, who are disinterested and not related to the applicant, who have actual knowledge of the facts that the child was born, the date of her birth; that she was living on March 4, 1905, and that Adeline Fobb is her mother be filed in this office.

    The affidavit of William Bunnup to these facts has been filed. It will, therefore, be necessary that you secure a simular[sic] affidavit from another person.

Applications for Enrollment of Choctaw Newborn
Act of 1905   Volume XV

This matter should receive your immediate attention as no further action can be taken relative to the enrollment of your said child until the Commission has been furnished with this affidavit.

Respectfully,

[sic]

7-NB-1129

Muskogee, Indian Territory, July 25, 1905.

Simeon Fobb,
    Eagletown, Indian Territory.

Dear Sir:

Your attention is called to a communication addressed to you by the Commission to the Five Civilized Tribes under date of June 2, 1905, requesting you to supply additional information in the matter of the enrollment of your infant child, Nellis Fobb, born May 16, 1903.

In this letter you were requested to furnish the affidavit of one other person who has actual knowledge of the facts, that the child was born, that date of her birth, that she was living March 4, 1905, and that Adeline Fobb is her mother; you were also advised that the affidavit of William Bunnup to these facts has been filed and that a similar affidavit of one other person was required. No reply to yes letter has been received.

The matter should receive your immediate attention as no further action can be taken relative to the enrollment of your said child until the evidence requested has been supplied.

Respectfully,

Commissioner.

(The affidavit below typed as given.)

United States of America,
    Indian Territory,
Central District.

I   Tennessee Colbert   , on oath states that I am   30   years of age, that my post office address is   Eagletown I.T.   that I was personally acquainted with   Adline Fobb   , and know that there was born to her on the   16   day of   May   1903, a   Female   child, which child was living on the fourth of march 1905, and said to have been named Nellis Fobb

Applications for Enrollment of Choctaw Newborn
Act of 1905   Volume XV

Witness to mark
W H Beale
CA Bowers

his
Tennessee x Colbert
mark

Subscribed and sworn to before me this 4th day of Oct 1905.

Jeff Gardner
Notary Public.

My commission expire 23 December 1905.

United States of America,)
)
Indian Territory,) ss.
)
Central District.)

I, William Bunnup, on oath state that I am thirty-six years of age and a citizen by blood of the Choctaw Nation; that my post office address is Eagletown, Indian Territory; that I am personally acquainted with Adeline Fobb, wife of Simon Fobb, and during their married life, for the last six years have lived within one half mile of them, near Eagletown, Indian Territory, and have often visited their home; that I know of my own knowledge that on or about the 16th day of May, 1903, there was born to the said Adeline Fobb a female child; that said child is now living and is said to have been named Nellis Fobb.

William Bunnup

Subscribed and sworn to before me this 18th day of April, 1905.

Wirt Franklin
Notary Public.

Choc New Born 1130
　　　Lester Sockey
　　　(Born Aug. 1, 1904)

Applications for Enrollment of Choctaw Newborn
Act of 1905   Volume XV

7-8828-9

DEPARTMENT OF THE INTERIOR,
COMMISSION TO THE FIVE CIVILIZED TRIBES.
WISTER, IND. TER.,   APRIL 19, 1905.

In the matter of the application for the enrollment of Lester Sockey as a citizen by blood of the Choctaw Nation.

Malinda Sockey being first duly sworn testifies as follows:

EXAMINATION BY THE COMMISSION:
Q What is your name? A Malinda Sockey.
Q What is your age? A Thirty-one.
Q What is your post office address? A Fanshawe.
Q You have this day made application for the enrollment of your child Lester Sockey as a citizen of the Choctaw Nation; when was this child born? A First day of August 1904.
Q Who is the father of this child? A Ned Sockey.
Q Is this child living today? A Yes, sir.
Q Who attended you in the capacity of midwife or physician when this child was born? A Doctor.
Q Doctor who? A Nabors.
Q Where is that doctor today - where does he live? A I don't know.
Q Where was he located at the time this child was born? A Fanshawe.
Q Do you know where he is at the present time? A No, sir.
                    Witness excused.

Ned Sockey being first duly sworn testifies as follows:
EXAMINATION BY THE COMMISSION:
Q What is your name? A Ned Sockey.
Q What is your age? A Thirty-five.
Q What is your post office address? A Fanshawe.
Q Your wife has this day made application for the enrollment of Lester Sockey your infant child as a citizen of the Choctaw Nation; when was this child born? A First August 1904.
Q Was that child living on March 4, 1905? A Yes, sir.
Q Who attended your wife, Malinda Sockey, when this child was born? A Dr. Nabors.
Q Is it possible for you to secure his affidavit at this time showing that he attended your wife? A No, sir, I have been trying to find out where he does locate since this coming up and I never could locate where he does locate.
Q Since Dr. Nabors left Fanshawe you have been unable to locate him? A Yes, sir, been unable to locate him.
Q Was any other person present when this child was born?
A Albert Kelly was present.
                    Witness excused.

W. E. Emerson being first duly sworn testifies as follows:

EXAMINATION BY THE COMMISSION:

Applications for Enrollment of Choctaw Newborn
Act of 1905   Volume XV

Q What is your name? A W. E. Emerson.
Q What is your age? A Twenty-five.
Q What is your post office address? A Wister.
Q Are you acquainted with Ned Sockey and Malinda Sockey? A Yes, sir, been knowing them for about six or seven years there up there where I moved from, where they live now.
Q Where did you live prior to when you moved to Wister? A Fanshaw[sic].
Q Were you living there at the time of the birth of Lester Sockey? A Yes, sir.
Q When was he born? A August - first of August.
Q What year? A 1904.
Q How far did you live from Sockey's at the time of the birth of this child? A About mile and half.
Q Was this child living on March 4, 1905? A Yes, sir.

Witness excused.

Chas. T. Difendafer being first duly sworn states that the above and foregoing is a full, true and correct transcript of his stenographic notes taken in said cause on said date.

Chas. T. Difendafer

Subscribed and sworn to before me this 19th day of April 1905.

OL Johnson
Notary Public.

NEW BORN AFFIDAVIT

No

CHOCTAW ENROLLING COMMISSION

IN THE MATTER OF THE APPLICATION FOR ENROLLMENT as a citizen of the Choctaw Nation, of   Lester Sockey   born on the 1 day of   August   190 4

Name of father   Ned Sockey   a citizen of   Choctaw   Nation, final enrollment No.   8828
Name of mother   Malinda Sockey   a citizen of   Choctaw   Nation, final enrollment No.   8829

Fanshawe I.T.   Postoffice.

Applications for Enrollment of Choctaw Newborn
Act of 1905   Volume XV

AFFIDAVIT OF MOTHER

UNITED STATES OF AMERICA }
INDIAN TERRITORY
DISTRICT   Central

    I   Malinda Sockey   , on oath state that I am   31   years of age and a citizen by   blood   of the   Choctaw   Nation, and as such have been placed upon the final roll of the   Choctaw   Nation, by the Honorable Secretary of the Interior my final enrollment number being   8829   ; that I am the lawful wife of   Ned Sockey   , who is a citizen of the   Choctaw   Nation, and as such has been placed upon the final roll of said Nation by the Honorable Secretary of the Interior, his final enrollment number being   8828   and that a   Male   child was born to me on the   1   day of   August   190 4; that said child has been named   Lester Sockey   , and is now living.

WITNESSETH: Malinda Sockey
Must be two witnesses { Joseph Leflore
who are citizens   Willy Blue

    Subscribed and sworn to before me this, the   17   day of   February   , 190 5

                                           James Bower
                                              Notary Public.

My Commission Expires:
Apr 23-1907

Affidavit of Attending Physician or Midwife

UNITED STATES OF AMERICA, }
INDIAN TERRITORY,
Central   DISTRICT

    I,   Ned Sockey   a   Attendant on oath state that I attended on Mrs. Malinda Sockey   wife of Ned Sockey on the   1   day of   August   , 190 4, that there was born to her on said date a   male   child, that said child is now living, and is said to have been named   Lester Sockey

                                           Ned Sockey   M. D.

    Subscribed and sworn to before me this the   17   day of   February   1905

                                           James Bower
                                            Notary Public.

WITNESSETH:
Must be two witnesses { Joseph Leflore
who are citizens and
know the child.   Willy Blue

Applications for Enrollment of Choctaw Newborn
Act of 1905   Volume XV

We hereby certify that we are well acquainted with   Ned Sockey a Attendant   and know   him   to be reputable and of good standing in the community.

Must be two citizen witnesses. { Joseph Leflore
Willy Blue

(The affidavit below typed as given.)

Affadavit

I, Jessie Collins on oath state that I am 50 years of age and a citizen by blood of the Choctaw Nation.

On the 1st day of Aug 1904 there was borned to Malinda Sockey wife of Ned Sockey a male child. The said child is now living and is said to have been named Lester Sockey.

                            his
                      Jessie x Collins
Witness to mark   mark
Isaac Durant
James Jones

Subscribed and sworn to before me this 10th day of June 1905

                  W L Harris
My Com Exp 7/8/08.   Notary Public.

(The testimony given on April 19, 1905, given again.)

BIRTH AFFIDAVIT.   7- 8828 - 8829
DEPARTMENT OF THE INTERIOR.
COMMISSION TO THE FIVE CIVILIZED TRIBES.

IN RE APPLICATION FOR ENROLLMENT, as a citizen of the   Choc   Nation, of Lester Sockey   , born on the 1st   day of August   , 1904

Name of Father: Ned Sockey   a citizen of the   Choc   Nation.
Name of Mother: Malinda Sockey   a citizen of the   Choc   Nation.

                  Postoffice   Fanshawe I.T.

Applications for Enrollment of Choctaw Newborn
Act of 1905 Volume XV

AFFIDAVIT OF MOTHER.

UNITED STATES OF AMERICA, Indian Territory,
Central   DISTRICT.

I, Malinda Sockey , on oath state that I am 31 years of age and a citizen by blood , of the Choc Nation; that I am the lawful wife of Ned Sockey , who is a citizen, by blood of the Choc Nation; that a male child was born to me on 1st day of August , 1904; that said child has been named Lester Sockey , and was living March 4, 1905.

Malinda Sockey

Witnesses To Mark:

Subscribed and sworn to before me this 19th day of April , 1905

OL Johnson
Notary Public.

$W^m O. B.$

COMMISSIONERS:
TAMS BIXBY,
THOMAS B. NEEDLES,
C.R. BRECKINRIDGE.

DEPARTMENT OF THE INTERIOR,
COMMISSIONER TO THE FIVE CIVILIZED TRIBES.

REFER IN REPLY TO THE FOLLOWING:

7-NB-1130.

WM. O. BEALL
Secretary

ADDRESS ONLY THE
COMMISSION TO THE FIVE CIVILIZED TRIBES.

Muskogee, Indian Territory, June 2, 1905.

Ned Sockey,
   Fanshawe, Indian Territory.

Dear Sir:

Referring to the application for the enrollment of your infant child, Lester Sockey, born August 1, 1904, it is noted from the testimony taken on April 19, 1905, that you were unable to locate and secure the affidavit of Doctor Nabors, who attended upon your wife at the time of birth of the applicant.

If you cannot now secure his affidavit it will be necessary that the affidavits of two persons, who are disinterested and not related to the applicant, who have actual knowledge of the facts that the child was born, the date of his birth; that he was living on March 4, 1905, and that Malinda Sockey is his mother, be filed in this office.

Applications for Enrollment of Choctaw Newborn
Act of 1905   Volume XV

The testimony of W. E. Emerson, to the above mentioned facts, is on file in this office. It will, therefore, be necessary that you secure an affidavit from another person to the same facts.

This matter should receive your immediate attention, as no further action can be taken relative to the enrollment of your said child, until this affidavit is furnished the Commission.

Respectfully,
T.B. Needles
Commissioner in Charge.

---

7 NB 1130

Muskogee, Indian Territory, June 14, 1905.

Ned Sockey,
    Fanshawe, Indian Territory.

Dear Sir:

Receipt is hereby acknowledged of the affidavit of Jessie Collins to the birth of Lester Sockey, son of Malenda[sic] and Ned Sockey, August 1, 1904, and the same has been filed in the matter of the enrollment of said child.

Respectfully,

Chairman.

Choc New Born 1131
    Gussie Lee Sample
    (Born Nov. 1, 1904)

BIRTH AFFIDAVIT.

DEPARTMENT OF THE INTERIOR.
COMMISSION TO THE FIVE CIVILIZED TRIBES.

IN RE APPLICATION FOR ENROLLMENT, as a citizen of the Choctaw Nation, of Gussie Lee Sample , born on the 1st day of November , 1904

Name of Father: Clarence Sample   a citizen of the United States Nation.
Name of Mother: Fannie A[sic] Sample   a citizen of the Choctaw Nation.

Applications for Enrollment of Choctaw Newborn
Act of 1905   Volume XV

Postoffice   Hugo, Ind. Ter.

AFFIDAVIT OF MOTHER.

UNITED STATES OF AMERICA, Indian Territory, }
Central   DISTRICT. }

I, Fannie B. Sample , on oath state that I am 22 years of age and a citizen by blood , of the Choctaw Nation; that I am the lawful wife of Clarence Sample , who is a citizen, ~~by~~ of the United States ~~Nation~~; that a female child was born to me on 1st day of November , 1904; that said child has been named Gussie Lee Sample , and was living March 4, 1905.

Fannie B Sample

Witnesses To Mark:
{

Subscribed and sworn to before me this 19th day of April , 1905

Wirt Franklin
Notary Public.

AFFIDAVIT OF ATTENDING PHYSICIAN OR MID-WIFE.

UNITED STATES OF AMERICA, Indian Territory, }
Central   DISTRICT. }

I, Perry E.A. Fling , a physician , on oath state that I attended on Mrs. Fannie B. Sample , wife of Clarence Sample on the 1st day of November , 1904; that there was born to her on said date a female child; that said child was living March 4, 1905, and is said to have been named Gussie Lee Sample

Perry E.A. Fling

Witnesses To Mark:
{

Subscribed and sworn to before me this 19th day of April , 1905

Wirt Franklin
Notary Public.

Applications for Enrollment of Choctaw Newborn
Act of 1905   Volume XV

NEW BORN AFFIDAVIT

No _____

CHOCTAW ENROLLING COMMISSION

IN THE MATTER OF THE APPLICATION FOR ENROLLMENT as a citizen of the Choctaw Nation, of Gussie Lee Sample born on the 1st day of November 190 4

Name of father Clarence L Sample   ^ *not* a citizen of Choctaw Nation, final enrollment No............
Name of mother Fannie B Sample   a citizen of Choctaw Nation, final enrollment No. 4127

Hugo, Ind Ter   Postoffice.

AFFIDAVIT OF MOTHER

UNITED STATES OF AMERICA
  INDIAN TERRITORY
DISTRICT   Central

I Fannie B Sample , on oath state that I am 22 years of age and a citizen by blood of the Choctaw Nation, and as such have been placed upon the final roll of the Choctaw Nation, by the Honorable Secretary of the Interior my final enrollment number being 4127 ; that I am the lawful wife of Clarence L Sample , who is *not* a citizen of the Choctaw Nation, and as such has been placed upon the final roll of said Nation by the Honorable Secretary of the Interior, his final enrollment number being............. and that a Female child was born to me on the 1st day of November 190 4; that said child has been named Gussie Lee Sample , and is now living.

WITNESSETH: Fannie B Sample
  Must be two witnesses { W T Glenn
  who are citizens   { J C Kirkpatrick

Subscribed and sworn to before me this, the 2 day of March , 190 5

John F Larecy
Notary Public.

My Commission Expires: Feby 5 1907

Applications for Enrollment of Choctaw Newborn
Act of 1905   Volume XV

Affidavit of Attending Physician or Midwife

UNITED STATES OF AMERICA,
   INDIAN TERRITORY,
 Central   DISTRICT

I, Dr Perry Fling   a   Physician on oath state that I attended on Mrs. Fannie B Sample   wife of Clarence L Sample on the 1st day day of Nov , 190 4, that there was born to her on said date a Female child, that said child is now living, and is said to have been named Gussie Lee Sample

                    Perry Fling   M. D.

Subscribed and sworn to before me this the 2nd day of March   1905

                    John F Larecy
                      Notary Public.

WITNESSETH:
Must be two witnesses who are citizens and know the child. { W T Glenn
    J C Kirkpatrick

We hereby certify that we are well acquainted with   Perry Fling a   Physician   and know ....to be reputable and of good standing in the community.

              Must be two citizen{ WT Glenn
              witnesses.   J C Kirkpatrick

Choc New Born 1132
    Hattie Bennett
    (Born Aug. 25, 1903)

Applications for Enrollment of Choctaw Newborn
Act of 1905 Volume XV

BIRTH AFFIDAVIT.

DEPARTMENT OF THE INTERIOR.
COMMISSION TO THE FIVE CIVILIZED TRIBES.

IN RE APPLICATION FOR ENROLLMENT, as a citizen of the Choctaw Nation, of Hattie Bennett, born on the 25th day of August, 1903

Name of Father: John Bennett   a citizen of the United States ~~Nation~~.
Name of Mother: Mary Jane Bennett   a citizen of the Choctaw Nation.

Postoffice   Hugo, Ind. Ter.

AFFIDAVIT OF MOTHER.

UNITED STATES OF AMERICA, Indian Territory, Central DISTRICT.

I, Mary Jane Bennett, on oath state that I am 23 years of age and a citizen by blood, of the Choctaw Nation; that I am the lawful wife of John Bennett, who is a citizen, ~~by~~ .... of the United States ~~Nation~~; that a female child was born to me on 25th day of August, 1903; that said child has been named Hattie Bennett, and was living March 4, 1905.

                         Mary Jane Bennett

Witnesses To Mark:

Subscribed and sworn to before me this 19th day of April, 1905

                         Wirt Franklin
                         Notary Public.

AFFIDAVIT OF ATTENDING PHYSICIAN OR MID-WIFE.

UNITED STATES OF AMERICA, Indian Territory, Central DISTRICT.

I, L C Rucker, a physician, on oath state that I attended on Mrs. Mary Jane Bennett, wife of John Bennett on the 25th day of August, 1903; that there was born to her on said date a female child; that said child was living March 4, 1905, and is said to have been named Hattie Bennett

                         L.C. Rucker M.D.

Witnesses To Mark:

Applications for Enrollment of Choctaw Newborn
Act of 1905   Volume XV

Subscribed and sworn to before me this   19th   day of   April   , 1905

Wirt Franklin
Notary Public.

Choc New Born 1133
    Pearl Grubbs
    (Born Oct. 15, 1902)
    Mae Grubbs
    (Born Aug. 7, 1904)

BIRTH AFFIDAVIT.

DEPARTMENT OF THE INTERIOR,
COMMISSION TO THE FIVE CIVILIZED TRIBES.

IN RE Application for Enrollment, as a citizen of the   Choctaw   Nation, of   Pearl Grubbs   , born on the   15   day of   Oct   , 1902.

Name of Father: T.L. Grubbs   a citizen of the United States Nation.
Name of Mother: Ernestine Grubbs   a citizen of the   Choctaw   Nation.

Post-Office: Doaksmill I.T.

AFFIDAVIT OF MOTHER.

UNITED STATES OF AMERICA,
    INDIAN TERRITORY.
    Central   District.

I,   Ernestine Grubbs   , on oath state that I am   21   years of age and a citizen by   Blood   , of the   Choctaw   Nation; that I am the lawful wife of   T. L. Grubbs   , who is a citizen, by   by Marriage   of the Choctaw Nation; that a   female   child was born to me on   15   day of   Oct   , 1902, that said child has been named   Pearl Grubbs   , and is now living.

Ernestine Grubbs

WITNESSES TO MARK:

Applications for Enrollment of Choctaw Newborn
Act of 1905   Volume XV

Subscribed and sworn to before me this 6 *day of* Dec , 1902

R.L. Carter
NOTARY PUBLIC.

AFFIDAVIT OF ATTENDING PHYSICIAN OR MID-WIFE.

UNITED STATES OF AMERICA, }
   INDIAN TERRITORY.
   Central   District.

I, G Rosenthall[sic] , a father , on oath state that I ~~attended on~~ know of Mrs. Ernestine Grubbs , wife of T.L. Grubbs on the 15 day of Oct , 1902 ; that there was born to her on said date a female child; that said child is now living and is said to have been named Pearl Grubbs

Geo Rosenthal

WITNESSES TO MARK:

Subscribed and sworn to before me this 6 *day of* Dec , 1902

R.L. Carter
NOTARY PUBLIC.

Earnestine Grubbs
on roll as Ernestine
Rosenthal, No. 3845

Earnestine Grubbs
on roll as Ernestine
Rosenthal, No. 3845.

Mother will send
in physician's
affidavit later.

(illegible)

Affidavits that
(illegible) Mch 4-05

Applications for Enrollment of Choctaw Newborn
Act of 1905   Volume XV

BIRTH AFFIDAVIT.

DEPARTMENT OF THE INTERIOR.
COMMISSION TO THE FIVE CIVILIZED TRIBES.

_____

IN RE APPLICATION FOR ENROLLMENT, as a citizen of the   Choctaw   Nation, of Mae Grubbs   , born on the 7th   day of August   , 1904

Name of Father: T.L. Grubbs   a citizen of the United States ~~Nation~~.
Name of Mother: Earnestine Grubbs   a citizen of the   Choctaw   Nation.

Postoffice   Fulton, Arkansas.

_____

AFFIDAVIT OF ATTENDING PHYSICIAN OR MID-WIFE.

UNITED STATES OF AMERICA, Indian Territory, ⎱
    Northern   DISTRICT. ⎰

I,   H. S. Grant   , a   physician   , on oath state that I attended on Mrs. Earnestine Grubbs   , wife of   T. L. Grubbs   on the 7th   day of   August, 1904; that there was born to her on said date a   female   child; that said child was living March 4, 1905, and is said to have been named Mae Grubbs

                                  H. S. Grant
Witnesses To Mark:
   { J.T. Hodges
     Oliver Hodges

Subscribed and sworn to before me this   21   day of   April   , 1905

                                  John M. Plumlee
                                  Notary Public.
                                  First term

_____

BIRTH AFFIDAVIT.

DEPARTMENT OF THE INTERIOR.
COMMISSION TO THE FIVE CIVILIZED TRIBES.

_____

IN RE APPLICATION FOR ENROLLMENT, as a citizen of the   Choctaw   Nation, of Mae Grubbs   , born on the 7th   day of August   , 1904

Name of Father: T.L. Grubbs   a citizen of the United States ~~Nation~~.
Name of Mother: Earnestine Grubbs   a citizen of the   Choctaw   Nation.

Postoffice   Fulton, Arkansas.

Applications for Enrollment of Choctaw Newborn
Act of 1905   Volume XV

AFFIDAVIT OF MOTHER.

UNITED STATES OF AMERICA, Indian Territory, }
Central   DISTRICT.

I,   Earnestine Grubbs   , on oath state that I am   23   years of age and a citizen by   blood   , of the   Choctaw   Nation; that I am the lawful wife of   T. L. Grubbs   , who is a citizen, ~~by~~ .... of the   United States   ~~Nation~~; that a   female   child was born to me on   7th   day of   August   , 1904; that said child has been named   Mae Grubbs   , and was living March 4, 1905.

Ernestine Grubbs

Witnesses To Mark:
{

Subscribed and sworn to before me this   19th   day of   April   , 1905

Wirt Franklin
Notary Public.

BIRTH AFFIDAVIT.

DEPARTMENT OF THE INTERIOR.
COMMISSION TO THE FIVE CIVILIZED TRIBES.

IN RE APPLICATION FOR ENROLLMENT, as a citizen of the   Choctaw   Nation, of   Pearl Grubbs   , born on the   15th   day of   October   , 1902

Name of Father: T.L. Grubbs   a citizen of the United States ~~Nation~~.
Name of Mother: Earnestine Grubbs   a citizen of the   Choctaw   Nation.

Postoffice   Fulton, Arkansas.

AFFIDAVIT OF ATTENDING PHYSICIAN OR MID-WIFE.

UNITED STATES OF AMERICA, Indian Territory, }
Central   DISTRICT.

I,   E W Morrison   , a   physician   , on oath state that I attended on Mrs.   Earnestine Grubbs   , wife of   T. L. Grubbs   on the   15th   day of   October , 1902; that there was born to her on said date a   female   child; that said child was living March 4, 1905, and is said to have been named   Pearl Grubbs

EW Morrison MD

Applications for Enrollment of Choctaw Newborn
Act of 1905   Volume XV

Witnesses To Mark:
{

    Subscribed and sworn to before me this   19   day of   April   , 1905

                                        E.Q. Franklin
                                        Notary Public.

BIRTH AFFIDAVIT.

DEPARTMENT OF THE INTERIOR.
COMMISSION TO THE FIVE CIVILIZED TRIBES.

    IN RE APPLICATION FOR ENROLLMENT, as a citizen of the   Choctaw   Nation, of   Pearl Grubbs   , born on the   15th   day of   October   , 1902

Name of Father: T.L. Grubbs   a citizen of the United States ~~Nation~~.
Name of Mother: Earnestine Grubbs   a citizen of the   Choctaw   Nation.

                Postoffice   Fulton, Arkansas.

AFFIDAVIT OF MOTHER.

UNITED STATES OF AMERICA, Indian Territory, }
    Central   DISTRICT.

    I,   Earnestine Grubbs   , on oath state that I am   23   years of age and a citizen by   blood   , of the   Choctaw   Nation; that I am the lawful wife of   T. L. Grubbs   , who is a citizen, ~~by~~ .... of the   United States   ~~Nation~~; that a   female   child was born to me on   15th   day of   October   , 1902; that said child has been named   Pearl Grubbs   , and was living March 4, 1905.

                                      Earnestine Grubbs

Witnesses To Mark:
{

    Subscribed and sworn to before me this   19th   day of   April   , 1905

                                        Wirt Franklin
                                        Notary Public.

Applications for Enrollment of Choctaw Newborn
Act of 1905   Volume XV

7-1396.

Muskogee, Indian Territory, May 4, 1905.

Mrs. E. Grubbs,
    Fulton, Arkansas.

Dear Madam:

    Receipt is hereby acknowledged of your letter of April 26, transmitting the affidavit of H. S. Grant to the birth of Mae Grubbs, daughter of T. L. and Earnestine Grubbs, August 7, 1904, and the same has been filed with our records as an application for the enrollment of said child.

    The communication from H. S. Grant enclosed with your letter is herewith returned.

    Respectfully,

    Chairman.

DeB--1/4

7- NB-1133.

Muskogee, Indian Territory, June 10, 1905.

T. L. Grubbs,
    Fulton, Arkansas.

Dear Sir:

    Referring to the application for the enrollment of your infant child, Mae Grubbs, born August 7, 1904, it is noted that the attending physician, in his affidavit of April 21, 1905, heretofore filed in this office, fails to state that the applicant was living on March 4, 1904[sic].

    You will please secure his affidavit to this fact, but in the event he is unable to make this affidavit, it will be necessary that you file in this office the affidavits of two persons who are disinterested and not related to the applicant, who know that the child was born, the date of her birth, that she was living on March 4, 1905, and that Earnestine Grubbs is her mother.

    Respectfully,

    Chairman.

Applications for Enrollment of Choctaw Newborn
Act of 1905   Volume XV

7 NB 1133

Muskogee, Indian Territory, June 23, 1905.

Ernestine Grubbs,
    Idabel, Indian Territory.

Dear Madam:

    Receipt is hereby acknowledged of the affidavits of J. W. Grubbs, W. D. Adcock and Viola Adcock, to the birth of Mae Grubbs, daughter of Ernestine Grubbs, August 7, 1904, and the same have been filed in the matter of the enrollment of said child.

    Respectfully,

Chairman.

7-NB-1133

Muskogee, Indian Territory, September 30, 1905.

T. L. Grubbs,
    Idabel, Indian Territory.

Dear Sir:

    Receipt is hereby acknowledged of your letter of the 25th instant in which you request to be advised as to whether or not the enrollment of your minor daughter Mae Grubbs has been approved.

    In reply to your letter you are advised that the name of your said daughter appears upon a partial roll of new born citizens by blood of the Choctaw Nation opposite number 1504, which schedule has been forwarded to the Honorable Secretary of the Interior for approval on August 26, 1905. As soon as the same is approved by the Secretary you will be duly notified.

    Respectfully,

Commissioner.

Applications for Enrollment of Choctaw Newborn
Act of 1905   Volume XV

(The affidavit below typed as given.)

Affidavit

United States of America }
    Indian Territory   }
    Central District   }

    Before me, a Notary Public within and for said District and Territory personally appeared J.W. Grubbs of full age, who being duly sworn according to law doth depose and say that he is well acquainted with Mrs Earnestine Grubbs and her infant child Mae Grubbs, that Mae Grubbs in the heir of Earnestine Grubbs that she, the said Mae Grubbs was born August the 7, 1904, and she was alive and living March 4th, 1905.

J.W. Grubbs

Subscribed and sworn to before me this June 19, 1905

C.J. Stewart, Notary Public

My commission expires March 21, 1909

(The affidavit below typed as given.)

Affidavit

United States of America }
    Indian Territory   }
    Central District   }

    Before me a notary public within and for said District and Territory, personaly appeared W. D. Adcock of full age, who being duly sworn according to law doth depose and say that he is well acquainted with Mrs. Earnestine Grubbs and her infant child Mae Grubbs; that said Mae Grubbs was a live and living on the the 4th day of March 1905, and that Mae Grubbs the heir of said Mrs. Earnestine Grubbs.

W.D. Adcock

Subscribed and sworn to before me this June 19, 1905.

C.J. Stewart, Notary Public

My commission expires March 21, 1909.

Applications for Enrollment of Choctaw Newborn
Act of 1905   Volume XV

(The affidavit below typed as given.)

Affidavit

United States of America }
    Indian Territory }
    Central District }

    Before me, a notary Public within and for said District and Territory personally appeared Mrs. Viola Adcock, of full age, who being duly sworn according to law, doth depose and say that she is well acquainted with Mrs. Earnestine Grubbs and her infant child Mae Grubbs, and that Mae Grubbs was alive and living on the 4th day of March 1905.

                              Viola Adcock

Subscribed and sworn to before me this June 19, 1905.   C.J. Stewart,
                                                        Notary Public
My commission expires March 21, 1909.

<u>Choc New Born 1134</u>
    Sarah Hampton
    (Born March 20, 1904)

BIRTH AFFIDAVIT.
                          DEPARTMENT OF THE INTERIOR.
              COMMISSION TO THE FIVE CIVILIZED TRIBES.

        IN RE APPLICATION FOR ENROLLMENT, as a citizen of the   Choctaw   Nation, of Sarah Hampton   , born on the 20th day of   March , 1904

Name of Father: Isaac D. Hampton   a citizen of the   Choctaw   Nation.
Name of Mother: Frances Hampton   a citizen of the   Choctaw   Nation.

                          Postoffice   Hugo, Ind. Ter.

Applications for Enrollment of Choctaw Newborn
Act of 1905   Volume XV

AFFIDAVIT OF MOTHER.

UNITED STATES OF AMERICA, Indian Territory, }
Central   DISTRICT.

I, Frances Hampton, on oath state that I am 27 years of age and a citizen by blood, of the Choctaw Nation; that I am the lawful wife of Isaac D Hampton, who is a citizen, by blood of the Choctaw Nation; that a female child was born to me on 20th day of March, 1904; that said child has been named Sarah Hampton, and was living March 4, 1905.

            her
           Frances x Hampton
Witnesses To Mark: mark
 { Robert Anderson
  Vester W Rose

Subscribed and sworn to before me this 19th day of April, 1905

           Wirt Franklin
           Notary Public.

AFFIDAVIT OF ATTENDING PHYSICIAN OR MID-WIFE.

UNITED STATES OF AMERICA, Indian Territory, }
Central   DISTRICT.

I, Lizzie Bohanan, a mid-wife, on oath state that I attended on Mrs. Frances Hampton, wife of Isaac D Hampton on the 20th day of March, 1904; that there was born to her on said date a female child; that said child was living March 4, 1905, and is said to have been named Sarah Hampton

            her
           Lizzie x Bohanan
Witnesses To Mark: mark
 { Robert Anderson
  Vester W Rose

Subscribed and sworn to before me this 19th day of April, 1905

           Wirt Franklin
           Notary Public.

Applications for Enrollment of Choctaw Newborn
Act of 1905 Volume XV

Choc New Born 1135
    Charmian Vaughan Sanguin
    (Born Aug. 23, 1904)

NEW-BORN AFFIDAVIT.

Number..............

Choctaw Enrolling Commission.

IN THE MATTER OF THE APPLICATION FOR ENROLLMENT, as a citizen of the Choctaw Nation, of Charmian Vaughan Sanguin

born on the 23 day of August 190 4

Name of father Thomas E Sanguin   a citizen of   Choctaw
Nation final enrollment No 3850
Name of mother Zula C Sanguin   a citizen of   Choctaw
Nation final enrollment No 1397

                  Postoffice   Hugo, I.T.

AFFIDAVIT OF MOTHER.

UNITED STATES OF AMERICA,
   INDIAN TERRITORY,
  Central   DISTRICT

    I   Zula C Sanguin   on oath state that I am 28 years of age and a citizen by Ind. Mar. of the Choctaw Nation, and as such have been placed upon the final roll of the Choctaw Nation, by the Honorable Secretary of the Interior my final enrollment number being 1397 ; that I am the lawful wife of Thomas E Sanguin , who is a citizen of the Choctaw Nation, and as such has been placed upon the final roll of said Nation by the Honorable Secretary of the Interior, his final enrollment number being 3850 and that a Female child was born to me on the 23 day of August 190 4 ; that said child has been named Charmian Vaughan Sanguin , and is now living.

WITNESSETH: Zula C Sanguin
  Must be two   Joel Spring
  Witnesses who
  are Citizens.   H.L. Sanguin

    Subscribed and sworn to before me this   31   day of   Jany   190 5

                               W.T. Glenn
                                      Notary Public.

My commission expires   1907

Applications for Enrollment of Choctaw Newborn
Act of 1905 Volume XV

Affidavit of Attending Physician or Midwife

UNITED STATES OF AMERICA,
INDIAN TERRITORY,
Central DISTRICT

I, H.H. White a Practicing Physician on oath state that I attended on Mrs. Zula C Sanguin wife of Thomas E Sanguin on the 23 day of August, 190 4, that there was born to her on said date a Female child, that said child is now living, and is said to have been named Charmian Vaughan Sanguin

HH White M. D.

Subscribed and sworn to before me this the 31 day of Jany 1905

W.T. Glenn
Notary Public.

WITNESSETH:
Must be two witnesses who are citizens and know the child. { Joel Spring
H.L. Sanguin

We hereby certify that we are well acquainted with H.H. White a Practicing Physician and know him to be reputable and of good standing in the community.

Must be two citizen witnesses. { Joel Spring
H.L. Sanguin

BIRTH AFFIDAVIT.

DEPARTMENT OF THE INTERIOR.
COMMISSION TO THE FIVE CIVILIZED TRIBES.

IN RE APPLICATION FOR ENROLLMENT, as a citizen of the Choctaw Nation, of Charmian Vaughan Sanguin, born on the 23 day of August, 1904

Name of Father: Thomas E Sanguin a citizen of the Choctaw Nation.
Name of Mother: Zula C Sanguin a citizen of the Choctaw Nation.

Postoffice Hugo I.T.

Applications for Enrollment of Choctaw Newborn
Act of 1905   Volume XV

AFFIDAVIT OF MOTHER.

UNITED STATES OF AMERICA, Indian Territory, }
Central   DISTRICT. }

I, Zula C Sanguin , on oath state that I am 28 years of age and a citizen by Ind. Mar. , of the Choctaw Nation; that I am the lawful wife of Thomas E Sanguin , who is a citizen, by Blood of the Choctaw Nation; that a Female child was born to me on 23 day of August , 1904; that said child has been named Charmian Vaughan Sanguin , and was living March 4, 1905.

          Zula C Sanguin

Witnesses To Mark:
{

   Subscribed and sworn to before me this 17 day of April , 1905

          W.T. Glenn
           Notary Public.

AFFIDAVIT OF ATTENDING PHYSICIAN OR MID-WIFE.

UNITED STATES OF AMERICA, Indian Territory, }
Central   DISTRICT. }

I, H.H. White , a Physician , on oath state that I attended on Mrs. Zula C Sanguin , wife of Thomas E Sanguin on the 23 day of August , 1904; that there was born to her on said date a Female child; that said child was living March 4, 1905, and is said to have been named Charmian Vaughan Sanguin

          H.H. White M.D.

Witnesses To Mark:
{

   Subscribed and sworn to before me this 17 day of April , 1905

          W.T. Glenn
           Notary Public.

Applications for Enrollment of Choctaw Newborn
Act of 1905 Volume XV

Choc New Born 1136
    Willie Harley
    (Born Aug. 24, 1904)

BIRTH AFFIDAVIT.

DEPARTMENT OF THE INTERIOR,
COMMISSION TO THE FIVE CIVILIZED TRIBES.

In Re Application for Enrollment, as a citizen of the Choctaw Nation, of Willie Harley, born on the 24 day of August, 1904

Name of Father: Melford Harley   a citizen of the Choctaw Nation.
Name of Mother: Ennis Harley   a citizen of the Choctaw Nation.

Post-office   Garvin I.T.

AFFIDAVIT OF MOTHER.

UNITED STATES OF AMERICA,
    INDIAN TERRITORY,
Central   District.

I, Eunis[sic] Harley, on oath state that I am 18 years of age and a citizen by Blood, of the Choctaw Nation; that I am the lawful wife of Melford Harley, who is a citizen, by Blood of the Choctaw Nation; that a male child was born to me on 24th day of August, 1904, that said child has been named Willie Harley, and is now living.

                                                       Ennis Harley

WITNESSES TO MARK:
    Ephraim McKinney
    Melvina Taylor

Subscribed and sworn to before me this 12th day of April AD, 1905.

                                                      Simon Taylor
                                                       NOTARY PUBLIC.

Applications for Enrollment of Choctaw Newborn
Act of 1905   Volume XV

AFFIDAVIT OF ATTENDING PHYSICIAN OR MID-WIFE.

UNITED STATES OF AMERICA, }
　INDIAN TERRITORY,
Central　　　　District.

I, Patsey Tanitobbi, a Midwife, on oath state that I attended on Mrs. Ennis Harley, wife of Melford Harley on the 24 day of August, 1904; that there was born to her on said date a male child; that said child is now living and is said to have been named Willie Harley

　　　　　　　　　　　　　　her
　　　　　　　　　　　Patsey x Tanitobbi
WITNESSES TO MARK:　　　mark
{ Ephraim McKinney
　Melvina Taylor

Subscribed and sworn to before me this 12th day of April, 1905.

　　　　　　　　　Simon Taylor
　　　　　　　　　　NOTARY PUBLIC.

NEW-BORN AFFIDAVIT.

　　　　　Number............

Choctaw Enrolling Commission.

IN THE MATTER OF THE APPLICATION FOR ENROLLMENT, as a citizen of the Choctaw Nation, of Willie Herley[sic]

born on the 24 day of August 1904

Name of father   Montford Herley　　　a citizen of   Choctaw
Nation final enrollment No   2988
　　　　　　　　Tantubbee
Name of mother   Enos[sic] *now* Herley　　a citizen of   Choctaw
Nation final enrollment No   1788

　　　　　　　Postoffice   Garvin

Applications for Enrollment of Choctaw Newborn
Act of 1905   Volume XV

AFFIDAVIT OF MOTHER.

UNITED STATES OF AMERICA,
   INDIAN TERRITORY,
 Central   DISTRICT

    I   Enos Tantubbee now Herley   on oath state that I am 19 years of age and a citizen by ———— of the Choctaw Nation, and as such have been placed upon the final roll of the Choctaw Nation, by the Honorable Secretary of the Interior my final enrollment number being 1788 ; that I am the lawful wife of Montford Herley , who is a citizen of the Choctaw Nation, and as such has been placed upon the final roll of said Nation by the Honorable Secretary of the Interior, his final enrollment number being 2988 and that a male child was born to me on the 24 day of Aug 190 4 ; that said child has been named Willie Herley , and is now living.

                             Enos Tantubbee   now Herley

WITNESSETH:
  Must be two   Timothy J Cephus
  Witnesses who
  are Citizens.   Celia Wallace

    Subscribed and sworn to before me this 18 day of Jany 190 5

                             W T Glenn
                                      Notary Public.

My commission expires 1907

Affidavit of Attending Physician or Midwife.

UNITED STATES OF AMERICA
INDIAN TERRITORY
 Central   DISTRICT

    I, Bessie Wallace now Cephus   a   Midwife on oath state that I attended on Mrs. Enos Tantubbee now Herley wife of Montford Herley on the 24 day of August , 190 4 , that there was born to her on said date a Male child, that said child is now living, and is said to have been named Willie Herley

                                        her
                           Bessie Wallace now Cephus x   M.D.
                                       mark

    Subscribed and sworn to before me this, the 18 day of Jany 190 5

                             WT Glenn
                                    Notary Public.

WITNESSETH:
  Must be two witnesses   Timothy J Cephus
  who are citizens and
  know the child.   Celia Wallace

Applications for Enrollment of Choctaw Newborn
Act of 1905 Volume XV

We hereby certify that we are well acquainted with Bessie Wallace *now Cephus* a mid wife and know her to be reputable and of good standing in the community.

{ Timothy J Cephus
{ Celia Wallace

Choctaw 728.

Muskogee, Indian Territory, April 22, 1905.

Milford Harley,
    Garvin, Indian Territory.

Dear Sir:

    Receipt is hereby acknowledged of the affidavits of Ennis Harley and Patsey Tanitobbi to the birth of Willie Harley, son of Melford and Ennis Harley, August 24, 1904, and the same have been filed with our records as an application for the enrollment of said child.

Respectfully,

Chairman.

Choc New Born 1137
    (Florence Maud Vawter)
    (Born February 21, 1903)

BIRTH AFFIDAVIT.

DEPARTMENT OF THE INTERIOR.
COMMISSION TO THE FIVE CIVILIZED TRIBES.

IN RE APPLICATION FOR ENROLLMENT, as a citizen of the Choctaw Nation, of Florence Maud Vawter, born on the 21 day of February, 1903

Name of Father: James W. Vawter   a citizen of the Choctaw Nation.
Name of Mother: Martha A. Vawter   a citizen of the Choctaw Nation.

Postoffice   Erin Springs, I.T.

Applications for Enrollment of Choctaw Newborn
Act of 1905   Volume XV

AFFIDAVIT OF MOTHER.

UNITED STATES OF AMERICA, Indian Territory,
Southern DISTRICT.

I, Martha A. Vawter, on oath state that I am 31 years of age and a citizen by blood, of the Choctaw Nation; that I am the lawful wife of James W Vawter, who is a citizen, by Marriage of the Choctaw Nation; that a female child was born to me on 21st day of February, 1903; that said child has been named Florence Maud, and was living March 4, 1905.

Martha A Vawter

Witnesses To Mark:

Subscribed and sworn to before me this 18th day of Mch, 1905

FM Bell
Notary Public.

AFFIDAVIT OF ATTENDING PHYSICIAN OR MID-WIFE.

UNITED STATES OF AMERICA, ~~Indian Territory~~ *Oklahoma*,
Cleveland County ~~DISTRICT.~~

I, J. L. Hoshall, a physician, on oath state that I attended on Mrs. Martha A Vawter, wife of James W Vawter on the 21st day of February, 1903; that there was born to her on said date a female child; that said child was living March 4, 1905, and is said to have been named Florence Maud Vawter

J.L. Hoshall, M.D.

Witnesses To Mark:
HP Doughty
Geo W Carson

Subscribed and sworn to before me this 7th day of April, 1905

H.P. Doughty
Notary Public.

My Commission expires *(Illegible)* 1906

Applications for Enrollment of Choctaw Newborn
Act of 1905 Volume XV

7-NB-1137

Muskogee, Indian Territory, July 24, 1905.

J. W. Vawter,
    Erin Springs, Indian Territory.

Dear Sir:

    Replying to that portion of your letter of July 14, 1905, in which you ask if you will receive notice of the approval of the enrollment of your child, you are advised that the name of your child Florence Maud Vawter has been placed upon a schedule of citizens by blood of the Choctaw Nation which has been forwarded the Secretary of the Interior, and you will be notified when her enrollment is approved by him.

        Respectfully,

        Commissioner.

Choc New Born 1138
    Irene Norman
    (Born May 16, 1904)

BIRTH AFFIDAVIT.

DEPARTMENT OF THE INTERIOR.
COMMISSION TO THE FIVE CIVILIZED TRIBES.

IN RE APPLICATION FOR ENROLLMENT, as a citizen of the Choctaw Nation, of Irene Norman, born on the 16th day of May, 1904

Name of Father: Joshua Allen Norman   a citizen of the Choctaw Nation. (non)
Name of Mother: Ida Norman   a citizen of the Choctaw Nation.

    Postoffice   Palmer
                 Ind Ter

Applications for Enrollment of Choctaw Newborn
Act of 1905 Volume XV

AFFIDAVIT OF MOTHER.

UNITED STATES OF AMERICA, Indian Territory, }
Southern DISTRICT.

I, Ida Norman, on oath state that I am 28 years of age and a citizen by Blood, of the Choctaw Nation; that I am the lawful wife of Joshua Allen Norman, who is a ~~citizen, by~~ non citizen of the Choctaw Nation; that a Female child was born to me on 16th day of May, 1904; that said child has been named Irene Norman, and was living March 4, 1905.

Ida Norman

Witnesses To Mark:
{

Subscribed and sworn to before me this 17th day of April, 1905

Robt H Buchanan
Notary Public.
My commission expires Dec 18th 1907

AFFIDAVIT OF ATTENDING PHYSICIAN OR MID-WIFE.

UNITED STATES OF AMERICA, Indian Territory, }
Southern DISTRICT.

I, John Strather Norman, a Physician, on oath state that I attended on Mrs. Ida Norman, wife of Joshua Allen Norman on the 16th day of May, 1904; that there was born to her on said date a Female child; that said child was living March 4, 1905, and is said to have been named Irene Norman

John Strather Norman

Witnesses To Mark:
{

Subscribed and sworn to before me this 17th day of April, 1905

Robt H Buchanan
Notary Public.
My commission expires Dec 18th 1907

Applications for Enrollment of Choctaw Newborn
Act of 1905 Volume XV

7-301

Muskogee, Indian Territory, April 24, 1905

Ida Norman,
    Palmer, Indian Territory.

Dear Madam:

    Receipt is hereby acknowledged of your letter of April 17, 1905, enclosing affidavits of Ida Norman and John Strather Norman to the birth of Irene Norman, daughter of Joshua Allen Norman and Ida Norman, May 16, 1904, and the same have been filed with our records as an application for the enrollment of said child.

                  Respectfully,

                              Chairman.

Choc New Born 1139
    Roy E. Bullard
    (Born Aug. 5, 1903)
    Elmer D. Bullard
    (Born Feb. 23, 1905)

NEW BORN AFFIDAVIT

No ....

CHOCTAW ENROLLING COMMISSION

IN THE MATTER OF THE APPLICATION FOR ENROLLMENT as a citizen of the Choctaw Nation, of Roy E. Bullard born on the 5 day of August 190 3

Name of father Frank Bullard   a citizen of   white   Nation, final enrollment No. ——

Name of mother Susan F. Bullard   a citizen of   Choctaw   Nation, final enrollment No. 12779

Applications for Enrollment of Choctaw Newborn
Act of 1905 Volume XV

McAlester I.T.   Postoffice.

AFFIDAVIT OF MOTHER

UNITED STATES OF AMERICA }
INDIAN TERRITORY }
DISTRICT   Central }

I   Susan F. Bullard   , on oath state that I am   23   years of age and a citizen by   blood   of the   Choctaw   Nation, and as such have been placed upon the final roll of the   Choctaw   Nation, by the Honorable Secretary of the Interior my final enrollment number being   12779   ; that I am the lawful wife of   Frank Bullard   , who is a citizen of the   white   Nation, and as such has been placed upon the final roll of said Nation by the Honorable Secretary of the Interior, his final enrollment number being —— and that a   male   child was born to me on the   5   day of   August   190 3; that said child has been named   Roy E. Bullard   , and is now living.

WITNESSETH:
Must be two witnesses { *(Name Illegible)*
who are citizens   { N.B. Ainsworth

Susie Bullard

My Commission Expires:

Sept 23, 1907   Subscribed & sworn to before me this 15 day of March 1905.

James Bower
n. P.

Affidavit of Attending Physician or Midwife

UNITED STATES OF AMERICA, }
INDIAN TERRITORY, }
Central   DISTRICT }

I,   W.E. Abbott   a   Practicing Physician on oath state that I attended on Mrs. Susie Bullard   wife of Frank Bullard on the   5   day of   August   , 190 3, that there was born to her on said date a   male   child, that said child is now living, and is said to have been named   Roy E. Bullard

W.E. Abbott   M. D.

Applications for Enrollment of Choctaw Newborn
Act of 1905   Volume XV

Subscribed and sworn to before me this the   15   day of   March   1905

             James Bower
             Notary Public.

WITNESSETH:
Must be two witnesses who are citizens and know the child.   { *(Name Illegible)*
         N.B. Ainsworth

    We hereby certify that we are well acquainted with   W.E. Abbott   a   Physician   and know   him   to be reputable and of good standing in the community.

         Must be two citizen witnesses.   { *(Name Illegible)*
               N.B. Ainsworth

BIRTH AFFIDAVIT.

DEPARTMENT OF THE INTERIOR.
COMMISSION TO THE FIVE CIVILIZED TRIBES.

   IN RE APPLICATION FOR ENROLLMENT, as a citizen of the   Choctaw   Nation, of   Roy E. Bullard   , born on the   5   day of   August   , 1903

Name of Father: Frank Bullard   a citizen of the United States Nation.
Name of Mother: Susie Bullard   a citizen of the   Choctaw   Nation.

         Postoffice   McAlester I.T.

AFFIDAVIT OF MOTHER.

UNITED STATES OF AMERICA, Indian Territory, }
   Central   DISTRICT.

   I,   Susie Bullard   , on oath state that I am   23   years of age and a citizen by Blood   , of the   Choctaw   Nation; that I am the lawful wife of   Frank Bullard   , who is a citizen, by .... of the   United States   Nation; that a   male child was born to me on   5   day of   August   , 1903; that said child has been named Roy E. Bullard   , and was living March 4, 1905.

             Susan L Bullard

Witnesses To Mark:
{

Applications for Enrollment of Choctaw Newborn
Act of 1905 Volume XV

Subscribed and sworn to before me this 19 day of April, 1905

R.B. Coleman
Notary Public.

AFFIDAVIT OF ATTENDING PHYSICIAN OR MID-WIFE.

UNITED STATES OF AMERICA, Indian Territory,
Central DISTRICT.

I, W.E. Abbott, a Physician, on oath state that I attended on Mrs. Susie Bullard, wife of Frank Bullard on the 5 day of August, 1903; that there was born to her on said date a male child; that said child was living March 4, 1905, and is said to have been named Roy E Bullard

Dr W.E. Abbott

Witnesses To Mark:

Subscribed and sworn to before me this 19" day of April, 1905

R.B. Coleman
Notary Public.

NEW BORN AFFIDAVIT

No

CHOCTAW ENROLLING COMMISSION

IN THE MATTER OF THE APPLICATION FOR ENROLLMENT as a citizen of the Choctaw Nation, of Elmer D. Bullard born on the 23 day of February 190 5

Name of father Frank Bullard a citizen of white Nation, final enrollment No. ——

Name of mother Susan F. Bullard a citizen of Choctaw Nation, final enrollment No. 12779

McAlester I.T. Postoffice.

Applications for Enrollment of Choctaw Newborn
Act of 1905 Volume XV

AFFIDAVIT OF MOTHER

UNITED STATES OF AMERICA
INDIAN TERRITORY
DISTRICT   Central

I   Susan F. Bullard   , on oath state that I am   23   years of age and a citizen by   blood   of the   Choctaw   Nation, and as such have been placed upon the final roll of the   Choctaw   Nation, by the Honorable Secretary of the Interior my final enrollment number being   12779   ; that I am the lawful wife of   Frank Bullard   , who is a citizen of the   white   Nation, and as such has been placed upon the final roll of said Nation by the Honorable Secretary of the Interior, his final enrollment number being —— and that a   male   child was born to me on the   23   day of   February   190 5; that said child has been named   Elmer D. Bullard   , and is now living.

WITNESSETH: Susie Bullard

Must be two witnesses { *(Name Illegible)*
who are citizens   N.B. Ainsworth

Subscribed and sworn to before me this, the   15   day of   March   190 5

James Bower
Notary Public.

My Commission Expires:
Sept 23 1907

Affidavit of Attending Physician or Midwife

UNITED STATES OF AMERICA,
INDIAN TERRITORY,
Central   DISTRICT

I,   Nancy Nobles   a   Midwife on oath state that I attended on Mrs. Susie F. Bullard   wife of   Frank Bullard on the   23   day of   February   , 190 5, that there was born to her on said date a   male child, that said child is now living, and is said to have been named   Elmer D. Bullard

        her
Nancy x Nobler   M. D.
        mark

Subscribed and sworn to before me this the   15   day of   March   1905

James Bower
Notary Public.

WITNESSETH:

Must be two witnesses { *(Name Illegible)*
who are citizens and
know the child.   N.B. Ainsworth

Applications for Enrollment of Choctaw Newborn
Act of 1905   Volume XV

We hereby certify that we are well acquainted with Nancy Nobles a midwife and know her to be reputable and of good standing in the community.

Must be two citizen witnesses. { *(Name Illegible)* N.B. Ainsworth

BIRTH AFFIDAVIT.

DEPARTMENT OF THE INTERIOR.
COMMISSION TO THE FIVE CIVILIZED TRIBES.

IN RE APPLICATION FOR ENROLLMENT, as a citizen of the Choctaw Nation, of Elmer D. Bullard, born on the 23 day of Feby, 1905

Name of Father: Frank Bullard   a citizen of the United States Nation.
Name of Mother: Susie Bullard   a citizen of the Choctaw Nation.

Postoffice   McAlester I.T.

AFFIDAVIT OF MOTHER.

UNITED STATES OF AMERICA, Indian Territory, }
Central   DISTRICT.

I, Susie Bullard, on oath state that I am 23 years of age and a citizen by Blood, of the Choctaw Nation; that I am the lawful wife of Frank Bullard, who is a citizen, by .... of the United States Nation; that a male child was born to me on 23 day of February, 1905; that said child has been named Elmer D. Bullard, and was living March 4, 1905.

Susan L Bullard

Witnesses To Mark:
{

Subscribed and sworn to before me this 19 day of April, 1905

R.B. Coleman
Notary Public.

Applications for Enrollment of Choctaw Newborn
Act of 1905   Volume XV

AFFIDAVIT OF ATTENDING PHYSICIAN OR MID-WIFE.

UNITED STATES OF AMERICA, Indian Territory, }
Central   DISTRICT.

I, Nancy Nobles , a midwife , on oath state that I attended on Mrs. Susie Bullard , wife of Frank Bullard on the 23 day of February , 1905; that there was born to her on said date a male child; that said child was living March 4, 1905, and is said to have been named Elmer D Bullard

her
Nancy x Nobles
mark

Witnesses To Mark:
{ W R Stirlen
{ Mrs W R Stirlen

Subscribed and sworn to before me this 19 day of April , 1905

R.B. Coleman
Notary Public.

7-4621

Muskogee, Indian Territory, April 24, 1905.

Frank Bullard,
  McAlester, Indian Territory.

Dear Sir:

Receipt is hereby acknowledged of the affidavits of Susan L. Bullard and W. E. Abbott to the birth of Roy E. Bullard son of Frank and Susie Bullard, August 5, 1903; also affidavits of Susan L. Bullard and Nancy Noble[sic] to the birth of Elmer D. Bullard, son of Frank and Susie Bullard, February 23, 1905, and the same have been filed with our records as an application for the enrollment of said children.

Respectfully,

Chairman.

Applications for Enrollment of Choctaw Newborn
Act of 1905   Volume XV

7-NB-1139.

Muskogee, Indian Territory, June 10, 1905.

Frank Bullard,
    McAlester, Indian Territory.

Dear Sir:

    There is returned herewith application for the enrollment of your infant child, Elmer D. Bullard, born February 23, 1905, in which the Notary Public before whom it was acknowledged failed to attach the jurat and his signature to the affidavit of the attending midwife.

    You will please have the Notary Public complete the affidavit and attach his signature, and then return the application to this office.

    Respectfully,

    Chairman.

DeB-8.10

---

7 NB 1139

Muskogee, Indian Territory, June 21, 1905.

Frank Bullard,
    McAlester, Indian Territory.

Dear Sir:

    Receipt is hereby acknowledged of the application for the enrollment of Elmer D. Bullard corrected by having the Notary Public affix his jurat and seal to the affidavit of the attending midwife and the same has been filed in the matter of the enrollment of said child.

    Respectfully,

    Chairman.

Applications for Enrollment of Choctaw Newborn
Act of 1905   Volume XV

Choc New Born 1140
    Horace C. Rose
    (Born April 26, 1903)

NEW-BORN AFFIDAVIT.

    Number............

...Choctaw Enrolling Commission...

IN THE MATTER OF THE APPLICATION FOR ENROLLMENT, as a citizen of the Choctaw Nation, of Horace Clayton Rose

born on the 26th day of ____April____ 190 3

Name of father   James Rose   a citizen of   white
Nation final enrollment No. ....
Name of mother   Annie Rose   a citizen of   Choctaw
Nation final enrollment No. 7717

                                      Postoffice   Stegler[sic] IT

AFFIDAVIT OF MOTHER.

UNITED STATES OF AMERICA
INDIAN TERRITORY
Central   DISTRICT

I   Annie Rose   , on oath state that I am 32 years of age and a citizen by blood of the   Choctaw   Nation, and as such have been placed upon the final roll of the   Choctaw   Nation, by the Honorable Secretary of the Interior my final enrollment number being   7717 ; that I am the lawful wife of   James Rose , who is a citizen of the   Choctaw   Nation, and as such has been placed upon the final roll of said Nation by the Honorable Secretary of the Interior, his final enrollment number being —— and that a   male   child was born to me on the   26   day of   April   190 3; that said child has been named   Horace Clayton Rose , and is now living.

                                                      Annie Rose

Witnesseth.
    Must be two
    Witnesses who   William Goins
    are Citizens.   Wm Martin

Applications for Enrollment of Choctaw Newborn
Act of 1905   Volume XV

Subscribed and sworn to before me this   3   day of   Jan   190 5

James Bower
Notary Public.

My commission expires:
Sept 23-1907

AFFIDAVIT OF ATTENDING PHYSICIAN OR MIDWIFE

UNITED STATES OF AMERICA
INDIAN TERRITORY
_____ DISTRICT

I,   Dr Lant Stevens[sic]   a   physician on oath state that I attended on Mrs.   Annie Rose   wife of   James Rose   on the   26th day of   April   , 190 3 , that there was born to her on said date a   male child, that said child is now living, and is said to have been named   Horace Clayton Rose

L.K. Stephens, M.D.

Subscribed and sworn to before me this, the   10th day of   Jany   190 5

(Name Illegible)   Notary Public.

WITNESSETH:
Must be two witnesses { Henry Cooper
who are citizens   { J.S. Stigler

We hereby certify that we are well acquainted with   Dr Lant Stevens a   physician   and know   him   to be reputable and of good standing in the community.

Henry Cooper   _____

JS. Stigler   _____

BIRTH AFFIDAVIT.

DEPARTMENT OF THE INTERIOR.
COMMISSION TO THE FIVE CIVILIZED TRIBES.

Choctaw

IN RE APPLICATION FOR ENROLLMENT, as a citizen of the   ~~CREEK~~   Nation, of   Horace C. Rose   , born on the   26th day of   April   , 1903

Name of Father: James Rose   a citizen of the _____ Nation.
Name of Mother: Annie Rose   a citizen of the   Choctaw   Nation.

Applications for Enrollment of Choctaw Newborn
Act of 1905   Volume XV

Postoffice   Stigler, Ind. Ter.

AFFIDAVIT OF MOTHER.

UNITED STATES OF AMERICA, Indian Territory, }
Central   ~~WESTERN~~   DISTRICT.

I, Annie Rose , on oath state that I am _____ years of age and a citizen by Blood , of the Choctaw Nation; that I am the lawful wife of James Rose , who is a citizen, by _____ of the Choctaw Nation; that a male child was born to me on 26th day of April , 1903, that said child has been named Horace C. Rose , and is now living.

Annie Rose

Witnesses To Mark:
{ Henry Cooper
{ J.S. Stigler

Subscribed and sworn to before me this 8th day of April , 1905.

My Commission   Chas. T. Walker
Expires May 7th 1907   Notary Public.

AFFIDAVIT OF ATTENDING PHYSICIAN OR MID-WIFE.

UNITED STATES OF AMERICA, Indian Territory, }
Central   DISTRICT.

I, Landon K Stephens , a Physician , on oath state that I attended on Mrs. Annie Rose , wife of James Rose on the 26th day of April , 1903; that there was born to her on said date a male child; that said child is now living and is said to have been named Horace C Rose

Landon K. Stephens M.D.

Witnesses To Mark:
{ Henry Cooper

Subscribed and sworn to before me this 8th day of April , 1905.

My Commission   Chas. T. Walker
Expires May 7th 1907   Notary Public.

Applications for Enrollment of Choctaw Newborn
Act of 1905   Volume XV

7-2659

Muskogee, Indian Territory, April 24, 1905.

James Rose,
    Stigler, Indian Territory.

Dear Sir:

    Receipt is hereby acknowledged of your letter of April 14, 1905, addressed to the United States Indian Agent which has been by him referred to this Commission for appropriate action. Therein you inclose affidavits of Annie Rose, and Landon K. Stephens to the birth of Horace C. Rose, son of James and Annie Rose, April 26, 1903, and the same have been filed with our records as an application for the enrollment of said child.

        Respectfully,

        Chairman.

Choc New Born 1141
    John W. Lyles
    (Born April 25, 1904)

NEW-BORN AFFIDAVIT.

    Number

...Choctaw Enrolling Commission...

    IN THE MATTER OF THE APPLICATION FOR ENROLLMENT, as a citizen of the Choctaw Nation, of John W. Lyles

born on the 25" day of __April__ 190 4

Name of father   William A Lyles   a citizen of   Choctaw
Nation final enrollment No.   7629
Name of mother   Mary L Lyles   a citizen of   Choctaw
Nation final enrollment No.   646

        Postoffice   Fox IT

Applications for Enrollment of Choctaw Newborn
Act of 1905   Volume XV

AFFIDAVIT OF MOTHER.

UNITED STATES OF AMERICA
INDIAN TERRITORY
Central   DISTRICT

I   Mary L Lyles   , on oath state that I am 40 years of age and a citizen by marriage of the Choctaw Nation, and as such have been placed upon the final roll of the Choctaw Nation, by the Honorable Secretary of the Interior my final enrollment number being 646 ; that I am the lawful wife of William A Lyles , who is a citizen of the Choctaw Nation, and as such has been placed upon the final roll of said Nation by the Honorable Secretary of the Interior, his final enrollment number being 7629 and that a Male child was born to me on the 25" day of April 190 4; that said child has been named John W. Lyles , and is now living.

Mary L Lyles

Witnesseth.

Must be two Witnesses who are Citizens.   Louis Leflore
Leonidas C Merryman

Subscribed and sworn to before me this   31st day of   Dec   190 4

Edwin L Hickman
Notary Public.

My commission expires: February 19" 1905

AFFIDAVIT OF ATTENDING PHYSICIAN OR MIDWIFE

UNITED STATES OF AMERICA
INDIAN TERRITORY
Central   DISTRICT

I,   A P Thompson   a   Practicing Physician on oath state that I attended on Mrs. Mary L Lyles wife of William A Lyles on the   25" day of   April , 190 4 , that there was born to her on said date a male child, that said child is now living, and is said to have been named   John W. Lyles

Subscribed and sworn to before me this, the   31"   day of December   190 4   AP Thompson MD

Edwin L Hickman   Notary Public.

WITNESSETH:
Must be two witnesses who are citizens   Louis Leflore
Leonidas E Merryman

Applications for Enrollment of Choctaw Newborn
Act of 1905   Volume XV

We hereby certify that we are well acquainted with   A P Thompson a   Practicing physician   and know   him   to be reputable and of good standing in the community.

    Louis Leflore   _____

    Leonidas E Merryman   _____

BIRTH AFFIDAVIT.

DEPARTMENT OF THE INTERIOR.
COMMISSION TO THE FIVE CIVILIZED TRIBES.

    IN RE APPLICATION FOR ENROLLMENT, as a citizen of the   Choctaw   Nation, of John W. Lyles   , born on the 25th day of   April   , 1904

Name of Father: William A Lyles   a citizen of the   Choctaw   Nation.
Name of Mother: Mary L Lyles   a citizen of the   Choctaw   Nation.

                  Postoffice   Fox, I.T.

AFFIDAVIT OF MOTHER.

UNITED STATES OF AMERICA, Indian Territory,
    Central   **DISTRICT.**

    I,   Mary L Lyles   , on oath state that I am 40   years of age and a citizen by intermarriage   , of the   Choctaw   Nation; that I am the lawful wife of   William A Lyles   , who is a citizen, by blood   of the   Choctaw   Nation; that a male   child was born to me on 25th day of   April   , 1904; that said child has been named   John W Lyles   , and was living March 4, 1905.

                                  Mary L Lyles
Witnesses To Mark:

    Subscribed and sworn to before me this   18 day of   April   , 1905

                                  Lacey P Bobo
                                  Notary Public.

Applications for Enrollment of Choctaw Newborn
Act of 1905   Volume XV

AFFIDAVIT OF ATTENDING PHYSICIAN OR MID-WIFE.

UNITED STATES OF AMERICA, Indian Territory, }
Central   DISTRICT.

    I,   A.P. Thompson   , a Physician   , on oath state that I attended on Mrs. Mary L Lyles   , wife of   William A Lyles   on the 25th day of April , 1904; that there was born to her on said date a   male   child; that said child was living March 4, 1905, and is said to have been named John W. Lyles

A.P. Thompson

Witnesses To Mark:
{

    Subscribed and sworn to before me this 18 day of   April   , 1905

Lacey P Bobo
Notary Public.

7-2626

Muskogee, Indian Territory, April 24, 1905.

William A. Lyles,
    Fox, Indian Territory.

Dear Sir:

    Receipt is hereby acknowledged of the affidavits of Mary L. Lyles and A. P. Thompson to the birth of John W. Lyles son of William A. and Mary L. Lyles, April 25, 1904, and the same have been filed with our records as an application for the enrollment of said child.

Respectfully,

Chairman.

Applications for Enrollment of Choctaw Newborn
Act of 1905   Volume XV

7-NB-1141

Muskogee, Indian Territory, July 25, 1905.

W. A. Lyles,
    Fox, Indian Territory.

Dear Sir:

    Receipt is hereby acknowledged of your letter of July 14, 1905, asking if your child John W. Lyles has been approved.

    In reply to your letter you are and advised that the name of your child John W. Lyles has been placed upon a schedule of citizens by blood of the Choctaw Nation which has been forwarded the Secretary of the Interior and you will be notified when his enrollment is approved by the Department.

                    Respectfully,

                                    Commissioner.

Choc New Born 1142
    Edward Daniel Bench
    (Born March 4, 1903)

NEW-BORN AFFIDAVIT.

                Number

...Choctaw Enrolling Commission...

    IN THE MATTER OF THE APPLICATION FOR ENROLLMENT, as a citizen of the Choctaw Nation, of Edward Daniel bench

born on the 4 day of March 190 4[sic]

Name of father Daniel Bench a citizen of Choctaw
Nation final enrollment No. 10177
Name of mother Katie Dench[sic] a citizen of Choctaw
Nation final enrollment No. 974

Applications for Enrollment of Choctaw Newborn
Act of 1905 Volume XV

Postoffice   Boswell I.T.

AFFIDAVIT OF MOTHER.

UNITED STATES OF AMERICA
INDIAN TERRITORY
central[sic]   DISTRICT

I   Katie Bench   , on oath state that I am   25   years of age and a citizen by   Marriage   of the   Choctaw   Nation, and as such have been placed upon the final roll of the   Choctaw   Nation, by the Honorable Secretary of the Interior my final enrollment number being   974   ; that I am the lawful wife of   Daniel Bench   , who is a citizen of the   ~~Blood~~   Choctaw   Nation, and as such has been placed on the final roll of said Nation by the Honorable Secretary of the Interior, his final enrollment number being   10177   and that a   Male   child was born to me on the   4   day of   March   190 4[sic]; that said child has been named   Edward Daniel Bench   , and is now living.

Katie Bench

Witnesseth.

Must be two Witnesses who are Citizens. } G D Duncan
John T Brown

Subscribed and sworn to before me this   16   day of   **FEB**   190 **5**

AJ Markey
Notary Public.

My commission expires: **1/24/09**

AFFIDAVIT OF ATTENDING PHYSICIAN OR MIDWIFE

UNITED STATES OF AMERICA
INDIAN TERRITORY
Central   DISTRICT

I,   C.B. Smith   a   Physicean[sic] on oath state that I attended on Mrs.   Katie Bench   wife of   Daniel Bench on the   4   day of   March   , 190 4[sic] , that there was born to her on said date a   Male child, that said child is now living, and is said to have been named   Edward Daniel Bench

C.B. Smith   𝑚.𝒟.

Subscribed and sworn to before me this, the   16   day of **Feb**   190 **5**

WITNESSETH:
Must be two witnesses who are citizens { G D Duncan
John T Brown

A J Markey   Notary Public.

Applications for Enrollment of Choctaw Newborn
Act of 1905 Volume XV

We hereby certify that we are well acquainted with C.B. Smith a Physicean[sic] and know Him to be reputable and of good standing in the community.

G D Duncan _____

John T Brown _____

_____

BIRTH AFFIDAVIT.

DEPARTMENT OF THE INTERIOR.
COMMISSION TO THE FIVE CIVILIZED TRIBES.

_____

IN RE APPLICATION FOR ENROLLMENT, as a citizen of the Choctaw Nation, of Edward Daniel Bench , born on the 4th day of March , 1903

Name of Father: Daniel Bench   a citizen of the Choctaw Nation.
Name of Mother: Katie Bench   a citizen of the Choctaw Nation.

Postoffice Boswell, Ind. Ter.

_____

AFFIDAVIT OF MOTHER.

UNITED STATES OF AMERICA, Indian Territory, }
Central   DISTRICT. }

I, Katie Bench , on oath state that I am 25 years of age and a citizen by marriage , of the Choctaw Nation; that I am the lawful wife of Daniel Bench , who is a citizen, by blood of the Choctaw Nation; that a male child was born to me on 4th day of March , 1903; that said child has been named Edward Daniel Bench , and was living March 4, 1905.

Katie Bench

Witnesses To Mark:
{

Subscribed and sworn to before me this 19th day of April , 1905

Perry M. Clark
Notary Public.

Applications for Enrollment of Choctaw Newborn
Act of 1905   Volume XV

AFFIDAVIT OF ATTENDING PHYSICIAN OR MID-WIFE.

UNITED STATES OF AMERICA, Indian Territory,
Central   DISTRICT.

I,   C.B. Smith   , a   physician   , on oath state that I attended on Mrs.   Katie Bench   , wife of   Daniel Bench   on the 4th day of   March   , 1903; that there was born to her on said date a   male   child; that said child was living March 4, 1905, and is said to have been named   Edward Daniel Bench

C.B. Smith M.D.

Witnesses To Mark:

Subscribed and sworn to before me this   19th day of   April   , 1905

Perry M Clark
Notary Public.

My Commission Expires 2/27/09

BIRTH AFFIDAVIT.

DEPARTMENT OF THE INTERIOR.
COMMISSION TO THE FIVE CIVILIZED TRIBES.

IN RE APPLICATION FOR ENROLLMENT, as a citizen of the   Choctaw   Nation, of Edward Daniel Bench   , born on the 4   day of   March   , 1903

Name of Father: Daniel Bench   Roll 10177   a citizen of the   Choctaw   Nation.
Name of Mother: Katie Bench   Roll ?.W. 974   a citizen of the   Choctaw   Nation.

Postoffice   Boswell, Ind. Ter.

AFFIDAVIT OF MOTHER.

UNITED STATES OF AMERICA, Indian Territory,
Cent   DISTRICT.

I,   Katie Bench   , on oath state that I am   25   years of age and a citizen by marriage   , of the   Choctaw   Nation; that I am the lawful wife of   Daniel Bench, who is a citizen, by blood   of the   Choctaw   Nation; that a   male   child was born to me on   4th   day of   March   , 1903; that said child has been named Edward Daniel Bench   , and was living March 4, 1905.

Katie Bench

Applications for Enrollment of Choctaw Newborn
Act of 1905   Volume XV

Witnesses To Mark:

$\left\{\rule{0pt}{2em}\right.$

    Subscribed and sworn to before me this 10th day of June, 1905

                         Perry M. Clark
                         Notary Public.

AFFIDAVIT OF ATTENDING PHYSICIAN OR MID-WIFE.

UNITED STATES OF AMERICA, Indian Territory,
Cent   DISTRICT.

    I, C.B. Smith, a Physician, on oath state that I attended on Mrs. Katie Bench, wife of Daniel Bench on the 4th day of March, 1903; that there was born to her on said date a male child; that said child was living March 4, 1905, and is said to have been named Edward Daniel Bench

                         C.B. Smith M.D.

Witnesses To Mark:

$\left\{\rule{0pt}{2em}\right.$

    Subscribed and sworn to before me this 10th day of June, 1905

                         Perry M. Clark
                         Notary Public.
        My Com Exp 2/27/09

                                     7-3602.

            Muskogee, Indian Territory, April 24, 1905.

Daniel Bench,
    Boswell, Indian Territory.

Dear Sir:

    Receipt is hereby acknowledged of the affidavits of Katie Bench and C. B. Smith, to the birth of Edward Daniel Bench, child of Daniel and Katie Bench, March 4, 1903, and the same has been filed with our records as an application for the enrollment of said child.

                       Respectfully,

                                    Chairman.

Applications for Enrollment of Choctaw Newborn
Act of 1905   Volume XV

7-NB-1142.

Muskogee, Indian Territory, June 2, 1905.

Daniel Bench,
    Boswell, Indian Territory.

Dear Sir:

There is enclosed you herewith for execution application for the enrollment of your infant child, Edward Daniel Bench.

In the affidavits of February 16, 1905, the date of the applicant's birth is given as March 4, 1904, while in those of April 19, 1905, this date is given as March 4, 1903. In the enclosed application the date of birth is left blank. Please insert the correct date and, when the affidavits are properly executed, return them to this office.

In having these affidavits executed care should be exercised to see that all names are written in full, as they appear in the body of the affidavit, and in the event that either of the persons signing the affidavit are unable to write, signatures by mark must be attested by two witnesses. Each affidavit must be executed before a Notary Public and the notarial seal and signature of the officer must be attached to each separate affidavit.

Respectfully,

VR 2/8.   [sic]

---

7 NB 1142

Muskogee, Indian Territory, June 15, 1905.

Daniel Bench,
    Boswell, Indian Territory.

Dear Sir:

Receipt is hereby acknowledged of the affidavits of Kattie[sic] Bench and C. B. Smith to the birth of Edward Daniel Bench son of Daniel and Katie Bench, March 4, 1903, and the same have been filed in the matter of the enrollment of said child.

Respectfully,

Chairman.

Applications for Enrollment of Choctaw Newborn
Act of 1905   Volume XV

Choc New Born 1143
    Edward Wilson
    (Born Oct. 23, 1902)

BIRTH AFFIDAVIT.

DEPARTMENT OF THE INTERIOR.
COMMISSION TO THE FIVE CIVILIZED TRIBES.

IN RE APPLICATION FOR ENROLLMENT, as a citizen of the Choctaw Nation, of Edward Wilson, born on the 23rd day of October, 1902

Name of Father: William P Wilson   a citizen of the Choctaw Nation.
Name of Mother: Littie Wilson   a citizen of the Choctaw Nation.

Postoffice   **LUKFATA IND TER**

AFFIDAVIT OF MOTHER.

UNITED STATES OF AMERICA, Indian Territory, }
    Central   DISTRICT. }

I, Little Wilson, on oath state that I am 25 years of age and a citizen by Blood, of the Choctaw Nation; that I am the lawful wife of William P Wilson, who is a citizen, by Blood of the Choctaw Nation; that a male child was born to me on 23rd day of October, 1902; that said child has been named Edward Wilson, and was living March 4, 1905.

                                  her
                            Little x Wilson
Witnesses To Mark: mark
  { Jesse Bunch
    W.A. Julian

Subscribed and sworn to before me this 17th day of April, 1905

                          J.W. Costelow
                              Notary Public.

Applications for Enrollment of Choctaw Newborn
Act of 1905   Volume XV

AFFIDAVIT OF ATTENDING PHYSICIAN OR MID-WIFE.

UNITED STATES OF AMERICA, Indian Territory, }
   Central   DISTRICT. }

    I, Soki Apotetubbi, a midwife, on oath state that I attended on Mrs. Littie Wilson, wife of William P Wilson on the 23rd day of October, 1902; that there was born to her on said date a male child; that said child was living March 4, 1905, and is said to have been named Edward Wilson

                                      Soki Apotetubbi

Witnesses To Mark:
  { Jesse Bunch
  { W.A. Julian

    Subscribed and sworn to before me this 17th day of April, 1905

                                      J.W. Costelow
                                            Notary Public.

(The letter below does not belong with the current applicant.)

7-NB-1243

                              Muskogee, Indian Territory, January 4, 1906.

Chief Clerk,
    Choctaw Land Office,
        Atoka, Indian Territory.

Dear Sir:

    You are advised that a red line has this day been drawn through the name of Jesse Thompson No. 1, on Choctaw NB care 1243. The large cancelled stamp has been placed across the face of the card and a notation in red ink placed thereon as follows:

        "Transferred to Chickasaw NB 546."

    You are therefore directed to make like change upon the duplicate Choctaw NB care 1243 in the possession of your office.

                              Respectfully,

                                                   Commissioner.

Applications for Enrollment of Choctaw Newborn
Act of 1905   Volume XV

(The letter below does not belong with the current applicant.)

7-NB-1243

Muskogee, Indian Territory, January 4, 1906.

Chief Clerk,
  Chickasaw Land Office,
    Ardmore, Indian Territory.

Dear Sir:

You are advised that a red line has this day been drawn through the name of Jesse Thompson No. 1, on Choctaw NB care 1243. The large cancelled stamp has been placed across the face of the card and a notation in red ink placed thereon as follows:

"Transferred to Chickasaw NB 546."

You are therefore directed to make like change upon the duplicate Choctaw NB care 1243 in the possession of your office.

Respectfully,

Commissioner.

Choc New Born 1144
  Minnie May Kirby
  (Born Nov. 27, 1903)

NEW-BORN AFFIDAVIT.

Number............

...Choctaw Enrolling Commission...

IN THE MATTER OF THE APPLICATION FOR ENROLLMENT, as a citizen of the Choctaw Nation, of Minnie May Kirby

born on the 27 day of ____Nov____ 190 3

Applications for Enrollment of Choctaw Newborn
Act of 1905   Volume XV

Name of father   Ed Kirby   a citizen of   Choctaw
Nation final enrollment No. 2996
Name of mother   Elizabeth Kirby   a citizen of   Choctaw
Nation final enrollment No. 809

Postoffice   Harris I.T

AFFIDAVIT OF MOTHER.

UNITED STATES OF AMERICA
INDIAN TERRITORY
   Central   DISTRICT

I   Elizabeth Kirby   , on oath state that I am 19 years of age and a citizen by intermarriage of the Choctaw Nation, and as such have been placed upon the final roll of the Choctaw Nation, by the Honorable Secretary of the Interior my final enrollment number being   809 ; that I am the lawful wife of   Ed Kirby   , who is a citizen of the Choctaw Nation, and as such has been placed upon the final roll of said Nation by the Honorable Secretary of the Interior, his final enrollment number being   2996   and that a   female   child was born to me on the   27   day of   Nov   190 3; that said child has been named   Minnie May Kirby   , and is now living.

Lizzie Beth Kirby

Witnesseth.
   Must be two Witnesses who are Citizens.   J B McFarland
   S.E. Morris

Subscribed and sworn to before me this   21   day of   Jan   190 5

W.A. Shoney
Notary Public.

My commission expires:

AFFIDAVIT OF ATTENDING PHYSICIAN OR MIDWIFE

UNITED STATES OF AMERICA
INDIAN TERRITORY
_____DISTRICT

I,   Laura Smith   a   midwife on oath state that I attended on Mrs. Lizzie Kirby   wife of Ed Kirby on the_____day of _____, 190____, that there was born to her on said date a   female   ~~Minnie May Kirby~~   child, that said child is now living, and is said to have been named   Minnie May Kirby   her
                                                              Laura Smith   x
                                                                                    mark

Applications for Enrollment of Choctaw Newborn
Act of 1905 Volume XV

Subscribed and sworn to before me this, the 21 day of Jan 190 5

WITNESSETH:
Must be two witnesses who are citizens

{ J B McFarland
S.E. Morris

W A Shoney   Notary Public.

We hereby certify that we are well acquainted with Laura Smith a midwife and know her to be reputable and of good standing in the community.

J B McFarland _____

S.E. Morris _____

BIRTH AFFIDAVIT.

DEPARTMENT OF THE INTERIOR.
COMMISSION TO THE FIVE CIVILIZED TRIBES.

IN RE APPLICATION FOR ENROLLMENT, as a citizen of the Choctaw Nation, of Minnie May Kirby, born on the 27th day of November, 1903

Name of Father: Ed Kirby   a citizen of the Choctaw Nation.
Name of Mother: Lizzie Kirby   a citizen of the Choctaw Nation.

Postoffice Harris, I.T.

AFFIDAVIT OF MOTHER.

UNITED STATES OF AMERICA, Indian Territory,
Central DISTRICT.

I, Lizzie Kirby, on oath state that I am 17 years of age and a citizen by marriage, of the Choctaw Nation; that I am the lawful wife of Ed Kirby, who is a citizen, by blood of the Choctaw Nation; that a female child was born to me on 27th day of November, 1903; that said child has been named Minnie May Kirby, and was living March 4, 1905.

Lizzie Kirby

Witnesses To Mark:

Applications for Enrollment of Choctaw Newborn
Act of 1905 Volume XV

Subscribed and sworn to before me this 12th day of April , 1905

                                   Wirt Franklin
                                   Notary Public.

AFFIDAVIT OF ATTENDING PHYSICIAN OR MID-WIFE.

UNITED STATES OF AMERICA, Indian Territory, }
   Central   DISTRICT. }

I, Laura Smith , a Midwife , on oath state that I attended on Mrs. Lizzie Kirby , wife of Ed Kirby on the 27th day of November , 1903; that there was born to her on said date a Female child; that said child was living March 4, 1905, and is said to have been named Minnie May Kirby

                                her
                          Laura x Smith
Witnesses To Mark: mark
   { E H Williams
   { B.S. Harris

Subscribed and sworn to before me this 17 day of April , 1905

                                   N.P. Hutchinson
                                   Notary Public.

Choc New Born 1145
      Soloman[sic] McGee
      (Born Feb. 20, 1905)

Birth affidavit.

DEPARTMENT OF THE INTERIOR,
COMMISSION TO THE FIVE CIVILIZED TRIBES.

IN RE APPLICATION FOR ENROLLMENT, as a citizen of the Choctaw Nation, of Solomon McGee , born on the 20th day of February 1905

Name of Father	Jesse McGee	a citizen of Choctaw	Nation
Name of mother	Licksey McGee	a citizen of Choctaw	Nation

                        Postoffice   Eagletown, I.T.

Applications for Enrollment of Choctaw Newborn
Act of 1905   Volume XV

AFFIDAVIT OF MOTHER.

UNITED STATES OF AMERICA, |
INDIAN TERRITORY, | ss.
Central   DISTRICT. |

I, Licksey McGee, on oath state that I am 35 years of age and a citizen by blood of the Choctaw Nation   blood   of the   Choctaw   Nation; that I am lawful wife of Jesse McGee   who   is   a   citizen   by   blood   of   the Choctaw   Nation; that a   Male   child was born to me on   20th day of   February 1905. that said child has been named   Solomon McGee, and was living March 4, 1905.

Licksey McGee

WITNESSES TO MARK:
Battiest Totubbe
  his
Toto x Jackson
  mark

Subscribed and sworn to before me this   14th day of April   1905.

William P. Wilson
Notary Public.

AFFIDAVIT OF ATTENDING PHYSICIAN OR MIDWIFE.

UNITED STATES OF AMERICA, |
INDIAN TERRITORY, | ss.
Central   DISTRICT. |

I, ~~Battiest Totubbe~~ *Joe Ben*, a   Midwife, on oath state that I attended on Mrs. Licksey McGee, wife of   Jesse McGee   on the   20th day of February, 1905 ; that there was born to her on said date a   Male   child; that said child was living March 4, 1905, and is said to have been named   Solomon McGee.

Joe Ben
~~Battiest Totubbe~~

WITNESSES TO MARK:
Battiest Totubbe
  his
Toto x Jackson
  mark

Subscribed and sworn to before me this   14th day of April   1905.

W. P. Wilson
Notary Public.

Applications for Enrollment of Choctaw Newborn
Act of 1905   Volume XV

BIRTH AFFIDAVIT.

DEPARTMENT OF THE INTERIOR.
COMMISSION TO THE FIVE CIVILIZED TRIBES.

IN RE APPLICATION FOR ENROLLMENT, as a citizen of the   Choctaw   Nation, of Solomon McGee   , born on the   20th day of   Feby   , 1905

Name of Father: Jesse McGee   Roll 2970   a citizen of the   Choctaw   Nation.
Name of Mother: Licksey McGee   " 2971   a citizen of the   Choctaw   Nation.

Postoffice   Eagletown, I.T.

AFFIDAVIT OF MOTHER.

UNITED STATES OF AMERICA, Indian Territory, }
Central   DISTRICT.

I,   Licksey McGee   , on oath state that I am   35   years of age and a citizen by   blood   , of the   Choctaw   Nation; that I am the lawful wife of   Jesse McGee   , who is a citizen, by   blood   of the   Choctaw   Nation; that a male   child was born to me on   20th day of   February   , 1905; that said child has been named   Solomon McGee   , and was living March 4, 1905.

                                            her
                              Licksey x McGee
Witnesses To Mark: mark
{ Lenas Wesley
{ Jackson McKinney

Subscribed and sworn to before me this   12th day of   June   , 1905

                                W.P. Wilson
                                    Notary Public.
My commission expires Dec. 1st 1905

AFFIDAVIT OF ATTENDING PHYSICIAN OR MID-WIFE.

UNITED STATES OF AMERICA, Indian Territory, }
Central   DISTRICT.

I,   Joe Bent[sic]   , a   midwife   , on oath state that I attended on Mrs.   Licksey McGee   , wife of   Jesse McGee   on the   20th day of   February   , 1905; that there was born to her on said date a   male   child; that said child was living March 4, 1905, and is said to have been named   Solomon McGee

Applications for Enrollment of Choctaw Newborn
Act of 1905   Volume XV

his
Joe x Ben
mark

Witnesses To Mark:
  { Lenas Wesley
    Jackson McKinney

Subscribed and sworn to before me this 12th day of   June   , 1905

W.P. Wilson
Notary Public.

My commission expires Dec. 1st 1905

7-NB-1145

Muskogee, Indian Territory, August 15, 1905.

Jesse McGee,
    Eagletown, Indian Territory.

Dear Sir:

    Receipt is hereby acknowledged of the affidavits of Licksey McGee and Joe Ben to the birth of Solomon McGee, son of Jesse and Licksey McGee, February 20, 1905, and the same have been filed in the matter of the enrollment of said child.

Respectfully,

Acting Commissioner.

7-NB-1145.

Muskogee, Indian Territory, June 2, 1905.

Jesse McGee,
    Eagletown, Indian Territory.

Dear Sir:

    There is enclosed you herewith for execution application for the enrollment of your infant child, Solomon McGee, born February 20, 1905.

    In the affidavits heretofore filed in this office it appears that the Notary Public, William P. Wilson, signed the affidavit purported to be executed by Licksey McGee, mother, and Joe Ben, the attending midwife. It is also noted that one of the attesting witnesses to these signatures signed his name by mark.

Applications for Enrollment of Choctaw Newborn
Act of 1905   Volume XV

     In having these affidavits executed care should be exercised to see that all names are written in full, as they appear in the body of the affidavit. Persons signing the affidavits who are able to write must sign in their own hand, but in the event that either of them are unable to write, signatures by mark must be attested by two witnesses who can write. Each affidavit must be executed before a Notary Public and the notarial seal and signature of the officer must be attached to each separate affidavit.

                         Respectfully,

VR 2-9.   [sic]

7-NB-1145

                                      Muskogee, Indian Territory, July 25, 1905.

Jesse McGee,
     Eagletown, Indian Territory.

Dear Sir:

     There is returned herewith application, dated June 12, 1905, for the enrollment of Solomon McGee, born February 20, 1905, it is noted that the Notary Public before whom the affidavits were executed signed the names of the mother and midwife. The affidavits can not be accepted in this form.

     The mother and midwife, if they can write, must sign in their own hand, and in the event they can not write, signatures by mark must be attested by two witnesses.

     You are requested to have the affidavits re-executed and forward to this office immediately, as no further action can be taken relative to the enrollment of your said child until these affidavits are, in due form, filed in this office.

                         Respectfully,

LM 25/8   Commissioner.

Choc New Born 1146
        Fostan Tushka
        (Born April 24, 1903)

Applications for Enrollment of Choctaw Newborn
Act of 1905 Volume XV

BIRTH AFFIDAVIT.

DEPARTMENT OF THE INTERIOR.
COMMISSION TO THE FIVE CIVILIZED TRIBES.

IN RE APPLICATION FOR ENROLLMENT, as a citizen of the Choctaw Nation, of Fostan Tushka, born on the 24 day of April, 1903

Name of Father: Levi Tushka a citizen of the Choctaw Nation.
Name of Mother: Eliza Tushka a citizen of the Choctaw Nation.

Postoffice **LUKFATA IND TER**

AFFIDAVIT OF MOTHER.

UNITED STATES OF AMERICA, Indian Territory, }
Central DISTRICT. }

I, Eliza Tushka, on oath state that I am 24 years of age and a citizen by Blood, of the Choctaw Nation; that I am the lawful wife of Levi Tushka, who is a citizen, by Blood of the Choctaw Nation; that a Male child was born to me on 24th day of April, 1903; that said child has been named Fostan Tushka, and was living March 4, 1905.

            her
            Eliza x Tushka
Witnesses To Mark: mark
  { H.L. Stiff
  { W.A. Julian

Subscribed and sworn to before me this 18th day of April, 1905

            J.W. Costelow
            Notary Public.

AFFIDAVIT OF ATTENDING PHYSICIAN OR MID-WIFE.

UNITED STATES OF AMERICA, Indian Territory, }
Central DISTRICT. }

I, Lina Tamka, a Midwife, on oath state that I attended on Mrs. Eliza Tushka, wife of Levi Tushka on the 24th day of April, 1903; that there was born to her on said date a Male child; that said child was living March 4, 1905, and is said to have been named Fostan Tushka

            her
            Lina x Tamka
            mark

Applications for Enrollment of Choctaw Newborn
Act of 1905 Volume XV

Witnesses To Mark:
{ H.L. Stiff
{ W.A. Julian

Subscribed and sworn to before me this 18th day of April , 1905

J.W. Costelow
Notary Public.

NEW-BORN AFFIDAVIT.

Number..............

Choctaw Enrolling Commission.

IN THE MATTER OF THE APPLICATION FOR ENROLLMENT, as a citizen of the Choctaw Nation, of Foston[sic] Tushka

born on the 24 day of April 190 3

Name of father   Levi Tushka   a citizen of   Choctaw
Nation final enrollment No   2649
Name of mother   Laisa[sic] Tushka   a citizen of   Choctaw
Nation final enrollment No   1432

Postoffice   Eagletown Ind Ter

AFFIDAVIT OF MOTHER.

UNITED STATES OF AMERICA,
  INDIAN TERRITORY,
  Central   DISTRICT

I   Laisa Tushka   on oath state that I am 24 years of age and a citizen by Blood of the Choctaw Nation, and as such have been placed upon the final roll of the Choctaw Nation, by the Honorable Secretary of the Interior my final enrollment number being 1432 ; that I am the lawful wife of Levi Tushka , who is a citizen of the Choctaw Nation, and as such has been placed upon the final roll of said Nation by the Honorable Secretary of the Interior, his final enrollment number being 2649 and that a Male child was born to me on the 24th day of April 190 3 ; that said child has been named Foston Tushka , and is now living.   her
                                                                                                   Laise x Tushka
WITNESSETH: mark

  Must be two   } (Name Illegible)
  Witnesses who }
  are Citizens.   (Name Illegible)

Applications for Enrollment of Choctaw Newborn
Act of 1905   Volume XV

Subscribed and sworn to before me this   21   day of   January   190 5

Jeff Gardner
Notary Public.

My commission expires   23rd Dec 1905

Affidavit of Attending Physician or Midwife

UNITED STATES OF AMERICA,
   INDIAN TERRITORY,
Central   DISTRICT

I, Lina Tonehka   a   Midwife on oath state that I attended on Mrs. Laise Tushka   wife of Levi Tushka on the 24th   day of April, 190 3, that there was born to her on said date a   male   child, that said child is now living, and is said to have been named   Foston[sic] Tushka

Lina x Tonehka   *Midwife*

Subscribed and sworn to before me this the   21   day of   January   1905

My commission   Jeff Gardner
expires 23rd Dec 1905   Notary Public.

WITNESSETH:

Must be two witnesses who are citizens and know the child. { *(Name Illegible)* / *(Name Illegible)* }

We hereby certify that we are well acquainted with   Lina Tonehka   a   midwife   and know   her   to be reputable and of good standing in the community.

Must be two citizen witnesses. { *(Name Illegible)* / *(Name Illegible)* }

Choc New Born 1147
   Elliston Apotatubbi[sic]
   (Born Feb. 8, 1904)

Applications for Enrollment of Choctaw Newborn
Act of 1905 Volume XV

BIRTH AFFIDAVIT.

DEPARTMENT OF THE INTERIOR,
COMMISSION TO THE FIVE CIVILIZED TRIBES.

IN RE *Application for Enrollment,* as a citizen of the Choctaw Nation, of Elliston Apototubbi, born on the 8th day of February, 1904

Name of Father: Greeks Apototubbi   a citizen of the Choctaw Nation.
Name of Mother: Eliza Apototubbi   a citizen of the Choctaw Nation.

Post-Office: Lukfata, Ind. Ter.

AFFIDAVIT OF MOTHER.

UNITED STATES OF AMERICA, }
   INDIAN TERRITORY.
   Central District.

I, Eliza Apototubbi (Anderson), on oath state that I am 27 years of age and a citizen by blood, of the Choctaw Nation; that I am the lawful wife of Greeks Apototubbe, who is a citizen, by Blood of the Choctaw Nation; that a male child was born to me on 8th day of February, 1904, that said child has been named Elliston Apototubbi, and is now living.

                        her
                Eliza x Apototubbi (Anderson)
WITNESSES TO MARK: mark
   { Anderson Gardner
     Billy Boling

Subscribed and sworn to before me this 9th *day of* June, 1905.

                        W.P. Wilson
                          NOTARY PUBLIC.

AFFIDAVIT OF ATTENDING PHYSICIAN OR MID-WIFE.

UNITED STATES OF AMERICA, }
   INDIAN TERRITORY.
   Central District.

I, Louisa Anderson, a midwife, on oath state that I attended on Mrs. Eliza Apototubbi, wife of Greeks Apototubbi on the 8th day of

Applications for Enrollment of Choctaw Newborn
Act of 1905   Volume XV

February   , 1904 ; that there was born to her on said date a   male   child; that said child is now living and is said to have been named   Elliston Apototubbi

her
Louisa x Anderson
mark

WITNESSES TO MARK:
{ Anderson Gardner
  Billy Boling

Subscribed and sworn to before me this   9th *day of*   June   , 1905.

W.P. Wilson
NOTARY PUBLIC.
My commission expires Dec. 1st 1905

Birth Affidavit.

DEPARTMENT OF THE INTERIOR,
COMMISSION TO THE FIVE CIVILIZED TRIBES.

IN RE APPLICATION FOR ENROLLMENT, as a citizen of the   Choctaw   Nation, of   Elliston Apototubbi   , born on the   8th day of   February 1904

Name of Father: Greeks Apototubbi   a citizen of the   Choctaw   Nation.
Name of Mother: Eliza Anderson   a citizen of the   Choctaw   Nation.

Post Office   Lukfata, I.T.

AFFIDAVIT OF MOTHER.

United States of America, |
Indian Territory, | ss.
Central   District. |

I,   Eliza Anderson   , on oath state that I am   27   years of age and a citizen by blood of the Choctaw Nation   Blood   , of the   Choctaw   Nation; that I am lawful wife of   Greeks Apototubbi   , who is a citizen, by   Blood   of the   Choctaw   Nation; that a   Male   child was born to me on   8th day of   Feby 1904 that said child has been named   Elliston Apototubbi   , and was living March 4, 1905.

Eliza Anderson

Witness to Mark:
    Louis Anderson
    Lenas Wesley

Applications for Enrollment of Choctaw Newborn
Act of 1905   Volume XV

Subscribed and sworn to before me this 17th day of April   1905.

                    W.P. Wilson
                    NOTARY PUBLIC.

AFFIDAVIT OF ATTENDING PHYSICIAN OR MIDWIFE.

United States of America, |
Indian Territory, | ss.
Central   District. |

    I,   Louisa Anderson   , a   midwife   , on oath state that I attended on Mrs.   Eliza ~~Anderson~~ *Apotulli*[sic], wife of   Greeks Apototubbi   on the 8th day of   February   1904   that there was born to her on said date a   male   child; that said child was living March 4, 1905, and is said to have been named   Elliston Apototubbi

                    Louisa Anderson

WITNESES[sic] TO MARK:
Louis Anderson
Lenas Wesley

Subscribed and sworn to before me this   17th day of   April   1905.

                    W.P. Wilson
                    NOTARY PUBLIC.

        Sub   7-NB-1147.

            Muskogee, Indian Territory, June 5, 1905.

Greeks Apototubbi,
    Lukfata, Indian Territory.

Dear Sir:

    There is enclosed you herewith for execution application for the enrollment of your infant child, Elliston Apototubbi, born February 8, 1904.

    It appears from the affidavits heretofore filed in this office that W. P. Wilson, the Notary Public before whom they were executed, signed the names of Eliza Anderson, the mother, Louisa Anderson, the midwife, and Lenas Wesley, one of the attesting witnesses. It will, therefore, be necessary that this application be re-executed.

Applications for Enrollment of Choctaw Newborn
Act of 1905   Volume XV

In having these affidavits executed care should be exercised to see that all names are written in full, as they appear in the body of the affidavit, and in the event that either of the persons signing the affidavit are unable to write, signatures by mark must be attested by two witnesses. Each affidavit must be executed before a Notary Public and the notarial seal and signature of the officer must be attached to each separate affidavit.

Respectfully,

VR 3-10.   [sic]

---

7 NB 1147

Muskogee, Indian Territory, June 14, 1905.

Greeks Apototubbi,
    Lukfata, Indian Territory.

Dear Sir:

    Receipt is hereby acknowledged of the affidavits of Eliza Apototubbi (Anderson) and Louisa Anderson to the birth of Ellison[sic] Apototubbi, son of Greeks and Eliza Apototubbi, February 8, 1904, and the same have been filed in the matter of the enrollment of said child.

Respectfully,

Chairman.

7-NB-1147

Muskogee, Indian Territory, July 25, 1905.

Greeks Apototubbi,
    Lukfata, Indian Territory.

Dear Sir:

    Referring to the application heretofore made to the Commission to the Five Civilized Tribes for the enrollment of your infant child Elliston Apototubbi, born February 8, 1904, it is noted that in the affidavit of the mother, it is alleged that you are a citizen by blood of the Choctaw Nation.

    If this is correct, you are requested to state when, where and under what name you were listed for enrollment, the names of your parents and other members of your family for whom application was made at the same time, and if you have selected an allotment, please give your roll number as it appears upon your allotment certificate.

Applications for Enrollment of Choctaw Newborn
Act of 1905   Volume XV

You are requested to give this matter your immediate attention as no further action can be taken relative to the enrollment of your said child until the evidence requested is supplied.

Respectfully,

Commissioner.

7-NB-1147

Muskogee, Indian Territory, September 30, 1905.

Eliza Anderson (or Apototubi[sic]),
   Lukfata, Indian Territory.

Dear Madam:

Receipt is hereby acknowledged of your letter of the 20th instant giving further information relative to the name under which you are finally enrolled, which information is furnished in the matter of the enrollment of your minor son Elliston Apototubi as a citizen by blood of the Choctaw Nation.

You are advised that the name of said child has been placed upon a partial roll of new born citizens by blood of the Choctaw Nation, which schedule was forwarded the Honorable Secretary of the Interior for approval on August 26, 1905. As soon as the enrollment of said child is approved you will be duly notified.

Respectfully,

Commissioner.

Choc New Born 1148
   Rhoda Wesley
   (Born June 14, 1904)

Applications for Enrollment of Choctaw Newborn
Act of 1905   Volume XV

Birth Affidavit.

DEPARTMENT OF THE INTERIOR,
COMMISSION TO THE FIVE CIVILIZED TRIBES.

IN RE APPLICATION FOR ENROLLMENT, as a citizen of the Choctaw Nation, of Rhoda Wesley , born on the 14th day of June   1904

Name of Father: Lenas Wesley   a citizen of the Choctaw Nation.
Name of Mother: Salean Wesley   a citizen of the Choctaw Nation.

Post Office   Lukfata, I.T.

AFFIDAVIT OF MOTHER.

United States of America, |
Indian Territory, | ss.
Central   District. |

I, Salean Wesley , on oath state that I am 24 years of age and a citizen by Blood of the Choctaw Nation Blood , of the Choctaw Nation; that I am lawful wife of Lenas Wesley , who is a citizen, by Blood of the Choctaw Nation; that a Female child was born to me on 14th day of June   1904 that said child has been named Rhoda Wesley , and was living March 4, 1905.

Salean Wesley

WITNESSES TO MARK:
  Lenas Wesley
  Tom Wilson

Subscribed and sworn to before me this 17 day of April   1905.

W.P. Wilson
Notary Public.

AFFIDAVIT OF ATTENDING PHYSICIAN OR MIDWIFE.

United States of America, |
Indian Territory, | ss.
Central   District. |

I,   Louisa Ben   , a   midwife   , on oath state that I attended on Mrs. Salean Wesley , wife of Lenas Wesley on the 14th day of June 1904 that there was born to her on said date a Female   child; that said child was living March 4, 1905, and is said to have been named Rhoda Wesley

Applications for Enrollment of Choctaw Newborn
Act of 1905 Volume XV

Louisa Ben

WITNESSES TO MARK:
Lenas Wesley
Tom Wilson

Subscribed and sworn to before me this 17 day of April 1905.

W.P. Wilson
Notary Public.

BIRTH AFFIDAVIT.

DEPARTMENT OF THE INTERIOR.
COMMISSION TO THE FIVE CIVILIZED TRIBES.

IN RE APPLICATION FOR ENROLLMENT, as a citizen of the Choctaw Nation, of Rhoda Wesley, born on the 14 day of June, 1904.

Name of Father: Lenas Wesley Roll 3400 a citizen of the Choctaw Nation.
Name of Mother: Salean Wesley nee Tonchka a citizen of the Choctaw Nation.
Roll 7393

Postoffice Lukfata I.T.

AFFIDAVIT OF MOTHER.

UNITED STATES OF AMERICA, Indian Territory,
Central DISTRICT.

I, Salean Wesley, nee Tonchka, on oath state that I am 24 years of age and a citizen by blood, of the Choctaw Nation; that I am the lawful wife of Lenas Wesley, who is a citizen, by blood of the Choctaw Nation; that a female child was born to me on 14th day of June, 1904; that said child has been named Rhoda Wesley, and was living March 4, 1905.

her
Salean x Wesley
mark

Witnesses To Mark:
Barnett Wade
Anderson Gardner

Subscribed and sworn to before me this 17th day of June, 1905

W. P. Wilson
Notary Public.
My commission expires Dec. 1st 1905

Applications for Enrollment of Choctaw Newborn
Act of 1905   Volume XV

AFFIDAVIT OF ATTENDING PHYSICIAN OR MID-WIFE.

UNITED STATES OF AMERICA, Indian Territory, }
Central   DISTRICT.

I, Louisa Ben, a Midwife, on oath state that I attended on Mrs. Salean Wesley, wife of Lenas Wesley on the 14th day of June, 1904; that there was born to her on said date a female child; that said child was living March 4, 1905, and is said to have been named Rhoda Wesley

her
Louisa x Ben
mark

Witnesses To Mark:
{ Barnett Wade
{ Anderson Gardner

Subscribed and sworn to before me this 17th day of June, 1905

W. P. Wilson
Notary Public.
My commission expires Dec. 1st 1905

7-897.

Muskogee, Indian Territory, April 24, 1905.

Lenas Wesley,
    Lukfata, Indian Territory.

Dear Sir:

    Receipt is hereby acknowledged of the affidavits of Salean Wesley and Louisa Ben, to the birth of Rhoda Wesley, child of Lenas and Salean Wesley, June 14, 1904, and the same have been filed with our records as an application for the enrollment of said child.

                  Respectfully,

                                      Chairman.

Applications for Enrollment of Choctaw Newborn
Act of 1905   Volume XV

7-NB-1148.

Muskogee, Indian Territory, June 2, 1905.

Lenas Wesley,
    Lukfata, Indian Territory.

Dear Sir:

    There is enclosed you herewith for execution application for the enrollment of your infant child, Rhoda Wesley, born June 14, 1904.

    In the application heretofore filed in this office it appears that the Notary Public, W. P. Wilson, before whom the affidavits were executed, signed the names of Salean Wesley, the mother, Louisa Ben, the attending midwife, and Lenas Wesley, on[sic] of the attesting witnesses. It will, therefore, be necessary that the enclosed application be re-executed.

    In having these affidavits executed care should be exercised to see that all names are written in full, as they appear in the body of the affidavit, and in the event that either of the persons signing the affidavit are unable to write, signatures by mark must be attested by two witnesses. Each affidavit must be executed before a Notary Public and the notarial seal and signature of the officer must be attached to each separate affidavit.

                      Respectfully,

VR 2-10.   Commissioner in Charge.

---

7 NB 1148

Muskogee, Indian Territory, June 22, 1905.

Lenas Wesley,
    Lukfata, Indian Territory.

Dear Sir:-

    Receipt is hereby acknowledged of the affidavits of Salean Wesley and Louisa Ben to the birth of Rhoda Wesley, daughter of Lenas and Salean Wesley, June 14, 1904, and the same have been filed with our records in the matter of the enrollment of said child.

                      Respectfully,

                                                Chairman.

Applications for Enrollment of Choctaw Newborn
Act of 1905   Volume XV

7-NB-1148

Muskogee, Indian Territory, July 26, 1905.

Lenas Wesley,
    Lukfata, Indian Territory.

Dear Sir:

    There is returned to you herewith the affidavits of Salean Wesley, the mother, and Louisa Ben, midwife, executed June 17, 1905, before W. P. Wilson, Notary Public, forwarded to this office in compliance to a communication addressed to you by the Commission to the Five Civilized Tribes under date of June 2, 1905, it appears that W. P. Wilson the Notary before whom this application was executed, signed the name[sic] of the mother and midwife to the said affidavits.

    The affidavits can not be accepted in this form; the mother and midwife, if they can write, must sign in their own hand, in the event they can not write, signatures by mark must be attested by two witnesses.

    You are requested to give this matter your attention, have the affidavits re-executed in conformity with instructions herein and return to this office as early as possible, as no further action can be taken relative to the enrollment of the applicant until the affidavits in due form are filed in this office.

    Respectfully,

LM 26/1

Commissioner.

7-NB-1148

Muskogee, Indian Territory, August 10, 1905.

Lenas Wesley,
    Lukfata, Indian Territory.

Dear Sir:

    Receipt is hereby acknowledged of the affidavits of Salean Wesley and Louisa Ben to the birth of Rhoda Wesley daughter of Lenas Wesley and Salean Wesley nee Tomhka, June 14, 1904, and the same have been filed with the records of this office in the matter of the enrollment of said child.

    Respectfully,

Acting Commissioner.

Applications for Enrollment of Choctaw Newborn
Act of 1905 Volume XV

Choc New Born 1149
    Donald Oakes
    (Born July 20, 1904)

BIRTH AFFIDAVIT.

DEPARTMENT OF THE INTERIOR.
COMMISSION TO THE FIVE CIVILIZED TRIBES.

IN RE APPLICATION FOR ENROLLMENT, as a citizen of the   Choctaw   Nation, of Donald Oakes   , born on the 20th day of July, 1904

Name of Father: George W. Oakes   a citizen of the Choctaw Nation.
Name of Mother: Rosa E. Oakes   a citizen of the Choctaw Nation.

    Postoffice   Hamden, Ind. Ter.

AFFIDAVIT OF MOTHER.

UNITED STATES OF AMERICA, Indian Territory,
Central   DISTRICT.

    I, Rosa E. Oakes, on oath state that I am 25 years of age and a citizen by marriage, of the Choctaw Nation; that I am the lawful wife of George W. Oakes, who is a citizen, by blood of the Choctaw Nation; that a male child was born to me on 20th day of July, 1904; that said child has been named Donald Oakes, and was living March 4, 1905.

                            Rosa E Oakes
Witnesses To Mark:
{

    Subscribed and sworn to before me this 17th day of April, 1905

                            Wirt Franklin
                            Notary Public.

AFFIDAVIT OF ATTENDING PHYSICIAN OR MID-WIFE.

UNITED STATES OF AMERICA, Indian Territory,
Central   DISTRICT.

    I, J D Brown, a physician, on oath state that I attended on Mrs. Rosa E Oakes, wife of George W. Oakes on the 20th day of July,

Applications for Enrollment of Choctaw Newborn
Act of 1905   Volume XV

1904; that there was born to her on said date a   male   child; that said child was living March 4, 1905, and is said to have been named   Donald Oakes

J.D. Brown, M.D.

Witnesses To Mark:
{

Subscribed and sworn to before me this 18th   day of   April   , 1905

JB Moreland
Notary Public.
Com Exp Oct 21-1905

~~7-1590.~~

Muskogee, Indian Territory, April 24, 1905.

George W. Oakes,
Hamden, Indian Territory.

Dear Sir:

Receipt is hereby acknowledged of the affidavits of Rosa E. Oakes and J. D. Brown to the birth of Donald Oakes, child of George W. and Rosa E. Oakes, July 20, 1904, and the same have been filed with our records as an application for the enrollment of said child.

Respectfully,

Chairman.

Choc New Born 1150
    Gilbert N. Wall
    (Born Jan. 28, 1905)

Applications for Enrollment of Choctaw Newborn
Act of 1905   Volume XV

BIRTH AFFIDAVIT.

DEPARTMENT OF THE INTERIOR.
COMMISSION TO THE FIVE CIVILIZED TRIBES.

IN RE APPLICATION FOR ENROLLMENT, as a citizen of the   Choctaw   Nation, of Gilbert N. Wall   , born on the 28   day of Jan , 1905

Name of Father: Chris Wall   a citizen of the   Choctaw   Nation.
Name of Mother: Delila Wall   a citizen of the   Choctaw   Nation.

Postoffice   Roff, Ind. Ter.

AFFIDAVIT OF MOTHER.

UNITED STATES OF AMERICA, Indian Territory, }
    Southern   DISTRICT.

I,   Delila Wall   , on oath state that I am 36 years of age and a citizen by blood , of the   Choctaw   Nation; that I am the lawful wife of   Chris Wall , who is a citizen, by   intermarriage   of the   Choctaw   Nation; that a   male   child was born to me on   28   day of   January   , 1905, that said child has been named   Gilbert N. Wall   , and ~~is now~~ *was* living. *March 4ᵗʰ 1905*

Delila Wall

Witnesses To Mark:
{

Subscribed and sworn to before me this 20   day of April   , 1905.

My Commission Expires Jan. 30, 1907.   J.C. Little
                                              Notary Public.

AFFIDAVIT OF ATTENDING PHYSICIAN OR MID-WIFE.

UNITED STATES OF AMERICA, Indian Territory, }
    Southern   DISTRICT.

I,   Sarah J Hammack   , a   mid-wife   , on oath state that I attended on Mrs. Delila Wall   , wife of Chris Wall   on the 28   day of January , 1905; that there was born to her on said date a   male   child; that said child is now living and is said to have been named   Gilbert N Wall

                                    her
                        Sarah J x Hammack
                                    mark

Applications for Enrollment of Choctaw Newborn
Act of 1905 Volume XV

Witnesses To Mark:
{ J D Moon
{ Tomay Dodd

Subscribed and sworn to before me this 20 day of April , 1905.

My Commission Expires Jan. 30, 1907.   J.C. Little
                                         Notary Public.

7-5573.

Muskogee, Indian Territory, April 24, 1905.

Chris Wall,
    Roff, Indian Territory.

Dear Sir:

Receipt is hereby acknowledged of the affidavits of Delila Wall and Sarah J. Hammack, to the birth of Gilbert N. Wall, child of Chris and Delila Wall, January 28, 1905, and the same has been filed with our records as an application for the enrollment of said child.

Respectfully,

Chairman.

Choc New Born 1151
    Lottie May Vice
    (Born April 30, 1904)

BIRTH AFFIDAVIT.

DEPARTMENT OF THE INTERIOR.
COMMISSION TO THE FIVE CIVILIZED TRIBES.

IN RE APPLICATION FOR ENROLLMENT, as a citizen of the   Choctaw   Nation, of
Lottie May Vice   , born on the 30 day of April , 1904

Name of Father: Robert Vice   a citizen of the Choctaw   Nation.
Name of Mother: May Vice   a citizen of the Choctaw   Nation.

Applications for Enrollment of Choctaw Newborn
Act of 1905   Volume XV

Postoffice   Folsom I T

AFFIDAVIT OF MOTHER.

UNITED STATES OF AMERICA, Indian Territory, }
Central   DISTRICT.

I, May Vice, on oath state that I am 19 years of age and a citizen by Blood, of the Choctaw Nation; that I am the lawful wife of Robert Vice, who is a citizen, by Blood of the Choctaw Nation; that a Female child was born to me on 30 day of April, 1904; that said child has been named Lottie May Vice, and was living March 4, 1905.

May Vice

Witnesses To Mark:
{

Subscribed and sworn to before me this 8 day of April, 1905

J.G. Reeder
Notary Public.

AFFIDAVIT OF ATTENDING PHYSICIAN OR MID-WIFE.

UNITED STATES OF AMERICA, Indian Territory, }
Central   DISTRICT.

I, W.W. Sames, a physician, on oath state that I attended on Mrs. May Vice, wife of ———— on the 30th day of April, 1904; that there was born to her on said date a female child; ~~that said child was living March 4, 1905, and is said to have been named~~

W.W. Sames

Witnesses To Mark:
{

Subscribed and sworn to before me this 1st day of April, 1905

Wm J Hulsey
Notary Public.

Applications for Enrollment of Choctaw Newborn
Act of 1905   Volume XV

BIRTH AFFIDAVIT.

DEPARTMENT OF THE INTERIOR.
COMMISSION TO THE FIVE CIVILIZED TRIBES.

IN RE APPLICATION FOR ENROLLMENT, as a citizen of the Choctaw Nation, of Lottie May Vice, born on the 30ᵗʰ day of April, 1904

Name of Father: Robert Vice   Roll 11675   a citizen of the Choctaw Nation.
Name of Mother: May Vice   " 14389   a citizen of the Choctaw Nation.
            (Illegible)
                    Postoffice   Folsom Ind Ter

AFFIDAVIT OF MOTHER.

UNITED STATES OF AMERICA, Indian Territory,
Central   DISTRICT.

I, May Vice, on oath state that I am 19 years of age and a citizen by blood, of the Choctaw Nation; that I am the lawful wife of Robert Vice, who is a citizen, by blood of the Choctaw Nation; that a female child was born to me on 30 day of April, 1904; that said child has been named Lottie May Vice, and was living March 4, 1905.

                    May Vice
Witnesses To Mark:

    Subscribed and sworn to before me this 23 day of August, 1905

                    J.G. Reeder
                        Notary Public.

AFFIDAVIT OF ATTENDING PHYSICIAN OR MID-WIFE.

UNITED STATES OF AMERICA, Indian Territory,
Central   DISTRICT.

                    are acquainted with
~~We   W. T. Askew and~~, a ...., on oath state that *we* ~~attended on Mrs.   May Vice, wife of Robert Vice on or about~~ the 30ᵗ day of April ~~, 1904; that there was born to her on said date a   female~~ child; that said child was living March 4, 1905, and is said to have been named Lottie May Vice

                    W T Askew

Applications for Enrollment of Choctaw Newborn
Act of 1905   Volume XV

Witnesses To Mark:

{ ....
{ ....

Subscribed and sworn to before me this ...... day of ...., 1905.

....
Notary Public.

(The affidavit below typed as given.)

Folsom IT
Sep 7 1905

This is to certify that we knew Robert Vice and May Krebbs before they were married knew them afterward we know there was a girl child born to them about the last of April 1904 they were not in this community at the time the child was born but come in hear soon after and are hear now the child has been named Lottie May Vice and is still living at this time

W T Askew
Bettie Askew

Subscribed and sworn to W T Askew and Bettie Askew this the 7 day of September AD 1905

J.G. Reeder
Notary Public

Childhood of Tom Davison

United States of America ⎫
Indian Territory   ⎬
   Central Jud Dist   ⎭

I, Tom Davison on oath state that I know personally Robert Vice an May Vice that there was born to them on April 30, 1904 a female child that said child is still living and is said to have been named Lottie May Vice Robert Vice and May Vice are Choctaw citizens by blood   Tom Davison

Subscribed and sworn to before me this 10 day of June 1905
Choctaw IT   JG Reeder Notary Pub
Central Dist   Notary Public

Affidavit of Beatrice Davison
I Beatrice Davison on oath state that I am personally acquainted with Robert Vice and may Vice. That there was born unto them a female child on April 30-1904 that said child is now living and is said to have been named Lottie May Vice
Robert Vice and May Vice are Choctaw citizens by blood

Applications for Enrollment of Choctaw Newborn
Act of 1905 Volume XV

JB Davison

J.G. Reeder
Notary Public

7-4159

Muskogee, Indian Territory, April 13, 1905.

Robert Vice,
Fulsom, Indian Territory.

Dear Sir:

Receipt is hereby acknowledged of the affidavits of May Vice and W. W. Sames to the birth of Lottie May Vice, daughter of Robert and May Vice, April 30, 1904.

It is stated in the affidavit of the mother that she is a citizen by blood of the Choctaw Nation. If this is correct you are requested to state the name under which she was enrolled, the names of her parents, and if she has selected an allotment of the lands of the Choctaw and Chickasaw Nations please give her roll number as it appears upon her allotment certificate.

Respectfully,

Commissioner in Charge.

7-NB-1151.

Muskogee, Indian Territory, June 3, 1905.

Robert Vice,
Folsom, Indian Territory.

Dear Sir:

Referring to the application for the enrollment of your infant child, Lottie May Vice, born April 30, 1904, it is noted that the physician failed to state that the applicant was living on March 4, 1905, and also failed to give her name.

In the event that he is unable to make affidavit to these facts it will be necessary that you secure the affidavits of two persons, who are disinterested and not related to the applicant, who have actual knowledge of the facts that the child was born, the date of her birth; that she was living on March 4, 1905, and that May Vice is her mother.

Respectfully,

Chairman.

Applications for Enrollment of Choctaw Newborn
Act of 1905   Volume XV

7 NB 1151

Muskogee, Indian Territory, June 16, 1905.

Robert Vice,
    Fulsom, Indian Territory.

Dear Sir:

    Receipt is hereby acknowledged of the affidavits of Tom Davison and Beatrice Davison to the birth of Lottie May Vice and the same are returned you herewith for the reason that the Notary Public before whom the affidavit of Beatrice Davison was executed has neglected to affix his jurat thereto. You are requested to have this jurat supplied and return the affidavit to this office as early as practicable.

Respectfully,

Chairman.

EB 1-16

---

7 NB 1151

Muskogee, Indian Territory, June 23, 1905.

Robert Vice,
    Fulsom, Indian Territory.

Dear Sir:

    Receipt is hereby acknowledged of the joint affidavit of Tom Davison and J. G. Reeder to the birth of Lottie May Vice, daughter of Robert and May Vice, April 30, 1904, and the same has been filed with our records in the matter of the enrollment of said child.

Respectfully,

Chairman,

Applications for Enrollment of Choctaw Newborn
Act of 1905   Volume XV

7-NB-1151

Muskogee, Indian Territory, August 4, 1905.

Robert Vice,
    Folsom, Indian Territory.

Dear Sir:

    There is inclosed you herewith for execution application for the enrollment of your infant child, Lottie May Vice, born April 30, 1904.

    In the affidavits heretofore filed in this case, it is noted that the Notary has failed to affix his notarial seal to the affidavit of the mother executed April 8, 1905; the Notary also failed to affix his official jurat to the affidavit of Tom Davison and J. B. Davison, executed June 10, 1905.

    In having the same executed, care should be exercised to see that all names written in full and in the event that either of the persons sign by mark, signatures must be attested by two witnesses, and the Notary Public before whom the affidavits are executed, must affix his notarial seal to each separate affidavit.

    This matter should receive your immediate attention as no further action can be taken relative to the enrollment of your said child until the evidence requested is supplied.

                        Respectfully,

LM 3/4   Commissioner.

7-NB-1151

Muskogee, Indian Territory, September 11, 1905.

Robert Vice,
    Folsom, Indian Territory.

Dear Sir:

    Receipt is hereby acknowledged of the affidavit of May Vice, the mother, and the joint affidavit of W. T. Askew and Bettie Askew, to the birth of your infant child, Lottie May Vice, born April 30, 1904, offered in support of the application for the enrollment of said child as a citizen by blood of the Choctaw Nation. The affidavits have been filed with the record in the matter of the enrollment of said child. this case.

                        Respectfully,

                                            Acting Commissioner.

Applications for Enrollment of Choctaw Newborn
Act of 1905   Volume XV

Choctaw N B
1151

Muskogee, Indian Territory, October 4, 1905.

May Vice,
    Allen, Indian Territory.

Dear Madam:

    Receipt is hereby acknowledged of your letter of September 27, asking if your baby has been enrolled. You also desire information relative to the sale of your land.

    In reply to your letter you are advised that the name of your child, Lottie May Vice, has not yet been placed upon a schedule of citizens by blood of the Choctaw Nation prepared for forwarding to the Secretary of the Interior, but you will be notified when her enrollment is approved.

    Replying to that portion of your letter in regard to the sale of your lands you are advised that this is a matter which is not within the jurisdiction of this office, and it is impracticable to give you any information on this subject.

                        Respectfully,

                                Commissioner.

7-NB-1151

Muskogee, Indian Territory, February 3, 1906.

May Vice,
    Folsom, Indian Territory.

Dear Madam:

    Your letter of January 15, 1906, addressed to the Secretary of the Interior has been by him referred to this office for consideration and appropriate action. Therein you ask the status of the enrollment of your child Lottie May Vice.

    In reply to your letter you are advised that the name of this child has been placed upon a schedule of new born citizens of the Choctaw Nation which has been forwarded the Secretary of the Interior and you will be advised when her enrollment is approved by the Department.

Applications for Enrollment of Choctaw Newborn
Act of 1905   Volume XV

Respectfully,

Acting Commissioner.

7-NB-1151

Muskogee, Indian Territory, April 30, 1906.

May Vice,
    Folsom, Indian Territory.

Dear Madam:

Your letter of March 25, 1906, addressed to the Secretary of the Interior has been by him referred to this office for consideration and appropriate action. Therein you ask regarding the enrollment of your child Lottie May Vice.

In reply to your letter you are advised that on March 14, 1906, the Secretary of the Interior approved the enrollment of your child Lottie May Vice as a new born citizen of the Choctaw Nation and selection of allotment may now be made in her behalf in accordance with the rules and regulations governing the selection of allotments and the designation of homesteads in the Choctaw and Chickasaw Nations.

Respectfully,

Commissioner.

Choc New Born 1152
    Edmond Krebbs
    (Born Jan. 27, 1905)

BIRTH AFFIDAVIT.
DEPARTMENT OF THE INTERIOR.
COMMISSION TO THE FIVE CIVILIZED TRIBES.

IN RE APPLICATION FOR ENROLLMENT, as a citizen of the Choctaw Nation, of Edmond Krebbs, born on the 27 day of Jan, 1905

Name of Father: John W. Krebbs   a citizen of the Choctaw Nation.
Name of Mother: Provi Lee Krebbs   a citizen of the .... Nation.

Applications for Enrollment of Choctaw Newborn
Act of 1905   Volume XV

Postoffice   Folsom, I.T.

AFFIDAVIT OF MOTHER.

UNITED STATES OF AMERICA, Indian Territory, }
Western   DISTRICT.

I, Provi Lee Krebbs, on oath state that I am 21 years of age and a citizen by .... of the .... Nation; that I am the lawful wife of John W Krebbs, who is a citizen, by blood of the Choctaw Nation; that a male child was born to me on 27 day of Jan., 1905; that said child has been named Edmond Krebbs, and was living March 4, 1905.

                                        her
                              Provi x Lee Krebbs
Witnesses To Mark: mark
  { JW Campbell
    Pat E Trent

Subscribed and sworn to before me this 25th day of April, 1905

                            J.B. Campbell
                                Notary Public.

AFFIDAVIT OF ATTENDING PHYSICIAN OR MID-WIFE.

UNITED STATES OF AMERICA, Indian Territory, }
Western   DISTRICT.

I, Mollie Farmer, a midwife, on oath state that I attended on Mrs. Provi Lee Krebbs, wife of John W Krebbs on the 27 day of Jan, 1905; that there was born to her on said date a male child; that said child was living March 4, 1905, and is said to have been named Edmond Krebbs

                                        her
                              Mollie x Farmer
Witnesses To Mark: mark
  { JW Campbell
    Pat E Trent

Subscribed and sworn to before me this 25th day of April, 1905

                            J.B. Campbell
                                Notary Public.

Applications for Enrollment of Choctaw Newborn
Act of 1905   Volume XV

Choc New Born 1153
Fisher Washington Morris
(Born Jan. 2, 1903)

NEW-BORN AFFIDAVIT.

Number..................

...Choctaw Enrolling Commission...

IN THE MATTER OF THE APPLICATION FOR ENROLLMENT, as a citizen of the Choctaw Nation, of Fisher Washington Morris

born on the 2d day of ___January___ 190 3

Name of father   Allington Morris   a citizen of   Choctaw
Nation final enrollment No. 11653
Name of mother   Emma Morris   a citizen of   Choctaw
Nation final enrollment No. 11654

Postoffice   Stringtown I.T.

AFFIDAVIT OF MOTHER.

UNITED STATES OF AMERICA
INDIAN TERRITORY
Central Judicial DISTRICT

I   Emma Morris   , on oath state that I am 45 years of age and a citizen by blood of the Choctaw Nation, and as such have been placed upon the final roll of the Choctaw Nation, by the Honorable Secretary of the Interior my final enrollment number being   11654 ; that I am the lawful wife of   Allington Morris   , who is a citizen of the Choctaw Nation, and as such has been placed upon the final roll of said Nation by the Honorable Secretary of the Interior, his final enrollment number being   11653   and that a   Male   child was born to me on the   second   day of   January   190 3; that said child has been named   Fisher Washington Morris   , and is now living.

Emma E. Morris

Witnesseth.
Must be two Witnesses who are Citizens.   Isaac A Billy
Thomas L Wood

Applications for Enrollment of Choctaw Newborn
Act of 1905   Volume XV

Subscribed and sworn to before me this   28th   day of   Feby   190 5

D. Skennedy
Notary Public.

My commission expires: Nov 1st 1905

AFFIDAVIT OF ATTENDING PHYSICIAN OR MIDWIFE

UNITED STATES OF AMERICA
INDIAN TERRITORY
Central Judicial DISTRICT

I,   Mary Randolph   a   Midwife on oath state that I attended on Mrs.   Emma Morris   wife of   Allington Morris   on the second day of January, 190 3, that there was born to her on said date a   male   child, that said child is now living, and is said to have been named   Fisher Washington Morris

Mary Randolph   M.D.

WITNESSETH:

Must be two witnesses who are citizens and know the child.
{ Isaac A Billy
  Thomas L Wood }

Subscribed and sworn to before me this, the   28   day of   Feby   190 5

D. Skennedy   Notary Public.

We hereby certify that we are well acquainted with   Mary Randolph   a   midwife   and know................to be reputable and of good standing in the community.

{ Isaac A. Billy
  Thomas L. Wood }

BIRTH AFFIDAVIT.

DEPARTMENT OF THE INTERIOR.
COMMISSION TO THE FIVE CIVILIZED TRIBES.

IN RE APPLICATION FOR ENROLLMENT, as a citizen of the   Choctaw   Nation, of   Fisher Washington Morris   , born on the 2nd day of Jan, 1903

Name of Father: Allington Morris   a citizen of the   Choctaw   Nation.
Name of Mother: Emma Morris   a citizen of the   Choctaw   Nation.

Applications for Enrollment of Choctaw Newborn
Act of 1905   Volume XV

Postoffice   Stringtown Ind Terr

AFFIDAVIT OF MOTHER.

UNITED STATES OF AMERICA, Indian Territory, }
Central   DISTRICT.

I, Emma Morris, on oath state that I am 45 years of age and a citizen by Blood, of the Choctaw Nation; that I am the lawful wife of Allington Morris, who is a citizen, by Blood of the Choctaw Nation; that a male child was born to me on 2nd day of January, 1903; that said child has been named Fisher Washington Morris, and was living March 4, 1905.

Emma Morris

Witnesses To Mark:
{

Subscribed and sworn to before me this 17th day of April, 1905

C B Prather
Notary Public.

AFFIDAVIT OF ATTENDING PHYSICIAN OR MID-WIFE.

UNITED STATES OF AMERICA, Indian Territory, }
Central   DISTRICT.

I, Mary Randolph, a Midwife, on oath state that I attended on Mrs. Emma Morris, wife of Allington Morris on the 2nd day of Jan, 1903; that there was born to her on said date a male child; that said child was living March 4, 1905, and is said to have been named Fisher Washington Morris

Mary Randolph

Witnesses To Mark:
{

Subscribed and sworn to before me this 18th day of April, 1905

C B Prather
Notary Public.

Applications for Enrollment of Choctaw Newborn
Act of 1905 Volume XV

7-4156

Muskogee, Indian Territory, April 24, 1905.

Allington Morris,
    Stringtown, Indian Territory.

Dear Sir:

    Receipt is hereby acknowledged of the affidavits of Emma Morris and Mary Randolph to the birth of Fisher Washington Morris, son of Allington and Emma Morris, January 2, 1903, and the same have been filed with our records as an application for the enrollment of said child.

                      Respectfully,

                                Chairman.

Choc New Born 1154
    David Baker
    (Born Feb. 24, 1904)

NEW-BORN AFFIDAVIT.

        Number............

...Choctaw Enrolling Commission...

    IN THE MATTER OF THE APPLICATION FOR ENROLLMENT, as a citizen of the Choctaw Nation, of David Baker

born on the 21st[sic] day of ___Feby___ 190 4

Name of father Logan Baker   a citizen of Choctaw
Nation final enrollment No. 9348
Name of mother Mary Baker   a citizen of Choctaw
Nation final enrollment No. 9349

                          Postoffice   Stringtown, I.T.

Applications for Enrollment of Choctaw Newborn
Act of 1905   Volume XV

AFFIDAVIT OF MOTHER.

UNITED STATES OF AMERICA
INDIAN TERRITORY
Central Judicial DISTRICT

I   Mary Baker   , on oath state that I am 26   years of age and a citizen by   blood   of the   Choctaw   Nation, and as such have been placed upon the final roll of the   Choctaw   Nation, by the Honorable Secretary of the Interior my final enrollment number being   9349 ; that I am the lawful wife of   Logan Baker   , who is a citizen of the   Choctaw   Nation, and as such has been placed upon the final roll of said Nation by the Honorable Secretary of the Interior, his final enrollment number being   9348   and that a   Male   child was born to me on the 21st[sic]   day of   Feby   190 4; that said child has been named   David Baker   , and is now living.

Mary Baker

Witnesseth.
Must be two Witnesses who are Citizens. } John Baker
Benj F. Baker

Subscribed and sworn to before me this   24th day of   Feby   190 5

D Skennedy
Notary Public.

My commission expires: Nov 1st 1905

AFFIDAVIT OF ATTENDING PHYSICIAN OR MIDWIFE

UNITED STATES OF AMERICA
INDIAN TERRITORY
Central Judicial DISTRICT

I,   Katie Baker   a   Midwife on oath state that I attended on Mrs.   Mary Baker   wife of   Logan Baker on the   21st[sic]   day of Feby   , 190 4 , that there was born to her on said date a   male child, that said child is now living, and is said to have been named   David Baker

her
Katie x Baker $m.D.$
mark

Subscribed and sworn to before me this, the   24   day of   Feby   190 5

WITNESSETH:
Must be two witnesses who are citizens { John Baker
Benj F. Baker

D. Skennedy   Notary Public.

322

Applications for Enrollment of Choctaw Newborn
Act of 1905   Volume XV

We hereby certify that we are well acquainted with   Katie Baker   a   Midwife   and know   her   to be reputable and of good standing in the community.

_____   Benj F. Baker

_____   James Baker

BIRTH AFFIDAVIT.

DEPARTMENT OF THE INTERIOR.
COMMISSION TO THE FIVE CIVILIZED TRIBES.

IN RE APPLICATION FOR ENROLLMENT, as a citizen of the   Choctaw   Nation, of David Baker   , born on the 24   day of February   , 1904

Name of Father: Logan Baker   a citizen of the   Choctaw   Nation.
Name of Mother: Mary Baker   a citizen of the   Choctaw   Nation.

Postoffice   Ti, I.T.

AFFIDAVIT OF MOTHER.

UNITED STATES OF AMERICA, Indian Territory, }
   Central   DISTRICT.   }

I,   Mary Baker   , on oath state that I am 26   years of age and a citizen by blood   , of the   Choctaw   Nation; that I am the lawful wife of   Logan Baker   , who is a citizen, by blood   of the   Choctaw   Nation; that a   male   child was born to me on   24   day of   February   , 1904; that said child has been named David Baker   , and was living March 4, 1905.

                                        Mary Baker
Witnesses To Mark:
 {
 {
   Subscribed and sworn to before me this   10   day of   April   , 1905

                        OL Johnson
                           Notary Public.

Applications for Enrollment of Choctaw Newborn
Act of 1905   Volume XV

AFFIDAVIT OF ATTENDING PHYSICIAN OR MID-WIFE.

UNITED STATES OF AMERICA, Indian Territory, }
Central   DISTRICT.

I, Katie Baker, a midwife, on oath state that I attended on Mrs. Mary Baker, wife of Logan Baker on the 24 day of February, 1904; that there was born to her on said date a male child; that said child was living March 4, 1905, and is said to have been named David Baker

            her
            Katie x Baker
Witnesses To Mark: mark
 { Thomas M Bell
  George Kemp

  Subscribed and sworn to before me this 20th day of April, 1905

       D. Skennedy
        Notary Public.

BIRTH AFFIDAVIT.

DEPARTMENT OF THE INTERIOR.
COMMISSION TO THE FIVE CIVILIZED TRIBES.

IN RE APPLICATION FOR ENROLLMENT, as a citizen of the Choctaw Nation, of David Baker, born on the 21st[sic] day of Feby, 1904

Name of Father: Logan Baker   a citizen of the Choctaw Nation.
Name of Mother: Mary A Baker a citizen of the Choctaw Nation.

      Postoffice   Ti, Ind. Ter.

AFFIDAVIT OF MOTHER.

UNITED STATES OF AMERICA, Indian Territory, }
Central   DISTRICT.

I, Mary A. Baker, on oath state that I am 26 years of age and a citizen by blood, of the Choctaw Nation; that I am the lawful wife of Logan Baker, who is a citizen, by blood of the Choctaw Nation; that a male child was born to me on 21st[sic] day of Feby, 1904; that said child has been named David Baker, and was living March 4, 1905.

       Mary A Baker

Applications for Enrollment of Choctaw Newborn
Act of 1905   Volume XV

Witnesses To Mark:
{

    Subscribed and sworn to before me this   27th day of   June   , 1905

                                D Skennedy
                                Notary Public.

AFFIDAVIT OF ATTENDING PHYSICIAN OR MID-WIFE.

UNITED STATES OF AMERICA, Indian Territory, }
   Central   DISTRICT. }

    I,   Katie Baker   , a midwife   , on oath state that I attended on Mrs.   Mary A Baker   , wife of   Logan Baker   on the   21st[sic] day of   Feby , 1904; that there was born to her on said date a   male   child; that said child was living March 4, 1905, and is said to have been named   David Baker

                              her
                        Katie x Baker
Witnesses To Mark: mark
{ Thos M Bell
{ *(Name Illegible)*

    Subscribed and sworn to before me this   30th day of   June   , 1905

                                D. Skennedy
                                Notary Public.

                                         7-3241.

                Muskogee, Indian Territory, April 24, 1905.

Logan Baker,
    Ti, Indian Territory.

Dear Sir:

    Receipt is hereby acknowledged of the affidavits of Mary Baker and Katie Baker, to the birth of David Baker, child of Logan and Mary Baker, February 24, 1904, and the same have been filed with our records as an application for the enrollment of said child.

                        Respectfully,

                                Chairman.

Applications for Enrollment of Choctaw Newborn
Act of 1905 Volume XV

7--NB--1154

Muskogee, Indian Territory, June 2, 1905.

Logan Baker,
    Ti, Indian Territory.

Dear Sir:

    There is enclosed you herewith for execution application for the enrollment of your infant child, David Baker.

    In the affidavits executed February 21, 1905, the date of the applicant's birth is given as February 21, 1904, while in the affidavits executed April 20, 1905, this date is given as February 24, 1904. In the enclosed application the date of birth is left blank. Please insert the correct date of birth and when the affidavits are properly executed return them to this office.

    In having the enclosed affidavits executed care should be exercised to see that all names are written in full, as they appear in the body of the affidavits and in the event that either of the persons signing the affidavit are unable to write, signatures by mark must be attested by two witnesses. Each affidavit must be executed before a Notary Public and the notarial seal and signature of the officer must be attached to each separate affidavit.

    This matter should receive your immediate attention as no further action can be taken relative to the enrollment of said child until the Commission has been furnished these affidavits.

                            Respectfully,

                                                Commissioner in Charge.

Enc-FVK-16.

ABBOTT
  Dr W E 264
  W E 262,263,264,267
  W E, MD 262
ADCOCK
  Viola 247,249
  W D 247,248
AINSWORTH, N B 262,263,265,266
AIRINGTON
  Benjamin F 201,202,203
  Jesse 202
  Jessie 200
  Make 200,201,203
  Willie 201,202,203
ALEXANDER
  Henry 114,115
  R S 127,128
ALLEN
  David 190
  Emily 70
  Isom 190,191
  L D 172
  Rufus 190,191
ALVIS
  R H 151
  R H, MD 151
ANDERSON
  Alsi 154
  Deborah 8,9,10
  Eliza 295,296,297,298,299
  Ella 8,9,10
  Lou 216,217
  Louis 296,297
  Louisa 295,296,297,298
  Mack 8,9,10
  Robert 13,21,38,39,41,42,44,45,
    50,51,53,54,56,57,58,69,111,222,250
  Susan 130,131,132,133
  Thelma 130,131,132,133
  Wesley 130,131,132,133
ANGELL, W H 28,29,100,102,175,
  176,218,219,220
APOTATUBBI, Elliston 294
APOTETUBBI, Soki 283
APOTOTUBBI
  Eliza 295,298
  Ellison 298

  Elliston 295,296,297,298
  Greeks 295,296,297,298
APOTOTUBI
  Eliza 299
  Elliston 299
APOTUBBI, Eliza 297
ARMSTRONG, Moses 146,147
ARNETT
  Leizy 169
  Lizzie 169
  Lizzy 168
ARRINGTON
  Benjamin F 200,201,202
  Jessie 202
  Make 200,201
  Willie 200,201,202
ASKEW
  Bettie 311,314
  W T 310,311,314
AUSTIN, Louie 80
AYERS, Fred H 179
BAGGETT
  John 16
  John L 15,16
  John O 15,16
  Mattie 15,16
BAKEN, L E 137
BAKER
  Benj F 322,323
  David 321,322,323,324,325,326
  Jackson 80
  James 323
  John 322
  Katie 322,323,324,325
  Logan 321,322,323,324,325,326
  Mary 321,322,323,324
  Mary A 325
BALDWIN, Jno D 97,101
BATTIEST, L G 11,12
BEAL
  Albert 103,104
  A B 103,104
  George 104
BEALE, W H 222,223,230
BEARDEN
  Bessie 33,34,35
  Beulah Bell 32

Index

Beulah Belle 33,34,35
Chas E 31,32,33,34,35
BELL
   F M 258
   Thomas M 324
   Thos M 325
BELVIN
   Eliza 119
   Lizie 119
BELVING
   James 119
   Jimmie 119
   Margaret 121
BEN
   Joe 288,290
   Louisa 300,301,302,303,304
BENCE, Alice 118
BENCH
   Alice 118,119,120,121,122
   Daniel 276,277,278,279,280,281
   Edward Daniel 276,277,278,279,
   280,281
   Katie 277,278,279,280
   Kattie 281
   Margaret 119,121,122
   Margarett 118,120
   Margret 119
   Sam 118,119,120,121,122
BENDLEY, R A 159
BENNETT
   Hattie 239,240
   John 240
   Mary Jane 240
BENT, Joe 289
BILLS, R C 113
BILLVIN, Makeslit 121
BILLY
   Eastman 92
   Elizabeth 175
   Emily 11
   Isaac A 318,319
   Joseph 10,11
   Lymon 82
   Millie 95
   Milly 92
   Mily 91,94
   Rebecca 176

Sidney 91,92,94,95
Susan 82
Wilkin 11,12
BINST, Sam 121
BIXBY, Tams 15,73,87,88,94,210,
213,214
BLUE, Willy 233,234
BOATRIGHT, J L 154
BOBO, Lacey P 86,135,155,210,223,
224,225,274,275
BOHANAN
   Benjamin 224,225
   Green 190,191
   H J 47
   Lizzie 250
BOHANON, Lucinda 7
BOLING, Billy 295,296
BOND, Emma 193,194
BOWER, James .. 18,233,262,263,265,270
BOWERS, C A 230
BOWMAN, William 223
BRADFORD, M S 9,10,154
BRANSFORD, C D 147
BRASHEARS, Tobias 171
BREEDING, O J 201
BROWN
   J D 22,23,24,305,306
   J D, MD 23,306
   John T 277,278
   Mary 18
   Sampson 1,2
BUCHANAN, Robt H 260
BULLARD
   Elmer D 261,264,265,266,267,268
   Frank 261,262,263,264,265,266,
   267,268
   Roy E 261,262,263,264,267
   Susan F 261,262,264,265
   Susan L 263,266,267
   Susie 262,263,264,265,266,267
   Susie F 265
BUNCH, Jesse 282,283
BUNNUP, William 228,229,230
BURCHFIEL
   Annie 166
   Annie E 165
BURNDAGE, Clarence B 124

Index

BURNS
  Alice 155,156,157,158
  Joseph 155,156,157,158
  Willie Jewell 155,156,157,158
BURRIS
  Lucy 14
  Martha Ann 13
  Marvin J 177
BURWELL, W P 52
BYINGTON
  Annie 58,59,60,61,62,63,65
  Lillie 58,60,61,62,63,64,65
  Mary 58,59,63,64
  Moody 58,59,60,61,62,63,64,65
  Thomas 59,60
BYRD, George F 177
CAMDEN
  A B 101,102
  Ida B 101,102
  Leroy H 101,102
CAMPBELL
  C M 151,152
  J B 317
  J M 222,223
  J W 317
CAREY, Al 122
CARNES
  Lewis 1,2
  Sinie... 122
CARNEY
  Al 123,124,125,126
  Allen 123,124,125,126
  Ella 124,125,126
  Ellar 123,125,126
  Screna 123,125,126
CARSON
  Geo W 258
  T J 150
CARTER, R L 242
CARTLIDGE, Nancy 160
CATLIN, J D 98,99
CEPHUS
  Bessie 256,257
  Timothy J 256,257
CHRISTIE, Edward 137
CHRISTY, Jesse 43,44,192,194
CLARK, Perry M 278,279,280

COLBERT
  Alexander 186,187,188,189,190
  Eliza 185,186,187,188,189,190,191
  Martha 186,187,188,189,190,191
  Susie May 185,186,187,188,189, 190,191
  Tennessee 227,229,230
COLE, Joseph......................37,38,40,113
COLEMAN
  Lou Anna 163,164
  R B 264,266,267
  Thompson 50,185
COLLINS
  Jessie..234,236
  Joseph 33,34
  L Jake 174
COMBS
  Edward 45,46,47,48
  Sarah...................................45,46,47,48
  Thomas L E 45,46
  Thomas Lee Edward....................47,48
  Thomas S E 45
CONSER
  Anie 132
  Peter.. 132
  Susan 132,133
COOPER
  Henry 270,271
  M M 143
COSTELOW, J W 14,282,283,292,293
COURTS, Joseph T 124,125
COVINGTON, W P ..86,135,210,224,225
CRAWFORD
  Barnett 70,71,72,75,76
  G B 73,74
  Lizzie 70,71,72,75
  Willie Arthur 70,71,72,75,76
CROWDER
  Louis.. 122
  Louisa 120,121
  Martin B 204,211
  Robert 120,121,122
CUNNINGHAM, Wm H.................... 218
CURRY, Guy A................................. 125
DALTON, E M 129
DANIEL, John 136
DAVISON

Index

Beatrice 311,313
J B 312,314
Tom 311,313,314
DAY, Nannie 77
DENCH, Katie 276
DENISON, Sue 17,18
DIFENDAFER, Chas T 93,95,186,187, 188,232
DILLS
    Eugene 102,103,104,105
    Loney Burton 105
    Lonie Burton 104
    Lonnie Burton 102,103,104,105
    Rosa 103,104,105
    Rosy 105
DODD, Tomay 308
DONALD, Bennie 195,196
DOUGHTY, H P 258
DOWLAND, Myrtle Lee 122
DRISKELL, Alice 6
DRISKILL, Allice 6
DUNCAN, G D 147,277,278
DURANT
    Isaac 234
    W F 25,26
DWIGHT, E T 147
DYER
    James, Jr 225,226
    Laura 225,226
EMERSON, W E 231,232,236
EVERIDGE, E M 207
EVINS, Elsiea 207
FANNIN, E J 73,74,98,99
FARMER, Mollie 317
FIZER, James 167
FLING
    Dr Perry 48,239
    Perry 48,205,239
    Perry E A 46,206,237
    Perry, MD 48,205,239
FOBB
    Adeline 221,222,223,224,225, 226,227,228,229,230
    Adline 222,226,229
    Nellie 221,223,224,225,226,227,228
    Nellis 221,222,223,224,228,229,230
    Philliston 227

Simeon 227,229
Simon .. 221,222,223,224,225,226,227, 228,230
FOLK, J W 201
FOLSOM
    Ara D 27
    A E 217
    Joseph 127,128
    Lena 39,41,42
    Linn 184,185
    Sim 41,42
    Sweeney 41,42
FOSTER & DALTON 130
FOWLER
    H L 136,137,139,193
    Hosea L 142,143,144,145,194
    Josephine 142,143,144,145
    Lillian B 142,143,144,145
    Lillian Beatrice 142,143
FRANKLIN
    E Q 245
    Wirt 13,14,19,21,30,35,36,37,38,39, 41,42,44,45,46,51,53,54,56,57,58,60, 61,62,68,69,70,72,77,78,102,111,206, 215,222,230,237,240,241,244,245, 250,287,305
FRASHER, Faney 67
FRAZIER
    Fannie 68
    Ross 25
FULSOM, Lena 37,38
FULTON, J S 102
GAINES, A W 150
GARDNER
    Alfred 78,79,80
    Anderson 295,296,301,302
    E J 80,81
    Edmond 142,143
    Jeff 223,230,294
    Mattie 78,79,80
    Susie M 78,80
    Susie Mattie 78,79
GARLAND
    Columbus 195,196,197,198,199,200
    Leo 195,196,197,198,199,200
    Lettie 196,197,198,199,200
    Little 195

Index

Ward, Jr 195,196
GENTRY
   I L 121,122
   J L, MD 119
GIBSON, Wilson 216,217
GILLIAM, A S 150
GLENN, W T 204,205,211,238,239, 251,252,253,256
GOING, Simeon 14
GOINS, William 269
GOODING, Chas H 212
GORDON, James M 201,202,203
GRANT, H S 243,246
GREEN, G B, MD 19
GRIGGS
   Tom, Jr 31
   W M 204
GRUBBS
   Earnestine 242,243,244,245,246, 247,248,249
   Ernestine 241,242,247
   J W 247,248
   Mae 241,243,244,246,247,248,249
   Mrs E 246
   Pearl 241,242,244,245
   T L 241,242,243,244,245,246,247
GRYDER, J M 71,72,75
HAIOPATUBBI, Sibbie 43,44
HALL
   Alice 115
   Fannie 115,116,117
   Joshua 114,115,116,117
   Sidney 114,115,116,117
HALLS, T J 167
HAMMACK, Sarah J 307,308
HAMPTON
   Frances 249,250
   Isaac D 249,250
   Sarah 249,250
HARGAVE
   Dr J H 25,26
   J H, MD 25
HARLEY
   Ennis 254,255,257
   Eunis 254
   Melford 254,255,257
   Milford 257

Willie 254,255,257
HARRIS
   B S 287
   W L 234
HARRISON, Rev J D 121
HATINGER, Emily 103,105
HAYES
   Dora Frances 182
   Rosa 182
   Thomas 182
HAYS
   Dora Frances 180,181
   Rosa 180,181
   Thomas 180,181
HEATHCOCK, H C 215
HERLEY
   Enos 255,256
   Montford 255,256
   Willie 255,256
HIBBEN
   Mary 66,67,68
   Mary Gertrude 66,67,68
   Sophie 66,67
   Thomas D 66,68
   Tomas D 67
HICKMAN, Edwin L 273
HICKS
   Minerva 1
   Minervia 1,3,4
HILL, C W 22,23
HODGES
   J T 243
   Oliver 243
HOFFMAN, Susie 153
HOGUE, R J 99
HOLBROOK, W H 156,158
HOLBROOKS, W H 156
HOLLOWAY, Ola 152,153
HOMER
   Jacob 84,85,133,134,224
   Silan 20,21
   Sissie 20,21
   Solomon 20,21
HOMES, J W 225
HOOPER
   I W 182
   I W, MD 181

Index

HOPKINS, D W 159,160,161
HOPSON
   Gensie 81,82,83,84,85,86,87, 88,89,90
   Ginsie 88
   Lena 81,82,83,85,86,87,88,89,90
   Rayson 88
   Reason 83,84,86,89,90
   Reyson 81,82,88
HORSTMAN, Charlie H 202
HORTON, L D 118,119,120,121,122
HOSHALL
   J L 258
   J L, MD 258
HOTINLUBBEE, Lina 21
HOWARD
   John H 202
   John H, MD 202
HUDSON
   Alice 12,13,14
   Calvin 12,13
   Charley 111,112,113
   Cleo 12,13,14
   Leeana 106,107,109
   P W 191
   Peter W 131
   Roar 12,13,14,15
   W M 113
HUFFMAN, Susie 151,152
HUFFMANN, Susie 152
HUGHES, Harley 183
HULSEY, Wm J 309
HUNTER, Mary 16
HUTCHINSON, N P 162,287
JACKSON
   Ben 127,128,129,130
   Bessie 126,127,128,129,130
   H J 91,92
   J H 227,228
   Joseph 174
   L T 71,75
   L T, MD 75
   Lorena 127,128,129,130
   Toto 288
JACOB
   Ben 133,135,136,137,138,139, 140,141

Eastman 136,137,139,140,141
Eman 138
Esman 135,136
Esmon 138
H B 43,44,192,194
Rhoda 136,137,139,140
Rhoda Meshaya 140
Rhoda Mishaia 137
JACOBS
   Ben 134,135
   Eastman 134
   Houston B 133,134
   Rhoda 134
JAMES
   Ada Ann 48,50,51
   Ada Anna 48,49
   Benjamen 49
   Benjamin 49,50,51
   Gincy 174
   Jackson 173,174
   Jinsie 174
   Maimie 59,60
   Rose 173,174
   Wicey 173,174
   Winnie 49,50,51
JEFFERSON
   Allice 116,117
   Fannie 114,115
   Ninnie 116
JEFFREYS, Martha J 34,35
JOEL, Hampton 52,55
JOHNSON
   Dr E 172
   E 171,173
   E, MD 171,172
   O L 16,93,95,172,186,187,188, 232,235,323
JOLLEY, Lizzie 74
JOLLY, Lizzie 73
JONES
   C C 195,196,197,198,199,200
   C C, MD 196
   Dr C C 196
   Ella 126
   Isaac 52,55
   J N 196,197,199
   J O 106

Index

James 234
   Robinson 7,8
JULIAN, W A 282,283,292,293
KAISER, John 201
KELLY, Albert 231
KEMP
   George 324
   Nelson 11
KING
   Allington 63
   Arlington 59,60,63,65
   Ida May 166,167
   Iler May 166,168,169
   Sarah 169
   Sarah J 168,169
   Sarah Jane 166,167
   William S 166,167,168,169
KIRBY
   Ed 285,286,287
   Elizabeth 285
   J H 116,117
   Lizzie 286,287
   Minnie May 284,285,286,287
KIRKPATRICK
   J C 238,239
   J O 211,212
KIZER, F M 103,104,105
KREBBS
   Edmond 316,317
   John W 316,317
   May 311
   Provi Lee 316,317
LABOR
   Alexander 145,146,147,148,149
   Earl Lee 145,146,147,148,149
   Eria 145,146,149
   Erie 147,148
LACEY, Frank 25,26
LAN, James 167
LARECY
   John F 238,239
   W E 37,40,112,113,183,184,185
LAYON, Thompson 116
LEFLORE
   J W 156,157
   Joseph 233,234
   Louis 273,274

LESTER, C L 7,8
LEWIS
   Calvin 1,2,3,4
   J L 157
   Jas L 156
   Mary 1,2,4
   Porter J 1,2,3,4
   Porter John 1
LILLARD, Minnie 177
LITTLE, J C 177,307,308
LOGAN, Joel 60,63
LOMAN, Elizabeth 45,58
LONG, Thomas J 179
LORING
   Albert Homer 24,25
   Elbert Homer 24,26,27
   Sallie 24,25,26,27
   William H 24,25,26,27
LYLE, J W 3
LYLES
   John W 272,273,274,275,276
   Mary L 272,273,274,275
   W A 276
   William 273
   William A 272,273,274,275
MANSFIELD, MCMURRAY &
   CORNISH 88,214
MARKEY, A J 277
MARKHAM, S S 183
MARTIN
   Kizzie 128,129,130
   W H 219,220
   William 129
   Wm 269
MCALESTER, W B 159
MCBRIDE
   J Bennett 201,203
   J Bennett, MD 201
MCCOY, Allis 15
MCDONALD
   A A 19
   Arthur 109
   Authar 109
   Author 106,107,108
   Authur 110
   Leeana 107,108,109,110
   Leeanna 109

Index

Onie 106,107,108,109
Pealy 109
Pearle 110
Pearlie 110
Pearly 106,107,108,109,110
MCFARLAND
   Abbie 164
   Abbie L 161,162,163
   Florence Glenn 161,162,163
   J B 161,162,163,164,285,286
MCGEE
   Jesse 287,288,289,290,291
   Licksey 287,288,289,290
   Soloman 287
   Solomon 287,288,289,290,291
MCGINNIS
   J C 131,132,133
   J C, MD 131
MCINTOSH, John 32,205
MCKINNEY
   Ephraim 254,255
   Jackson 289,290
   Louise 174
MCNEELEY, Cleo A 97
MCNEELY
   Cleo A 97,100
   Miss W M 99
   W M 98
MERRY, J L 107,108
MERRYMAN
   Leonidas C 273
   Leonidas E 274
MILTON
   Mila 92,93,94,95
   Sidney 90,92,93,94
MISHAIA
   Rhoda 134,135,136,139
MITCHELL, R P 226
MOON, J D 308
MOORE
   Ada Bell 104
   Emily 11
   H M 170,171
   Olive M 178,179,180
   R M 180
   Robert 180
   Robert M 178,179

Sylvan G 178,179,180
Thomas M 180
MORELAND, J B 306
MORRIS
   Allington 318,319,320,321
   Emma 318,319,320,321
   Fisher Washington 318,319,320,321
   Robert 94
   S E 163,164,285,286
MORRISON
   E W 244
   E W, MD 244
MURPHY
   Ed G W 175,176
   Elizabeth 175,176
   Robinson 175,176
MYRICK, Albert 16
NABORS, Dr. 231,235
NAIL
   Dollie M 182,183,184,185
   J O 37,38,40
   Joe 182,183,184,185
   Paralee 182,183
   Parley 184,185
NEEDLES, T B 220,236
NEHKA, Lena 83,85,89
NEKHA, Lena 86
NELSON
   B A 22,24
   Emma 22,23,24
   Isaac 22,23,24
   James 22,23,24
NOBLES, Nancy 265,266,267
NOBLE, Nancy 267
NORMAN
   Ida 259,260,261
   Irene 259,260,261
   John Strather 260,261
   Joshua Allen 259,260,261
OAKES
   Aurilla 212
   Charles D 36
   D F 208
   David 207
   David F 204,205,206,207,209, 210,211,212,213
   Donald 305,306

Index

Edward 203,207,208,209,210, 211,212,213,214
Elsie J 206
Elsie Jane 204,205,206,209,211, 212,213
George W 305,306
L E 33,34
Margaret A 36
Martha Ellen 36,37
Myrtle Grace.............203,205,206,209
Myrtle Grae 204
Rosa E 305,306
Rosie...36,37
T J... 113
Tom 185
Tom, Jr 113
OASCES, G W 207
OLIVER
    Josie.. 48
    Sam R 48
OSHTA, H... 122
PARISH, R M... 27
PARKER, J C 25
PARSONS, J U..................................... 185
PATTERSON, Carl 106,107,108
PAUDLUM, C J 11,12
PAYNE
    Sam C 67
    Sophie...66,67
PERKINS, J W 7,8
PERRY
    Liza..92,93,94
    Roberson................................91,92,94
PLUMLEE, John M........................... 243
POSEY, J W 74
PRATHER, C B................................... 320
QUINN, Thomas 91,92,93,94,95
RABON
    Ethel M 170,171,172,173
    J W 170,171
    Lynn 169,170,171,172,173
    Rufus 170,171,172,173
RANDOLPH, Mary...............319,320,321
RANOLDS, Eria.......................... 147,149
REED, James N 160,161
REEDER, J G 309,310,311,312,313
REYNOLDS

G A... 50
Nancy 50
RIDDLE
    Jack... 4
    Okemah 4
RIGGS, J J 91,92
ROBERT
    Artemissa.. 7
    Bassie 6,7
    Daniel 7
ROBUCK, Betsie 215
ROEBUCK
    Betsie..214,215
    Edward 214,215
    Minnie Lee 214,215
ROSE
    Annie 269,270,271,272
    Horace C...................269,270,271,272
    Horace Clayton........................269,270
    James 269,270,271,272
    Vester 50,51,69
    Vester W....... 13,21,38,39,41,42,44,45, 53,54,56,57,58,69,111,222,250
ROSENTHAL, Ernestine 242
ROSENTHALL
    G 242
    Geo 242
ROWELLS, R E 48
RUCKER
    L C 240
    L C, MD 240
RUSHING, Laura 28
RUTHERFORD
    B C 146,147,148
    B C, MD 146,148
SAMES, W W 309,312
SAMPLE
    Clarence..................................236,237
    Clarence L 238,239
    Fannie A 236
    Fannie B 237,238,239
    Gussie Lee 236,237,238,239
SAMPSON, Yahoke........................... 11
SANDERS
    George 37,38,39,40
    J M.. 177
    Robert.......................37,38,39,40,184

Index

Susan 38,39,42
SANGUIN
   Charmian Vaughan 251,252,253
   H L 251,252
   Thomas E 251,252,253
   Zula C 251,252,253
SCOTT
   Benjamin Thomas 176,177
   John P 176,177,178
   Phoebe 176,177,178
   S F 162
SELF
   Chas W 16,156
   Guy 164,165,166
   Joseph M 164,165,166
   Lillian O 164,165,166
   Price 16
SETTLE
   Dr J M 177
   J M 177
SEXTON
   Mary 1,2,3,4
   Porter John 2
SHANAFELT, Richard 218,219,220
SHONEY, W A 25,43,47,49,59,79, 115,143,163,164,192,194,285,286
SHOTUBE
   Charles 191,193,194
   Dickson 191,192,193,194
   Jane 191,193,194
SHOTUBY
   Charles 191,193,194
   Charley 192
   Dickson 192,193,194
   Jane 192,193,194
SHULL, Chas G 17
SIMMONS
   T W 30,32
   Thos W 32
   Thos W, MD 30,32
SKENNEDY, D 319,322,324,325
SMITH
   C B 277,278,279,280,281
   C B, MD 277,279,280
   Laura 162,163,164,285,286,287
   M S 146,147
SOCKEY

Lester 230,231,232,233,234,235,236
Malenda 236
Malinda 231,232,233,234,235
Ned 231,232,233,234,235,236
SPANN, F R 124,125
SPENCER, D O 144
SPRING
   Cicero 17,18,19,20
   Cisero 20
   Hattie 29,30,31,32
   Henry 17,18
   Joel 17,18,19,20,251,252
   Joel, Jr 19
   Julia Lee 29,30,31,32
   Willie 29,30,31,32
   Winnie 18
   Winnie R 17,18,19
STAMPS, F M 154
STEINSEIPPE, Gertrude 159
STEINSIPE, Gertrude 160
STEPHENS
   L K, MD 270
   Landon K 271,272
   Landon K, MD 271
STEVENS, Dr Lant 270
STEWART, C J 248,249
STIDHAM
   F R 153
   Frank R 150,151
   Laura 5,6
   Mr F R 151,152
   Pearley Ann 150,151
   Pearly Ann 153
   Susie Ann 150,151
   Willie 5,6
   Zachariah 5,6
STIFF
   H L 14,292
   J L 293
STIGLER, J S 270,271
STILES
   Ara D 27,28
   Bertie May 27,28,29
   H R 27,28
STIRLEN
   Mrs W R 267
   W R 267

Index

STONE, W B 73,74
SWINK, William W 79,142,143
TALBERT, Jno E 82,83,84
TAMKA, Lina 292
TANITOBBI, Patsey 255,257
TANTUBBEE, Enos 255,256
TAYLOR
    Jonas 136
    M J 71,75
    Melvina 254,255
    Mrs M J 75
    Simon 254,255
THOMAS
    Josephine 69,70
    Susan 49,50,51,69,70
    Wilson 49,50,69,70
THOMPSON
    Jesse 283,284
    A P 273,274,275
    A P, MD 273
THROHBE, Mary 158
TIMS, Columbus 83,84
TOLBERT, John E 84,85
TOM, Morris 83,84
TOMHKA, Salean 304
TOMPKINS, J J 122
TONEHKA
    Lina 294
    Salan 301
TOTUBBE, Battiest 288
TRAUBE
    Charley 160
    Elizabeth 160,161
    Mary 159,160
TRENT, Pat E 317
TRISHKA, Eliza 114,115
TROHBE
    Charles 158,159
    M L Elizabeth 158,159
    Mary 158,159
TUEY, L C 1,2,170,171
TUSHKA
    Eliza 292
    Fostan 291,292
    Foston 293,294
    Laisa 293
    Laise 294

Levi 292,293,294
USHER, E W 65
VARNELL
    J H 105
    R H 105
VAWTER
    Florence Maud 257,258,259
    J W 259
    James W 257,258
    Martha A 257,258
VICE
    Lottie May 308,309,310,311,312,
    313,314,315,316
    May 308,309,310,312,314,315,316
    Robert ... 308,309,310,311,312,313,314
WADE, Barnett 301,302
WALACE, W M 112,113,183,185
WALKER, Chas T 271
WALL
    Chris 307,308
    Delila 307,308
    Gilbert N 306,307,308
WALLACE
    Besse 256
    Bessie 257
    Celia 256,257
    Frank 127,128
    Lillian 192,193
    W M, MD 112,113,183,185
WALLS, Tandy 188,190
WARD
    Henry 96,97,98,99,100
    J M 96,97
    J P 33,34
    John S 96,97
    Nova Cleo 96,97,100
    Willia Maud 100
    Willie Maud 96,97
WATKINS
    Aaron 55,56
    Agnes 51,52,53,54,55
    Eliza 51,52,53,54,55
    Ennissie 56
    Joseph 51,52,53,54,55
    Sinsie 53,54
    W E 79
    Zona 55,56

Index

WATSON
  A.. 160
  Simon 55,56
WECHABIBIE
  Willie 66,67
  Williw 67
WESLEY
  Davis................................42,43,44,45
  Eliza.................................42,43,44,45
  Joseph 42,43,44,45
  Lenas 289,290,296,297,300,301,
  302,303,304
  Rhoda 299,300,301,302,303
  Salean 300,301,302,303,304
WEST, A T... 165
WHISTLER
  Arena 153,154
  Dora 9,10,153,154
  Robinson..................................153,154
WHITE
  H H 252,253
  H H, MD.....................................252,253
  J M.......................... 123,124,168,169
WHITEMAN, M J............................62,63
WILLIAM, Anna............................... 144
WILLIAMS
  Anna 145
  B W 26,27,146
  E H 162,287
  Henry 113
WILLIS
  Elmira 111,112,113
  Elmire 112
  Emerson D 57,58
  Louisa 57,58
  Martha 57,58
  Rebeca 112,113
  Rebecca 111,112,113
  Susan 37,39,40
WILLSON, Susan E 217
WILSON
  C W 3
  Edward 282,283
  Littie 282,283
  Narcissa 217,218,219,221
  Narsissa 216,217
  Noah J..................................216,217

Noel J..........216,217,218,219,220,221
S W 217,218,219,220,221
Silas W 216,217
Susan 218,219,221
Susan R.. 217
Susan W... 217
Tom 300,301
W A 5,6
W P 288,289,290,295,296,297,
300,301,302,303,304
William P..................282,283,288,290
WILTON, Silina............................... 177
WOOD
  John W... 77
  Julius Arthur 76,77
  Margaret 77
  Thomas L..................................318,319
WRIGHT
  C L 79,80
  C L, MD 79,80
  J P 160,161
YEAGER, J T 147
YOUNG, J F 152

www.ingramcontent.com/pod-product-compliance
Lightning Source LLC
Chambersburg PA
CBHW020243030426
42336CB00010B/586